Zidane Meriboute is a Senior Legal Consultant at the International Committee of the Red Cross (ICRC) in Geneva. He is also ICRC's Consultant for Global Affairs for Operations in the Muslim World. His first book, now published for the first time in English, is the winner of a major European literary prize.

'The author is to be lauded for pointing to the internal diversity of the Islamic tradition and the deep roots of tolerance, human rights, women's empowerment, and religious freedom embedded within it. Such concepts retrieved from within Islamic thought and practices represent the strongest rejoinder to the extremists and their distortion of Islamic history and doctrine. *Islam's Fateful Path* is a timely and eloquent appeal to both Muslims and non-Muslims to recognize their common values and the possibility for peaceful co-existence this shared heritage implies.'

– Asma Afsaruddin, Associate Professor of Arabic and Islamic Studies, University of Notre Dame

ISLAM'S FATEFUL PATH

THE CRITICAL CHOICES FACING MODERN MUSLIMS

Zidane Meriboute

TRANSLATED BY
JOHN KING

I.B. TAURIS

LONDON · NEW YORK

Published in 2009 by I.B.Tauris & Co Ltd
6 Salem Road, London W2 4BU
175 Fifth Avenue, New York NY 10010
www.ibtauris.com

Distributed in the United States and Canada Exclusively by
Palgrave Macmillan
175 Fifth Avenue, New York NY 10010

ISBN: 978 1 84511 741 2 (PB)
ISBN: 978 1 84511 740 5 (HB)

A full CIP record for this book is available from the British Library
A full CIP record is available from the Library of Congress

Library of Congress Catalog Card Number: available

Typeset in Palatino by
Ellipsis Books Limited, Glasgow

Printed and bound in Great Britain by
CPI Antony Rowe, Chippenham

CONTENTS

FOREWORD

Between 1986 and 2001 I visited many Muslim countries. This book is based on that personal experience, on my reading, and on ideas I have been able to share. In the Arab Maghreb and the Middle East, as well as in Pakistan, Kazakhstan, Turkey, Iran and various African countries, I was able to look closely at a range of tendencies within contemporary Islam, including radical Islam, the stance of moderation, secularism, Sufi mysticism and rationalism. I attempted to penetrate to the core of these schools of thought, hoping to demonstrate that Islam is in reality not a monolithic and indivisible entity, despite the contention of certain observers.

I have attempted to establish whether Islam is in truth a religion of fear, intolerance, fatalism, terrorism and contempt for the dignity of women, as is often supposed. Or, on the contrary, is it a faith that is misunderstood and stigmatised, whose true ethical message hostile observers have sought to distort, for political purposes, or even from personal prejudice?

In my analysis of diverse practices, ranging from strict Islam to the liberal interpretation of the faith found in some Muslim lands, I have striven to achieve an understanding of the practical consequences of the different schools of thought within Islam for various issues. These included women's rights, the wearing of the veil, the delicate question of sexuality in the Islamic world, the role of the individual in society, the status of Jewish and Christian minorities, and the so-called 'clash of civilisations'.

My intention has been that this book should be as useful to the general public as to specialist readers. With this in mind, I have attempted to make it easier for readers to find their way through the complexities of the world of Islam, which is as various as it is fascinating.

Finally, I wish to express my gratitude to the School of Oriental and African Studies of London University (SOAS). In 2002, the School kindly invited me to spend a year in London with the status of a visiting scholar. Without the opportunity afforded by this invitation I would have been unable to shape into their present form the results of the research I have undertaken and the ideas I have assembled over a number of years. I would also like to take the opportunity to thank the Prize Committee of the 'Prix Spiritualités d'Aujourdhui' for 2005, chaired by the distinguished Orientalist André Chouraqi. I am grateful for the special mention with which the committee honoured my book, and for their invitation to lecture on the book's subject matter at the Centre Méditerranéen de Littérature (CML) in Perpignan which awards this Prize for works in French.

Z.M.

ACKNOWLEDGEMENTS

I would like to express my heartfelt gratitude to all those who have helped and supported me in the research, writing and translation of this book. Special thanks are due to:

- Dr John King, who in addition to translating the book into English proposed changes that have left the book better adapted to an English-speaking readership.
- Annie D. for her meticulous and professional scrutiny of the French manuscript.
- Toufik, Mara and Sami-Mathias for their invaluable help with research.
- Saber Mansour, my editor at A. Fayard, and Alex Wright, my editor at I.B.Tauris, for their generous and unstinting advice.

PART ONE

INTRODUCTION

Islamist ideologists contend that after the failure of the crusades to subjugate the Orient by military means, and following the collapse of the colonialist enterprise in more recent times, the West has adopted a changed approach to the spiritual and economic conquest of the Orient. The strategy of the West has been, in their view, literally identical with that proposed in the thirteenth century by the crusading monarch King Louis IX of France, known as St Louis. Acknowledging in a secret testament that the Muslims could not be conquered by force, he ordained the adoption of other methods. Specifically he counselled his successors to employ the methods of cultural and spiritual domination.[1] Louis IX was a figure of great piety whose ambition had been the conquest of the Holy Places, including Jerusalem. His attack on Egypt, launched in 1248, was frustrated by his defeat at the battle of Mansura in 1250. He was taken prisoner and was later ransomed. Seeking revenge, Louis raised a second expedition but, on its arrival at Carthage on the coast of North Africa, his army was decimated by plague. He was himself also stricken by the disease, but before he succumbed he took his chance to urge the Christians to wage the struggle against the Muslim foe by means that would be non-violent but nonetheless effective. These methods were to include faith and education, as well as the critical study of Muslim theology and eastern languages. In his view, only thus would the West be able to halt the ferocious resistance of the Muslims and consolidate western domination.[2]

It was on the basis of principles identical to those laid down by St Louis that groups of Orientalists, students of Islam and Arabists came into existence, led by seasoned missionaries. Under the guise of scholarship, these groups developed into fully fledged academic institutions that were worthy of recognition on an international level. On the other hand, such scholars were always mistrusted by the Islamists, who suspected them of distortion of the holy texts in order to distract the Muslim community from the true message of the faith. Suspicious of the West's motivation for its interest in the religion and languages of the East, these Islamists have passed down to succeeding generations of Muslims the idea that the ultimate objective of the edicts of St Louis was the westernisation and secularisation of Islam. The goal of the West was nothing less than the infiltration and subjugation of the faith.

Such fundamentalist Islamists think in theocratic terms. They view the recommendations of St Louis as the equivalent of a 'fatwa', or religious edict, and therefore conclude that the Christian community will sooner or later be obliged to implement them in order to satisfy the will of God.[3] In fact, western society is secular, and in modern times would ascribe to these recommendations no more than a historical value. This stands in contrast to the belief of the fundamentalists that everything is subject to God's will. The basic cultural values of the Christians and the Islamists are therefore in diametrical opposition. This has led to a dialogue of the deaf, with misunderstandings and a visceral level of hostility between the world-views of the adherents of Christianity and Islam.

The antagonism between Islam and Christianity goes back to the most distant times. The overall picture, however, is clear enough. From its origins, Islam has startled the world with its vigour and universal ambition. Its irresistible force rolled across the globe: vast territories were seized from the Christians, from the Hindus, from the Sassanids of Persia and the Confucians of Asia. The vigour of its expansion has been an additional factor that has helped to explain why, over the centuries, Islam has attracted hostility on a global scale, especially from the Christian community. In addition, the Christians have stood alone among the defeated nations in seeing the Prophet Muhammad as an impostor, whom they accuse of shamefully plagiarising the message of Jesus Christ.[4]

In more general terms, the West has tended to view Islam as a bogeyman, festooned around with senseless, irrational, feudal and barbaric beliefs. On the other hand, the West also swiftly understood that its adversary was a religious power bloc, determined to achieve the privileged position among the nations of the world it believed was its right. Islam's egregious ambition aroused panic in the Western mind. From the last decade of the 1990s, the struggle between these two civilisations intensified, becoming a clash of cultures that has still the potentiality to become yet more violent in the future if the two sides continue to foment intolerance and mutual rejection. At the same time, inside the Muslim world, a violent confrontation may develop, pitting the fundamentalists against the rationalists, secularists and the adherents of Sufism.

My ambition is that the present study should to make a contribution, no matter how modest, towards the development of dialogue and tolerance between Muslims and the West, and the mitigation of sectarian hatred among the Muslims themselves. At present, however, the explicit and implicit signals sent by each side to the other tend to be more discouraging than not and afford no latitude for the construction of an intercultural dialogue that I would like to describe as global religious diplomacy, an idea I shall develop later. In January 1991, I was in Baghdad where I personally experienced the second Gulf War, in the aftermath of which religious crisis and confusion shook the Arab world. This led me to consider that it would be futile at that time to attempt to bridge the chasm which had opened up between the Muslims and the West. Communication between the two civilisations was virtually severed.

In addition, within the Islamic *umma*, hostility has raged for centuries. There is profound misunderstanding between Sunnis and Shi'ites. But there is also a clash between Salafists and Sufis. Sufis, especially, have often been stigmatised as heretics by both Salafist reformists and orthodox theologians. Their ordeal has not ceased since 922, when the Sufi Al-Hallaj was beheaded in Baghdad for the offence of having pronounced the words, 'I am the truth' (*'Ana ul-Haqq'*). (It should be understood that in Arabic the word 'truth' – *haqq* – can be used only of God.) Though Al-Hallaj's intention was to signify that he had achieved a direct and intimate relationship with God, the Muslim legal establishment, fiercely protective of the Shari'a, condemned this great Sufi as an apostate, meriting the penalty of death. In their view, he was in fact possessed by the Devil, and his objective was the destruction of the basis of the theological order eternally established by the pious ancestors (the *salaf*).

Today, after the events of September 11, 2001 and their political consequences, the Muslim world is again awash with resentment. This has grown out of the wars waged by the West against Iraq, Sudan, Somalia and Afghanistan, as well as the sanctions taken against Libya, the sufferings of the Chechens, and the misery of the Palestinians. Muslims find it hard to understand why it is always Muslim civilians who pay the price for this confrontation. They are aware that there is little concern in the wealthy countries about their fate, and go as far as to harbour the suspicion that the West has an urge to revert to the extremist posture of the medieval crusaders. To counter this real or imagined neo-crusader plot, the ideology of Islamism has quickly taken root in the mind of the Muslim populace.

If the fears of the Muslim masses are not assuaged, especially by an effort to rebuild trust, the Islamist challenge will become a fuse that will ignite the Middle East, followed by Africa, Asia, the Americas, and sooner or later Europe itself. In these circumstances, terrorism and armed conflict will run rife in the years to come. In addition, such methods of waging war as the manufacture of weapons, and especially chemical, biological and nuclear weapons, will be radically rethought in the Muslim world. No longer will there be large-scale arms-manufacturing plants easily targeted by enemy cruise missiles. Instead, such weapons will be produced on a small scale, outside state supervision but providing material usable by suicide bombers. The effects of such weapons, though less far-reaching, would be devastating. Classical western doctrines and concepts aimed at countering weapons of mass destruction will in consequence be outflanked. The events of September 11, 2001 have shown us what can happen. In future, who can predict whether radical Islamists may succeed in carrying small quantities of biological, chemical or radioactive weapons on board kamikaze aircraft? Meanwhile, minority religious ghettos will continue to flourish within the major western cities and may undergo attempts to subdue them by force, which will lead to brutal religious clashes.

Turning to demography, it would be an error, in the first decade of this new millennium, to underestimate the extent of Islam and its influence over the world's peoples. In January 2000, the number of Muslims in the world was estimated at more than a billion and a half,[5] and Islam appears increasingly to be taking root in the West. At the opening of the twenty-first century, it has been claimed that there are between five and six million American Muslims: possibly a larger minority within the country than its five million Jews.[6] (Other estimates, it should be said, put the number of Muslims in the United States lower, at not more than three million.) In France, Islam has overtaken Protestant Christianity. More precisely, French statistics revealed that in 2007 there were between four and five million Muslims in France as against something between 700,000 and 1.7 million Protestants, and 800,000 Jews.[7] In the United Kingdom, Islam presents a demographic challenge to the Roman Catholic Church.[8] The Pakistani and Indian communities are the nucleus of Muslim expansion in Britain, where there are more than 1.5 million Muslims.[9] Wider statistics show the strength of Islam across the world. There are a billion Muslims in Asia, more than 370 million in the Middle East and the Maghreb, and 443 million in Africa, where almost one African in two is a Muslim.[10]

At the same time, there exists the paradoxical phenomenon of the attraction Islam holds for some Christians, despite the overall hostility of the West. European Christians, in search of mystic eastern spirituality such as that offered by Sufism, with its contribution to the inner peace of the individual, have converted in small but significant numbers and have made no secret of their new faith. Another motive that has led some Europeans to convert is their sympathy with young Muslims who are the object of racist attacks. In 2003, it was estimated in an internal intelligence report that between 30,000 and 50,000 French citizens had become official converts to Islam.[11] In 2006, in the United Kingdom, a prominent British Muslim put the number of Muslim converts in Britain at 14,000.[12] In Germany in 2005, according to a government-sponsored Muslim organisation, the total number of converts was also 14,000.[13] In Switzerland, converts were estimated in 2002 at 8,000 out of a total of more than 300,000 resident Muslims, who made up 4 per cent of the country's population.[14] Nevertheless, despite the real attraction towards Islam experienced by some individuals, the vast majority in the West continue to experience profound unease faced by the enigma of Islam.

In western eyes, different aspects of Islam are conflated. Islam is deprecated as an outmoded faith promulgating repressive rules governing personal conduct, but it is also regarded as the vehicle for an aggressive and expansionist policy aimed at dominating the Christian world. Meanwhile, another view is that it is a religious system that oppresses untold millions of women behind the veil, subjecting them to the absurdity of an uncontrollable theological regime. The confusion in western minds arises from the way Islam has been translated and explained by certain western experts, the 'Islamologists'.[15] Prejudice and emotion have characterised the study of the subject. 'Islamology' has also often been confused with 'Orientalism', though these are in reality two distinct fields whose subject matter sometimes overlaps. To be precise, Orientalism is an expression of the intellectual power of the manipulative and dominating West.[16] Meanwhile, westerners find it hard to master Islamology, as its subject matter is elusive. Few Judaeo-Christian intellectuals have succeeded in pursuing to its conclusion the obstacle course that leads to Islam, and the resultant half knowledge of Islam in the West serves to feed the fear and prejudice of westerners towards the Muslim faith.

The subject matter of Islamology, in contrast to Orientalism, is not limited to the Arab world. It also spills over into the African and Asian continents and bubbles up inside Europe itself, for instance in Kosovo, Bosnia and Chechnya. Despite the extent of its geographical range, however, the study of Islam has remained the prerogative of a small handful of scholars, both Muslims and westerners, often linked to the established authorities. For some westerners, Islam still remains obscure and tends to be seen as a shadowy force that threatens humanistic civilisation. Some European intellectuals, despite their intellectual ability, seem bemused and unable to grasp the complexity of the phenomenon of contemporary Islamism, though this stricture does not universally apply. Most remain content to take their impression of Islamism exclusively through the 'prism' of the views of established local and western thinkers. The study of such partial and secondary sources restricts them to the role of passive and powerless observers. This is an unusual predicament for the western mind, which I should point out has not failed to impose its domination in the parallel and equally complex field of Orientalism.

It is clear that political Islamism disconcerts western intellectuals. Confronted with this nebulous adversary, the West has always reacted in an irrational way. Today, the West has apparently opted either to confront the ambitions of political Islam by military means in order either to eradicate it, or infiltrate it and undermine its cultural foundations. The West deludes itself today that it can impose its democratic blueprints, built up over patient centuries of endeavour in western countries, onto an alien religious terrain that is unreceptive to imported ideas and has since the fifteenth century gradually sunk into obscurantism and authoritarianism.

It should never be forgotten, however, that in historical terms Islam, in its earlier days, led the West in the fields of science, the arts and even in the development of democracy. From the seventh century, Muslim power presided over a brilliant civilisation based both on its own original efforts and on the translation of Greek and Latin humanistic texts. Islamic thought became the benchmark of its era. From the eleventh century onwards, Muslim culture was in its turn imitated and translated by the crusading West. This impetus facilitated the later appearance in the old continent of Europe of a glittering artistic, philosophical and scientific renaissance. Even as this was taking place, however, the Muslim world sank into stagnation and declined progressively into a medieval obscurantism. The exercise of power in the Muslim countries, once founded on democratic consultation (*shura*), underwent changes that led to the emergence of authoritarian oligarchies with absolute power. It is impossible for such oligarchies to coexist with civil society in the western style and they can only be sustained by an intrusive and repressive security apparatus. Corruption has sprung up as a way of life in this 'police society', which has become the preferred option of the modern Muslim world. Finally, it must be said that this social model comes equipped, for the sake of form, with complaisant and uncritical political parties, trades unions, media and men of culture.

There are positive and negative aspects of the understanding achieved by western Islamologists. On the basis of observations that are accurate in part but are nevertheless biased, certain Islamologists have tended on the basis of a limited comprehension of the evidence to leap to the conclusion that Islam is unable to adapt itself to modernity and humanistic thought. This false notion has induced the majority of westerners to demonise and spurn the Islamic faith. As a consequence, the image of Muslims has frequently been caricatured and dehumanised. In the view of such western observers, it is in the nature of a Muslim to be corrupt, hypocritical, treacherous and tyrannical to those weaker than himself. Once this attitude has been adopted, the positive qualities associated with Muslim culture and identity are deliberately ignored. The generosity of Muslims, their sense of justice and their magnanimity are brushed aside. Meanwhile, the West's debt to Muslim civilisation in the fields of philosophy, astronomy, medicine and mathematics goes virtually unacknowledged.[17]

At the same time, the Islamic world ought also to recognise the contribution made by certain western Islamologists whose understanding has been sufficient to show the Muslims the nature of their own culture, contributing significantly to the study of authors who, without these western experts, would have been condemned to languish in obscurity. Among these are Ibn Khaldun,[18] the famous Tunisian sociologist, whose reputation was resurrected by W.M. de Slane and Vincent Monteil; Jalaluddin Rumi, translated into English for the first time, by Reynold A. Nicholson, the distinguished British Orientalist;[19] and Al-Hallaj, revealed by the French Catholic and leftist intellectual Louis Massignon.[20] Ernest Renan, despite his excessive and regrettable hostility to the Semitic peoples, both the Arabs and the Jews, undertook a brilliant analysis of the rationalist philosophy of Averroes (Ibn Rushd); and Jacques Berque's French translation of the Qur'an is incomparable. Finally, such scholars as André Miquel, Maxime Rodinson, Bernard Lewis and Eva de Vitray-Meyerovitch have made exceptional studies of the trends of thought in the Muslim world.

Nevertheless, it also remains true that in addition to furnishing a broadly distorted image of the Muslims, western Islamologists have in general led the West to focus on a limited range of historical phenomena. One of these is the emergence of Saudi Wahhabism in the eighteenth century. It should be clarified, however, that the official Wahhabism espoused by the Saudi monarchy inclines towards a quietist posture, while the Wahhabism expounded by certain radical Saudi Imams who have made their presence felt in Afghanistan, in Africa and in Europe is more influenced by radical political ideas. Other focuses for the western Islamologists have included Jamal Ad-Din Al-Afghani's nineteenth-century revitalisation of Islamic thought, and the widespread proselytisation carried out in the twentieth century by Abul Ala Mawdudi in South Asia and Hassan Al-Banna in the Middle East. These phenomena are wrongly seen as the basis of contemporary political Islamism. At the same time, the impact of the liberal rationalists and the medieval Sufi mystics on Muslim society has often been neglected, and even viewed with suspicion.

This little-known area of study, however, is precisely what will be my focus in this present study. I intend to return to the origins of the three principal 'generations' in the history of Islamism, both to outline the differences between them and to underline the similarities in their ideas. I shall attempt to establish that, in parallel to the genealogy of fundamentalist Islam, a rationalist and Sufi school of thought has developed. This is an intellectual current that is both spiritual and tolerant, and includes the most brilliant minds within Islam. The Sufis have striven to disseminate their influence in the Muslim world, though great efforts have been made to eradicate their influence.

In the light of this, my plan will be to divide this book into two principal sections. In the first of these, I shall look at the three generations of fundamentalist Islamism. I shall strive to show that the origins of such ideas hark back to an earlier historical period than is generally accepted. I shall argue, in fact, that the first 'generation' of Islamist thought dates to the seventh century, with

11

the Prophet Muhammad himself. In Medina, the Prophet established not only the bases of the faith but also the earliest Islamic institutions. The theocratic state that Muhammad progressively constructed was, among other things, the product of a rebellion against the injustice, profanity and brutality of the tribal order in the pre-Islamic Arabian Peninsula.

However, it must not be forgotten that the theocracy of the founding phase of Islam had little in common with the two generations of Islamism that were to follow it. The second 'generation', identified with political Islam, was a phenomenon of the thirteenth century and reflected a conservative movement on the part of the Muslims, under the aegis of the unswerving moral rectitude of Ibn Taymiyya. Faced by the collapse of Muslim institutions under the unrelenting onslaught of the Mongols, Ibn Taymiyya's radical ideas triumphed. The religious rigour that later prevailed among the Wahhabis in Saudi Arabia stemmed directly from Ibn Taymiyya's ideas.

The third 'generation' of Islamism made its appearance at the beginning of the twentieth century. It was the direct result of the injustices of colonialism and the maladministration perpetrated by the post-colonial nationalist regimes. This 'generation' of thought, though essentially elitist in nature, presented itself as populist, claiming roots in the masses. It instrumentalised the Islamism of Mawdudi, from the Indian subcontinent, and later that of Egypt's Hassan Al-Banna, the founder of the Muslim Brotherhood, as well as Sayyid Qutb and others. These men exhorted the faithful to revolt against the alienation and devaluation of their personal values imposed by the West. Disciples of these fundamentalist Islamists appeared in due course in the Maghreb, in the shape of Sheikh Abassi Madani and Ali Belhadj in Algeria, as well as Rachid Ghannouchi in Tunisia and Abdessalam Yacine in Morocco. In parallel to these theorists, an 'operational' wing prepared to resort to acts of violence first made its appearance. The principal elements within this were Osama Bin Laden's group, the GIA and the GSPC in Algeria, and more recently Al-Qa'ida in the Maghreb, and Islamic Jihad in Egypt. Within the context of this study of the three 'generations' of theocratic Islam, it should be mentioned that I shall also examine the particular problems that relate to the status of women and the veil. In addition, I shall also look at issues concerned with human rights and problems arising out of the resort to armed conflict.

In the second section of the book, I shall try to show that in parallel to this fundamentalist Islam, whose ideas were particularly exemplified by Ibn Taymiyya, there has always existed another school of thought, liberal, rational, enlightened and tolerant. This flowed from the work of some of the most brilliant Muslim thinkers of the Middle Ages and from the Sufis. Such men included Ibn Rushd (Averroes), Ibn Sina (Avicenna), Al-Khawarizmi, Al-Hallaj, Ibn Al-Arabi and Rumi. Centuries later, Jamal Ad-Din Al-Afghani and Muhammad Abduh followed on from their work. Contemporary thinkers such as Egypt's Abdullah Badawi and Mohammed Al-Jabri in Morocco continue to play their part. It continues to be the only way in which Islam will be able to coexist with the West. Neither orthodox theologians nor Muslim politicians, however, have yet come to terms with these reformers and unconventional mystics whose activities tend to destabilise dogmatic Islam.

I shall also attempt to draw the attention of my readers to a further phenomenon. This is the way in which those Muslim states that have been hostile to the Sufi orders are also those that appear to have been most encroached on by radical Islam. Those Muslim states that have attempted to suppress the Sufi orders, including Egypt, Turkey, Algeria and Tunisia, have given ground significantly to Islamism. At the same time, those countries and regions that have made room for the Sufis within civil society – especially in West Africa, Tanzania and Morocco – have suffered much less, for the time being at least, from religious extremism.

What is original about this research as a whole, however, is not its classification of the Islamist phenomenon into three 'generations'. Nor is it my avoidance of the pitfall that has beset most Islamologists: that of concentrating on the third 'generation' of Islamism, from the thirteenth to the twenty-first centuries. Rather, it is my attempt to carry the investigation further, into the impact in practice of each of the three 'generations', as well as the ideas

13

of the rationalists and the Sufis, on the rights of Muslim women, the veil, the role of the individual within society, the status of minorities (the *dhimmis*) and the laws of war.

Finally, in the third and concluding section of my study, I have tried to give the reader some idea of the possibility that the current tensions between Islam and the West might be diminished, and that trust may even be restored.

1

ISLAM IN THE FIRST GENERATION: MUHAMMAD'S STATE FROM THE ASHES OF PRE-ISLAMIC SOCIETY

In 622, scarcely twelve years after the revelation of the first verses of the Qur'an to Muhammad, the earliest state in Muslim history came into existence in Medina. As some saw it, this state was an island of hope in an Arabian Peninsula riven by anarchy and disorder. This was an era when each group, clan and tribe clung to its own gods. The Arabs worshipped stones, carved rocks and statues, of which the most notorious was the Nabatean deity, a statue known as 'Hubal'. According to Al-Tabari, the pre-Islamic Arabs believed in a plethora of such idols as well as in a single supreme God, though the Muslims later refused to accept that this was the one God of whom Muhammad speaks in the Qur'an.[1] The Ka'aba, Mecca's holy edifice, was already a place of worship before the advent of Islam. The Quraysh, Muhammad's tribe, regarded Hubal as the most important idol situated inside the Ka'aba, and the Ka'aba was dedicated to it, though it was still regarded as inferior to the supreme God. Muhammad's earliest biographers, such as Ibn Ishaq, believed that Hubal was given by the Syrian *'Amaliq* tribe to the pagan merchant 'Amru ibn Luhayy, who 'returned to Mecca with the idol, set it up, and instructed the people to worship it and show it veneration'.[2]

Before Islam, the religion was brutal, society was violent, and morality was not highly regarded. It is said that the custom was to sacrifice children in the curtilage of the god-stones. The tribes of the Peninsula were locked in perpetual warfare, striving to wrest from each other women, flocks, herds and other booty. Their leaders were drawn from an aristocracy of wealthy merchants, whose fortunes were built on the exploitation of secure trade routes in the Red Sea in an era when the wars between Greece and Persia had made the Levant impassable. The upper classes of pre-Islamic Mecca were notorious for their laxness and moral depravity. For example, an inhabitant of Mecca, Abu Gubshan ibn Hulayl, entrusted with responsibility for the care of the Ka'aba, sold the keys to Qusayy ibn Kilab for a common skin of wine.[3] This transaction was indicative of the immorality and corruption that were rife in the pre-Islamic community. At the time, the Arabian Peninsula was untrammelled by the constraints of either organised government or established law. As Francesco Gabrieli remarks: 'They were a pastoral folk ... who pillaged neighbouring and better-founded States, or simply banded together in gangs working on their own account or that of their tribe.'[4]

This was the murky and violent environment in which the Prophet Muhammad lived. Once his status as a Prophet was secure, he determined to put an end to the prevailing state of anarchy and to the paganism that sustained it. His first assault was on Mecca's wealthy slave owners, who were compelled to free their slaves. The slaves, with their pride and their dignity restored, converted in large numbers to Islam, whose great attraction was the offer of equality and the promise of a future in Paradise. Muhammad fundamentally altered the practices of Mecca's ruling class. Specifically, he abruptly halted the situation in which the rich grew richer through their monopoly over trade at the same time as the poor grew poorer, gravitating to the bottom of the social ladder where slavery frequently became their lot. Among these classes, Muhammad found fertile ground in which to sow his new ideas, and his message of spirituality and egalitarianism easily prevailed. Among the first converts to his faith were his wife Khadija and his cousin Waraqa, who had been a Christian.

Over the space of a few years, Muhammad laid down a solid body of doctrine that embodied a highly rigorous ethical code obligatory on all believers on pain of condemnation either on this earth or in the world to come. The scale of punishment was calibrated with stern precision. In contradiction to what has been said by certain Orientalists such as Henri Lammens[5] and Ernest Renan,[6] Islam had no roots in 'superstition and violence': on the contrary, it rejected intolerance, anarchy and belligerence. After a fierce struggle, Islam succeeded in setting itself apart from the arbitrary rule, racial inequality, inquisitorial administration and servility that characterised the Byzantine and Persian regimes that at the time occupied the lands on what would become the frontiers of the Islamic world. Unfortunately, some Islamologists hostile to the Islamic faith have misrepresented the Prophet Muhammad's message, exaggerating the mistrust and antagonism between Muslims and other faiths. In reality, the Prophet's message did not seek either to challenge or undermine Christianity or Judaism, either at the time of the first generation of Islam in Medina or in subsequent ages. Its goal was the reform of the social and religious status quo, and this was the true reason for its intense conflict with the empires that bordered on Islam's lands. By the time of the Prophet's death in 632, Islam had already expanded impressively. As Francesco Gabrieli remarks, 'Muhammad's religion triumphed and would soon become a vast empire that extended from western Africa to the Indies. Over a space of centuries, Islam shaped the visage of the Arab world and exercised its influence far beyond.'[7]

In the light of this achievement, one question urgently demands to be answered: namely, what was it that drove a group of bedouin tribesmen to burst out of their arid Arabian deserts and to transform half of the ancient known world, from Jakarta to the fertile lands of France? The answer to this question will be the subject of this study. Two elements that shook the world can be pointed to from the outset, however. These are, first, Muhammad's powerful advocacy of a tolerant Islam, and second, the nature of Islam's Holy Book, the Qur'an.

THE 'SPIRITUAL ORPHAN' AND HIS 114 SERMONS THAT CHANGED THE WORLD: THE ORIGIN AND UNCHANGING ESSENCE OF THE QUR'AN

The 'Spiritual Orphan' to whom I refer is none other than Muhammad, a Prophet innocent of all suggestion of worldly motivation. Muhammad derived his legitimacy from two sources. The first of these was the Qur'an, which began to be revealed to him in 610 by the Angel Gabriel in a cave in the neighbourhood of Mecca, to which Muhammad had retired to meditate. Second, there was also the example set by his own ethical and moral behaviour, in the context of a bedouin society dominated by pillage and enslavement. His own tribe, the Quraysh, drove Muhammad out of Mecca, whereupon he fled to Medina, accompanied by a number of companions (*ansar*), establishing there a theocratic state of which he was the unchallenged leader.

Within this nascent Islamic State, Muhammad not only made the law, in his capacity as an infallible Prophet, but also offered practical counsel on the basis of his own fallible humanity. He never failed to draw the distinction between his prophetic vocation and his comportment as a human being, which was susceptible to error. It should be recalled that, as with the other faiths of its era, divine injunction within Islam was seen as taking constant precedence over temporal regulations imposed by human agency. Such divine laws seemed customarily to be conveyed to the faithful through the intermediary of a Prophet, expressly chosen by God as a messenger between Him and his servants. Each such Prophet, be it Moses, Jesus or Muhammad, was distinguished by his ability to give signs of his prophethood, or through visible miracles. Each 'Messenger' was also distinguished by having been, previous to his revelation, a good man, innocent, honest and just.[8]

In the case of Muhammad, as we have seen, the first revelations of the Qur'an were transmitted to him in 610 in Mecca. He continued to receive such messages over a period of 20 years, particularly at his place of exile in Medina, to which he had migrated after the persecution to which his own tribe, the Quraysh, subjected him. His peers took him to task for having shaken the foundations of the tribal social order, and even made a bid to induce him to change the direction of his preaching towards support of the traditional hierarchy. Muhammad, however, resisted all such blandishments, and his personal campaign to overturn the undesirable order of his day through his teaching ceased only with his death in 632. His message, as a whole, is what constitutes the Holy Book of Islam, known as the Qur'an. The extraordinary revelations made to Muhammad were later collected and presented to the Islamic community in their present form by the third Caliph, Othman, who reigned from 644 to 656.

While it is possible to read the Qur'an in a simplistic and literal way, it also harbours within it esoteric meanings that only the Sufi mystics and the theologians, known as the *ulema*, are able to discern.[9] The primary significance of the Qur'anic message, however, is that all human beings are seen as equal before God. There is no distinction between an Arab and a foreigner of some other ethnic origin, except in their degree of belief. To embrace Islam, all that is necessary is to pronounce, with conviction, the following verse: 'There is no God but God, and Muhammad is the Prophet of God.' It is also true, in contradiction to the general view, that only a small proportion of the Qur'an is of a juridical nature. In fact, its prescriptions and injunctions are mainly of a moral or ethical kind.[10]

The Qur'an is made up of 114 sections known as Suras, each of which is made up of a number of verses (*ayat*). After the initial Fatiha, whose seven verses make up the basic prayer of Islam, the other Suras are arranged in order of decreasing length. The first is *Al-Baqara* (The Cow), which occupies some 60 pages of text in the conventional edition, containing 286 verses, and concludes with *An-Nas* (The People), which occupies a solitary paragraph, six verses long. The 114 Suras are not transcribed logically in the chronological order of their revelation to Muhammad. Instead, they have simply been compiled according to their length into the Holy Qur'an as we know it, some thousand pages long, which Muslims attempt to learn by heart. The Qur'an is the core of the Muslim faith and guides Muslims in their social and spiritual life, as also in their everyday personal behaviour.

An idea of the power of the Qur'an can be gathered from some of its shorter Suras, many revealed early in Muhammad's Prophethood, which are strongly rhythmic and full of divine poetic bravura. Others are 'in a more placid and contemplative style, recounting moral tales from ancient Arabia or Biblical episodes',[11] while others again partake of symbolic mysticism and up to the present day remain as coded documents which no-one has so far deciphered. For instance, the two symbolic letters of the Arab alphabet placed before certain Suras – 'Ha Mim' – remain mysterious. Some of the longer Suras, on the other hand, revealed as Muhammad constructed his state at Medina, are replete with detailed injunctions to the Muslims as to how to live together. It should also be understood that no translation of any part of the Qur'an into another language can properly convey 'the cadenced balance of the phrases, the plethora of rhymes, the pattern of long and short syllables which enchants all who hear it recited. It is precisely this that makes God's word inimitable and unforgettable.'[12] From this springs the difficulty of access for non-Arabist researchers and readers.

To gain an idea of the power of the Qur'an's language, as well as its rhythm and religious import, I shall quote here the prayers embodied in Sura 81 (The Coiling Up) and in Sura 93 (The Forenoon). The first says:

> When the Sun shall be coiled up;
> And when the stars shall be scattered about;
> And when the mountains shall be set in motion;
> And when the camels in calf shall be discarded;
> And when the beasts shall be corralled;
> And when the seas shall rise mightily;
> And when souls shall be paired off;
> And when the buried infant shall be asked:
> 'For what sin was she killed?'
> And when the scrolls shall be unrolled;
> And when Hell shall be stoked;
> And when Paradise shall be brought near:
> Then each soul shall know what it had brought forth.

The second Sura, which is moving and was more personal to the Prophet, reads as follows:

> By the forenoon;
> And the night when it falls calmly,

Your Lord did not forsake you or scorn you.
Surely, the last day is better for you than the First,
Your Lord shall give you of his bounty; and so you shall be
    well-pleased,
Did he not find you an orphan and then gave you refuge?
Did he not find you in error and then guided you?
And find you in need and then enriched you?

Other Suras throw light on contemporary political and social conditions and set out the penalties for transgression of the Qur'an's instructions, while others, as do also the Bible and the Torah, reflect the joys of Paradise that await the obedient faithful and the infernal damnation reserved for those who disobey. As an example I quote part of Sura 87, The Most High:

Glorify the name of thy Lord, the Most High;
Who created and fashioned well;
And who fore-ordained and guided rightly . . .;
We shall make you recite; so you will not forget;
Except what God wishes . . .;
So remind, if the reminder will avail.
He who fears shall remember;
And the most wretched shall not;
He who shall roast in the Great Fire,
Then he shall neither die therein nor live.

Finally, Sura III, entitled The Fibre, commemorates the story of Muhammad's uncle Abu Lahab, a rich inhabitant of Mecca who refused to convert to Islam. It declares:

Perish the hands of Abu Lahab, and may he perish too,
Neither his wealth nor what he has earned will avail him
    anything.
He will roast in the flaming fire,
And his wife will be a carrier of firewood,
She shall have a rope of fibre around her neck.[13]

Islam permits no change, no matter how minor, in the verses of the Qur'an as they were revealed to the Prophet Muhammad. The Word of God has remained unchanged since the seventh century. The text of the Qur'an, in contrast to the Bible and the Torah, has never been revised in any way. In addition, only the text itself can be accepted as a basic source of the Shari'a (Islamic law), together with the consensus, or *ijmaa*, of the Muslim community regarding the Sunna: the record of the Prophet's deeds and words, which is now codified and regarded as an acceptable secondary source. In the Prophet's lifetime, however, only the Qur'an was set down in writing, and the Sunna remained unwritten. As Malek Bennabi explains, 'In his lifetime the Prophet vigorously forbade his Companions to write down his words, so that there should be no confusion between such words and the revealed verses. There was to be no confusion between the Tradition and the Qur'an.'[14] Only after the Prophet's death was the Sunna defined in writing in the 'traditions' (Hadith), which then became the supplementary source of Islamic law, after the Qur'an.

The Sunna is followed by the majority of Muslims throughout the world, with the exception of the Shi'ites, the Ismailis, the Syrian Alawis and the Alevis in Turkey, and some other Muslim minorities. All Muslims, however, accord primacy to the Qur'an, whatever their sect. The fact that it has remained untouched from the days of its seventh-century revelation to Muhammad, means that it is difficult to read for non-Muslims who come to it with a western rationalist mentality. On the phenomenon of the unchanging nature of the text of the Qur'an, Bennabi comments:

> The Qur'an has been handed down from generation to generation in a single and unique form known from Morocco to the frontiers of Manchuria. It is therefore the only religious text that in our time stands unchallenged in its authenticity. In regard to the Qur'an, there are no critical issues relating to its historicity, either in relation to its origins or the form it takes.[15]

This fundamental doctrine may be seen as the 'culmination of the current of monotheistic thought'.[16] It may also be viewed as a divine message rigidly fixed for many centuries. The logical consequence of the unchanging nature of the Qur'an is to differentiate Islamic scripture entirely from the texts of Judaism and Christianity. These have been revised over time, while the Qur'an has remained immutable. Its nature and its history are complex, and only a handful of qualified theologians at certain Islamic universities regard themselves as able to read it correctly, though it must be said their interpretations often differ from each other. In addition, without wishing unduly to complicate the issue, it should be said that, seen from certain aspects, the Qur'an carries mystic and philosophical messages that lie within the grasp of only the rationalist philosophers and the mystic Sufis.

In practice, two concepts of Islam have existed in parallel, coexisting to a greater or lesser degree. On the one hand, there is an official and consensual Islam, agreed upon by the theologians. On the other hand, there also exists a faith shared by the Sufi philosophers, such as the schools of Ibn Al-Arabi and Rumi, with the unwavering support of the international networks of mystic Sufi orders, which lie beyond the control of official authority. In fact, while the text of the Qur'an has been unmodified, it would be incorrect to say that the interpretation of the Qur'an has remained unaltered since the seventh century. After the Prophet's death, the divisions that appeared within Muslim society in fact hastened the appearance of various rationalist tendencies, as well as the Sufi mystics, who have interpreted the Qur'an in an adventurous and liberal manner. This was perhaps more appropriate to a new, multicultural and tolerant Islamic world, where the Arabs exercised relatively little control.

AFTER THE DEATH OF MUHAMMAD:
AN 'UMMA' IN CONSTANT TURMOIL

In Muhammad's lifetime, the Islamic community (the *umma*) was a single entity, held together by a juridical and moral system unambiguously embodied in the authority of the Prophet. Once the Prophet had passed on, however, the Muslims felt themselves to be disunited and relationships within the community began to deteriorate. There were many reasons for this inter-Islamic malaise, which has persisted down to our own era. First, there was the profound and ongoing crisis over the succession to the Caliphate, followed by the emergence of a deep cleavage within the *umma*, and by differences in the interpretation of Islamic dogma.

THE CLASH BETWEEN THE CALIPHS, AND THE FRAGMENTATION OF ISLAM

The first three Caliphs to succeed Muhammad after 632 were not 'Messengers', nor were they God's representatives on earth.[17] Their legitimacy as successors was called into question by many Muslims, as well as by the Prophet's own immediate family, in the shape of Ali, the fourth Caliph and the cousin and son-in-law of the Prophet, Ali's wife Fatima, Muhammad's daughter, and Aisha, the Prophet's favourite wife. It should be said here that the role played by the Caliphs has to some extent been exaggerated by Islamic tradition. In reality, they were guardians of the law and spiritual guides. The Caliph was the supreme 'Imam', but they had no privileged channel to God and could claim no right to express God's will on earth. Their role as guardians of the divine law did not empower them to formulate the law, as had sometimes been the case with Christian kings and emperors. Despite the exemplary piety they displayed, the early Caliphs faced constant challenges over the way in which they were chosen. Many fell victim to the murky stratagems of power and suffered assassination by members of their own community. For example, Abu Bakr, who reigned from 632 to 634, died in unexplained circumstances, and his successor Omar Ibn Al-Khattab (634–644) was murdered at a mosque in Medina after an internecine conspiracy. Othman (644–656) was accused of religious deviation and of nepotism towards his own Ummayad clan. He fell victim to a plot supposedly mounted by Aisha and Ali and was assassinated in his own palace.[18]

Even the Caliph Ali (656–661), who was greatly venerated in his capacity as the son-in-law and cousin of Muhammad, was obliged to fight against Aisha and Mu'awiya, then the governor of Syria, as these sought to establish the Ummayad Caliphate. Ali fell victim to a stratagem by Mu'awiya at the battle of Siffin in 657, losing both his power and the backing of an important faction of his erstwhile faithful supporters, who became the Kharijites. His enemies later ensured that he suffered a violent death. He was assassinated in 661 and was buried at Najaf, in modern-day Iraq, which has become a leading destination of Shi'ite pilgrimage. This is also true of Kerbala, where Hussein, Ali's son and the grandson of Muhammad, was buried after he was beheaded in 680. Hussein's death confirmed the split between the partisans of Ali, known as the Shi'ites, and the Sunni Muslims, who already exercised the real power over the vast Arab empire through the Umayyad Caliphate.[19] The Shi'ites are today dispersed throughout the Muslim world and are the majority in Iran. They believe the Caliphate should be hereditary. In other words, they maintain that Ali and his descendants are the sole true successors to the Prophet Muhammad.

At the time, however, pragmatism and the spirit of reconciliation held sway, and the majority of the Sunnis took the side of Mu'awiya, who was proclaimed Caliph in Damascus in 660. Though many Muslims gave their hearts and their prayers in secret to Ali, their swords and their worldly interests were on the side of Mu'awiya and the Umayyad Caliphate. Mu'awiya kept to the rules of bedouin warfare and distributed to his people the plunder amassed in the conquests outside the confines of Arabia. The Ummayad dynasty, from its seat in Damascus, ruled over the Muslim world from 660 to 750.[20] In the course of the eighth century, all the members of the dynasty except for Abd Al-Rahman met their deaths at the hands of members of the Abbasid clan, who were descended from Muhammad's uncle. In the reign of Abu Jaafar Al-Mansur, the Abbasids moved the capital to Baghdad, where it remained from 750 to 1258.[21] However, Abd Al-Rahman, the only Ummayad who had escaped, established an Umayyad Caliphate in Spain, which endured from 756 to 1031, with its capital in the Spanish city of Cordova.[22] The fate of the powerful Abbasid dynasty was itself sealed when in 1258 the Mongol invasion resulted in the brutal massacre of virtually all the Abbasids together with much of the population of Baghdad. The Mongol chieftain Hulagu was superstitious as well as savage. He feared that the earth itself might revolt in the shape of earthquakes, were it to be sullied by the 'sacred' blood of the Abbasid Caliph. A subterfuge was suggested to him to dispose of his illustrious prisoner. The Caliph Al-Musta'sim was rolled up in a carpet, and Hulagu's men trampled him until he died, without his blood touching the earth.

Despite the death of the Caliph, however, the institution of the Caliphate survived. In 1261, it was re-established in Egypt, where the Mamluk Sultan Baibars elevated the last survivor of the Abbasid dynasty to the rank of Caliph. In 1517, the Mamluks themselves were conquered and their dynasty toppled by the Turco-Ottoman Sultan Selim. Selim brought the last Abbasid Sultan, Mutawakkil, to Istanbul, where he was obliged to renounce the Caliphate in favour of the Ottoman ruler. After the Turkish conquest of Egypt, the Caliphate thus became an appanage of the Turkish Sultan. This disposition did not achieve international recognition until the Russo-Ottoman treaty of 1774. Thereafter the Caliphate remained in Turkish hands until March 1924, when it was finally suppressed by Turkey's new ruler, Kemal Ataturk, and Turkey's new Grand National Assembly.[23] A fact seldom mentioned is that the Hashemite Sherif Hussein of Mecca, the great-great-grandfather of Jordan's present King Abdullah II, then immediately laid claim to the Caliphate.[24] Hussein was a direct descendant of the Prophet Muhammad and had declared himself King of the Hejaz, in which lay the Holy Places of Islam, Mecca and Medina. Soon afterwards, however, Hussein was obliged to abandon his claim to this part of the Arabian Peninsula in favour of Ibn Saud's dynasty, backed by the Wahhabis. Hussein fled to Aqaba in October 1924. Nevertheless, the Caliphate, whose assumption by the Turks in 1517 was of dubious validity, had at last returned to its legitimate incumbents, the descendants of the Prophet. Henceforth, it fell to them alone to determine the fate of this much-contested institution.

THE CASE FOR A SUPREME RELIGIOUS COUNCIL AND
THE CONTROL OF UNAUTHORISED FATWAS

The question of whether there is a case for the restoration of the Caliphate in the modern Muslim world is highly controversial. In the view of some, and especially of the Islamists, the faith has always been identified with the State, and the proof of the necessity of the Caliphate is found in Sura 4 of the Qur'an (The Women), verses 59 and 83. In the words of verse 59:

Oh believers, obey God and obey the Messenger and those in authority among you.

Similarly in verse 83:

And when a matter of security or fear reaches them, they broadcast it; but had they referred it to the Messenger or the people in authority among them, those of them who investigate it would comprehend it.[25]

In addition, in a Hadith reported by Abu Hureira the Prophet Muhammad said:

... as to Prophets who may come after me, there will be none, but there will be Caliphs, and they will be numerous.[26]

A further issue is that in the various Muslim States that have succeeded each other since the time of the Prophet Muhammad, Islam has always been an essential element within the State. Bernard Lewis made the point succinctly when he wrote, 'Within Islam, God is Caesar.' On this basis, the partisans of the Caliphate have taken the view that it is imperative to re-establish the institution and to give the Islamic nation (the *umma*) a leader capable of defending it, and of leading it in the correct path. In the judgement of others, however, and especially the secularists, 'the Caliphate has no real basis in the fundamental sources of the Islamic faith [the Qur'an, the Sunna, and the communal consensus known as the *ijmaa*]'.[27] On this view, the Caliphate is simply a temporal monarchy maintained by force, and finds no justification in the founding principles of Islam or in the practice of the Prophet. It was imposed, in fact by violence. In other words, it is argued that the role of the Prophet was purely religious, pertaining to *din* (religion) and not to *dawla* (the state).

It should also be pointed out that the unilateral suppression of the Caliphate by Ataturk, seen from the Islamic point of view, was illegitimate, since it was justified by no recognised theologian nor by any fatwa binding on a Muslim State, however marginal. According to Islamic law, Ataturk had no juridical competence to take such an action without the support of a council of *ulema* representing the principal schools of Islamic thought. Ataturk's move caused a kind of paralysis within the Muslim world, and the vacuum created exacerbated existing tensions within the Muslim community, within which partisans and opponents of the Caliphate have since constantly clashed. Since 1924, furthermore, no proposal has been made to the Muslim community that might serve as an alternative to the Caliphate. The lack of an ultimate moral authority has split the Muslim world, whose unity was already fragile. The most regrettable consequence of this fragmentation has been the emergence of Islamic pseudo-States ruled by warlords (styling themselves 'Emirs') who rule through the pronouncement of unauthorised fatwas. These 'Emirs' are well aware that they are not qualified to utter fatwas, but claim that circumstances require them to do so, since they have no recognised Imams to whom they can turn.

As an example of the regrettable consequences of this situation, it is well established that the rules of Islamic humanitarian law forbid attacks on civilians. In 1999, even some of the leaders of the Algerian GIA for a time acknowledged this principle, after the Islamist Sheikh Nasiruddine El-Albani, of Albanian origin, pronounced a fatwa declaring the GIA's operations to be inconsistent with the Shari'a. In his fatwa, entirely motivated by Muslim law, he affirmed the Islamic principles that forbid the deaths of civilians and prohibit Muslims from killing each other. However, Sheikh El-Albani died later that year and the killing of civilians resumed in Algeria with even greater intensity. These atrocities were once again allegedly justified by unauthorised fatwas that displayed the ignorance of humanitarian Islamic law of those who originated them. Even worse, such unauthorised fatwas began to spread through the Muslim world. Day by day, they became ever more repressive, illogical and illegal.

This absence of any universal spiritual authority, in effect a total void, would in all likelihood not have come into being had there been within the Muslim community a ruling body made up of superior Imams that could have played the part of a Caliphate. To gain credibility, such a body, which should have a territorial base within some country to be selected, would need to represent all the schools within Islam, including Shi'ism, Kharijism, Islamism and the rest. The body should be elected by a college drawn half from Imams representing the 57 States which are members of the Organisation of the Islamic Conference, and half from Imams who officiate in recognised mosques in Europe, the Americas, Africa, Asia and Oceania. Each member of the governing body should serve as its President in rotation, for a two-year term. This 'Supreme Imamate' would not interfere in the sovereignty of States. However, it would serve as an ultimate moral and spiritual authority for the Muslims of the whole world, in a manner similar to the Vatican or the Protestant governing bodies that serve as guides for Christian communities around the world. A council of qualified Muftis would assist the supreme Imam to formulate fatwas in the light of Muslim law. He should also have available to him specialist departments of history, anthropology and philosophy, as well as units dedicated to the protection of minority rights and human rights in general. In addition he should maintain archives, a central library and a scholarly translation service on the lines of the 'House of Wisdom' set up by the Abbasid Caliph Abdallah Al-Ma'mun (813–833).

Despite the urgency of the need now felt, however, the issue of a Caliphate or Supreme Imamate continues to be a taboo subject in Muslim countries, and no Islamic conference has ever discussed it. The subject arouses passions and divides Muslims into two factions. On the one hand there are those who back the concept of a Caliphate in the full sense of the term which would manage religious affairs within the Muslim States according to the Shari'a. On the other hand, there are those who oppose the institution of such a Supreme Imamate, regarding it as an institution whose theocratic nature would potentially permit religious interference in the private lives of citizens. In practice, the choice has never been offered to Muslims. Instead, the question continues to be avoided, at a time when for practical reasons the need is increasingly felt for a symbolic moral authority separate from the power of the State. Nothing will be achieved by deferring the problem, which will only recur with greater intensity in the decades to come. The time has therefore come to consider the modalities of a legal status for an independent and symbolic 'Caliphate', democratically elected, whose minuscule sovereign territory, like the Vatican, would not exceed the size of a major university. Meanwhile, the realities of the Islamic world continue to cause concern. It presents the image of an *umma* which, from the days of the first Ummayad Caliph up to modern times, has known nothing but internal struggles, rivalries and regional interests.

'MY *UMMA* SHALL BE DIVIDED INTO SEVENTY-THREE GROUPS'

After the demise of the Prophet, theological consensus among the Muslims was short-lived. Muhammad himself foresaw the fragmentation of Islam and the potential for internal conflict when he said that after his death the Islamic *umma* would split into '73 factions' (*firka*). At the outset, virtually all adhered to the orthodox Sunni traditions. In other words, they followed to the letter the two principal sources of the Shari'a, the Qur'an and the 'Hadith' – the record of Muhammad's deeds and words. The Sunni tradition also refers to the views of the four 'rightly guided' Caliphs: Abu Bakr, Omar Ibn Al-Khattab, Othman and Ali. After the defeat of Ali, however, religious splits of the most serious kind took place, and a number of major schools of thought made their appearance.

The Kharijites
Literally, those who leave, i.e. the secessionists. These Muslim zealots rejected both the authority of the Ummayads and of Ali,

whom they castigated for his failure to stand up against the opposition to him. The Kharijites, who followed the Ibadi rite,[28] favoured the selection of the Caliph on personal merit. They flourished in the Maghreb, and particularly in Algeria, where Abd Al-Rahman Ibn Rustam established the Kingdom of Tahert in 761. The dynasty was finally expelled from Tahert in 909. Kharijites are found today in M'Zab (in Algeria), on the Tunisian island of Djerba, in Oman and on the Swahili coasts of Zanzibar.

The Shi'ites (The Partisans of Ali)

This is a major school of spiritual doctrine distinct from Sunni orthodoxy. Like the Sufis, the Shi'ites attempt to discover not merely the literal sense of the Qur'an but also its hidden spiritual meaning. They also have the additional belief that the succession to Muhammad should go to a recognised member of his immediate family. They gave their supreme leader the title of Imam, rather than Caliph, as the Sunnis do. The Shi'ite movement is for the most part 'Twelver', recognising Twelve Imams, beginning with Ali. The final Imam is regarded as still alive but is 'occulted'. It is believed he 'will return at the end of time as the Mahdi ... to bring justice to the world.'[29] It is often wrongly supposed that Shi'ism is confined to Iran alone. In fact its adherents are to be found in many Muslim countries, including Iraq, Syria, Lebanon, Pakistan and the Gulf States, as well as India. In addition, a not inconsiderable number of Sunnis convert to Shi'ism in order to benefit from the better position it accords to women, especially in the matter of inheritance. Within Shi'ism there are various sub-groups, including the Ismailis, the Druzes and the Alawis.

The Ismailis

The Ismailis give credence only to the first seven Imams, and are therefore known as 'Seveners'. This religious group originated as the result of a clash over the succession, which occurred after the death of the sixth Imam, Ja'far Al-Sadiq, who wanted to disinherit his elder son Ismail in favour of his second son Musa. Ismail, however, established his own schismatic faction and attracted followers spread throughout Persia, Iraq and Syria.[30] The movement has historical roots which go back to the eighth century. In the late eleventh century it was revitalised by the chieftain of the so-called *hashashin*, Hassan Ibn Sabah, who was dubbed 'The Old Man of the Mountain' because of his fortress on the mountain of Alamut in north-western Persia. From this vertiginous stronghold he held undivided sway over his followers in the mountains of Persia as well as the territories of Syria and Lebanon.[31] The *hashashin* practised a kind of mystical Shi'ism, and used terrorism as an effective weapon against the Sunni religious establishment and even against the secular rulers. Today, the spiritual guide of the Ismailis is the Aga Khan, whose family has a reputation for its intellectual and financial contributions to humanitarian causes and world peace. The Ismaili humanist network is found around the globe, especially in Europe, Central Asia and East Africa. Up to 5 per cent of the Pakistani Shi'ite population are Ismailis.[32]

The Druzes

The Druzes are also an offshoot of Ismailism. They take their name from Al-Darazi, who had spiritual links with Al-Hakim, the Shi'ite Fatimid Caliph. According to the Druzes, this Caliph was also a divine embodiment. He was 'occulted' in Cairo in 1021 and is supposed to return at the end of days.[33] In modern times, the Druze community lives almost entirely in the mountainous regions of Lebanon and Syria. In Lebanon, under the leadership of Walid Jumblatt, they have played an important role in the attempt to return to normality in that country, wracked by years of civil war and presently in a state of uneasy tension.

The Alawis

The Alawis are also part of the Shi'ite community. Their centre of population is the Syrian city of Latakia. They make up a minority of 12 per cent of Syria's 19.5 million people (according to a July 2007 estimate), of whom 74 per cent are Sunni.[34] Historically, the Alawis have long been persecuted as a sect that allegedly deifies Ali.[35] In 1970, the Alawis came to be the ruling group in Syria, when Hafez Al-Assad came to power at the head of the Baath Party. Assad's son, Bashar Al-Assad, continues to hold power. The

Sunni majority, which includes the sophisticated urban elite, represents a challenge to Alawi supremacy. The Alawis are more liberal than Syria's Sunnis in terms of their attitude to women, who may go unveiled. In the political sphere, the Alawis tend to ally themselves with other Shi'ite groups, for instance the ruling elite of Iran and Lebanese Hizbollah.

The Zaidis
Mention should finally be made of the Zaidis of Yemen. This group, separate from the others, recognises only five Imams. In contemporary Yemen, the Zaidis became popular because of their opposition to the regime in Sana'a under their spiritual leader Al-Houti, who was eventually killed by the Yemeni armed forces. The Al-Houti family continues to be opposed to the Yemeni regime.

THE DIVISION BETWEEN SUNNIS AND SHI'ITES OVER ISLAMIC DOCTRINE

Uniformity within Islam has been an equally elusive goal within the majority Sunni confession. Sunnis recognise different versions of the Shari'a, based on differing interpretations of the sacred texts. These variations have a strong geographical component, depending on whether the Muslim community in question is that of Turkey, Egypt, Indonesia or the Maghreb. The Shari'a was in practice adapted to local exigencies arising from the daily circumstances of the Muslim community, with the result that in due course four renowned jurists formalised the four principal Sunni schools of jurisprudence, each known as a *madhhab*.[36] These four jurists were as follows:

Abu Hanifa Al-Numan Ibn Thabit (699–767)
Abu Hanifa founded the oldest school of jurisprudence, known as the Hanafi school. It places the accent on human values and the protection of the vulnerable. Its followers are found in India and Pakistan, Central Asia, in Turkey, in China and south-east Asia, and in the Muslim republics that were formerly part of the Soviet Union.

Malik Ibn Abbas Al-Asbahi (713–795)

This jurist founded the Maliki school, which emphasises both individual opinion and the public interest. This is the *madhhab* followed by the inhabitants of North Africa and West Africa, as well as to some extent in Sudan and Upper Egypt, together with Kuwait and Bahrain.

Muhammad Ibn Idris Al-Shafi'i (767–820)

The Shafi'i school was established by Muhammad Ibn Idris Al-Shafi'i, who made an attempt to adapt some of the rules of Islamic law to contemporary circumstances. This school is present in Lower Egypt, Iraq, Palestine, Lebanon, Yemen, Indonesia and East Africa.

Ahmed Ibn Hanbal (780–855)

Ibn Hanbal founded the most austere school of jurisprudence. The Hanbali school's application of the Islamic Shari'a is the most rigorous of the four. This was the school which inspired Ibn Taymiyya (1263–1326), the founding father of Islamism down the ages, and of the Wahhabism of Saudi Arabia. In addition to Saudi Arabia, it has its adherents in Lebanon and Syria, and is individually followed by small groups of the faithful in the former Soviet Islamic Republics and in Chechnya.

These legal schools saw the light of day in the eighth century only after a long period of indecision, but succeeded in settling the difficulties experienced by Muslims in the domain of personal law, covering such matters as marriage, divorce and inheritance. Though they adapted themselves to local conditions, often influenced by local pre-Islamic practices, the establishment of the schools of law led to an increasing rigidity in Islamic teaching which expressed itself in restrictions on the freedom of thought.[37] In the end, the Muslim community came to accept without question the various exegeses offered by the four schools of jurisprudence. Perhaps it was no bad thing that lethargy and religious conformism were soon called into question by the free thinkers of the 'Mu'tazilite' movement, promoted by the Abbasid Caliph Al-Ma'mun, who reigned from 813 to 833. This enlightened Caliph made no secret of his interest in Persian culture. His personal inclination was to reject dogmatism, and he permitted the rationalist Mu'tazilite philosophers and the ascetic Sufis to undermine Ibn Hanbal's rigorous interpretations. It should be noted, however, that in due course Hanbali doctrine was adopted to the letter by such redoubtable Islamist thinkers as Ibn Taymiyya and Abd Al-Wahhab (the founder of Wahhabism).

CONCLUSIONS: THE FIRST GENERATION

In relation to Muhammad's original polity, it is significant that, before the advent of Islam, State authority did not exist in Medina and Mecca, or was at least in a chaotic condition. Islam invented the State, and established it in accordance with the rules of conduct and doctrines established by the Prophet. It was structured on the foundation of a strict religious hierarchy that was also based on consensus. There could be no legitimate leader without the implicit consent of the body of the faithful. The foundation stone of the first Muslim state was the principle that Islam is both religion and State (*Al islam din wa dawla*). These two dimensions are, in the eyes of the Islamists, inextricably linked. As Muhammad Talbi has sagely observed, 'In Mecca as well as in Medina, Caesar held no sway. There was no State, therefore there was nothing that was properly to be rendered unto him.'[38] The historian William Zartmann has commented:

> Up to this point, the argument had reflected a political thought based on divine revelation and intended to limit human excesses and put in place a more equitable system of socio-political relationships. All political philosophy based on religion has this function. But in Islam, where there was no distinction between God and Caesar, and where society, politics and even economics formed a religious whole, it became yet further accentuated. However, there are, by the same token, aspects of political thought where human behaviour is explained or justified in religious terms.[39]

This notion of the Muslim State, guided by divine laws based on the Qur'an and the Hadith, shaped the course of the Muslim institutions that came into existence after the Prophet's death. On this interpretation, the succeeding Caliphs were no more than simple mechanisms for the transmission of the divine sources. In practice, no separation of Mosque and State seemed ever to emerge under the Caliphs, up to the abolition of the Caliphate in 1924. In the words of René Kalinsky:

> ... as Muhammad held both the supreme Imamate of the community and the position of Head of State, it was not surprising that the Caliph, as his successor, also wielded countervailing power in both the religious and the political spheres. However, this absolute power had the drawback that it was transferable. The absence of hierarchy of all kinds positively encouraged . . . attempts to seize power at the very heart of the community. The Caliph was obliged to make a stronger show of power than was strictly necessary, to fend off the insurgence of Mahdist movements, impelled to rebel by the seductive prospect of power.[40]

Relations between the Ottoman Turks and Arab Muslims were characterised by mutual dislike and mistrust. While the Turks were in charge of the *umma*, the liberalism and dubious morals of their leaders led to a hardening of rigorous Arab attitudes, which brought in its train a return to fundamental Islamic values. The decadence and the racism of the Ottomans only served to encourage the radical Arab Wahhabism that took its inspiration from Ibn Taymiyya. The further excesses of Kemalism in Turkey up to 1924 and the suppression of the Caliphate, further frustrated the Arabs and nourished their demands for a return to their religious identity.

Relationships between Sunni Muslims and Shi'ites have always been anomalous. In practice, it has always verged on the taboo to discuss the Sunni view of Shi'ism and vice versa. Consequently, the myths accepted on both sides prevail. Sunni culture, for instance, in contrast with that of the Shi'ites, passes over in silence the family intrigues of the Prophet Muhammad's companions. No one will mention, for example, that Aisha, the Prophet's wife, detested the Shi'ite branch of the Prophet's family, made up of his daughter Fatima and his son-in-law Ali. Neither will attention be drawn to the apparent dislike of Abu Bakr, the future Caliph, for Fatima, from whom he took an inheritance left to her by Muhammad. Nor will it be mentioned that after Muhammad's death the future Caliph Omar is supposed to have attacked Fatima's house, with the result that she lost a child, named Muhsin, as the result of the wounds she had received. Contradictory stories abound relating to the five close members of the Prophet's family known as the 'Ahl Al-Bayt' (People of the House): Muhammad himself, his daughter Fatima, his son-in-law Ali and his two grandsons, Hassan and Hussein.[41] Depending on whether the stories are told by Shi'ites or by Sunnis, the Ahl Al-Bayt are either canonised or cut down to size.

All in all, the Muslim world is not monolithic. It brings together human societies which hold very different religious, moral and ethical values, within which, however, it is today the most radical factions that claim to speak for the silent and peaceful majority. The mistake of the West, shared with most Sunni clerics, is to approach Islam with simplistic ideas, even though it is potentially heterogeneous and even contradictory. If Islamic radicalism is not stifled in time, through education and professional development, it will in the end lead to profound conflict within Islamic civilisation. Even without the problem of radically divergent interpretations of Islam, especially those of the Shi'ites, Sunnis, fundamentalists, secularists and Sufis, the Muslim community is in any case an *umma* that is more virtual than real. Their solidarity is an observable phenomenon, but does not rise beyond the primitive emotional level and is rarely exercised in such contexts as economic relations or mutual defence. Today, when Muslims travel between the various Muslim countries, experience shows that it is better to hold a passport from a Christian western country than an Arab or Muslim one. In the latter case, permission to remain seems either to be systematically delayed, or flatly refused. Muslims must shed their schizophrenia, which leads them to experience irrational feelings of inferiority towards westerners, about whom they at the same time often speak ill.

THE SECOND GENERATION OF POLITICAL ISLAM: IBN TAYMIYYA AND IBN ABD AL-WAHHAB

IBN TAYMIYYA: THE FOUNDER OF POLITICAL ISLAM

Since the thirteenth century, the formidable conservative theologian Ibn Taymiyya (1263–1328) has been at all times a pervasive influence on the Islamists. Ibn Taymiyya militated for the establishment of an Islamic polity governed according to the fundamental precepts of the faith as laid down by the *salaf*, the pious ancestors. He also developed the idea of the Jihad, which he described as a 'canonical war for the triumph of the word of God'. He popularised the use of the fatwa, and issued many conservative rulings on specific points of the Shari'a. Finally, he was indefatigable in his exhortations to Muslim rulers to follow unswervingly the fundamental texts of the Qur'an and the Sunna. Ibn Taymiyya was certainly the most incisive Islamist propagandist of his own or any other era. Study of his writings makes it clear that he basically drew his ideas from the rigorous legal school of Ibn Hanbal. He was to leave his mark in turn on Sheikh Abd Al-Wahhab, the spiritual master of Saudi Wahhabism in the eighteenth century.

IBN TAYMIYYA'S IDEAS AND PERSONALITY

This exceptional thinker was born in Harran, in Syrian Mesopotamia. He was no more than five when he witnessed the Mongol sack of his native city in 1268 and fled with his family to Damascus, an experience he remembered angrily to the end of his life. His family was wealthy and educated, with a leaning towards the religious sciences. Both his father and grandfather were practitioners of the strict Hanbali school, within which they issued thoughtful legal rulings. The indications are that the young Ibn Taymiyya was brought up in a very strict religious atmosphere and that this was what led to his attachment to the fundamentals of Islam, as revealed to Muhammad and passed down unchanged to the *salaf*. He succeeded in revitalising Islamist spirituality on the basis of the dictum, 'God knows all and sees all'. His emphasis on unconditional respect for the fundamentals of Islam leads to the saying, 'No Hadith can be authentic unless endorsed by Ibn Taymiyya'.

Ibn Taymiyya's reputation as a Hanbali cleric based in Damascus soon spread beyond the bounds of Syria and Lebanon. The Egyptian Mamluks issued an honorific formal invitation to him to address religious seminars. However, his uncompromising conception of religion brought him serious trouble. A polemic he delivered at a Cairo seminar resulted in his being imprisoned by his adversary, the Egyptian judge Sheikh Shams Al-Din Ibn Adlan, who accused him of narrow-mindedness and fanaticism.[1] When he appeared before the court, Ibn Taymiyya refused to recognise Sheikh Shams Al-Din's authority as a judge, citing the principle that a party to a case may not be its judge. Angry at this challenge to his authority, Sheikh Shams Al-Din had him summarily arrested. In prison, Ibn Taymiyya found the inmates passing their time at games of chess and backgammon, and exhorted them instead to devote themselves to prayer and reading the Qur'an. This practice, known as *da'wa*, the 'call' to Islam, is still the preferred approach used by Islamists of all persuasions. Ibn Taymiyya adhered strictly to the teaching of the pious ancestors, who maintained that the Qur'an was not created but had been revealed to Muhammad. In addition, all was dependent on the will of God. These contentions were soon to be challenged by the rational philosophers and the Sufis, who preached the freedom of man's will and the 'created' nature of the Qur'an.

Ibn Taymiyya's thinking and teaching regarding the Qur'an left its mark on all later generations of Muslims. All Qur'anic schools (*madrasas*) in the Muslim world maintain, if unknowingly, the Qur'anic teaching methods established by Ibn Taymiyya in the thirteenth century. For instance, he simplified the burdens of those learning the Holy Book by arranging these tasks in order of priority.

As he saw it, the first stage was to learn the introduction – the Fatiha – which sums up the doctrine of the faith, and then Al-Ikhlas, which follows on from the Fatiha and, according to Ibn Taymiyya, is worth a third of the Qur'an on its own.[2] Ibn Taymiyya also prioritised the duties incumbent upon a Muslim. In his view, Jihad for the victory of the word of God was supreme. 'Prior to everything comes Islam; its pillar is prayer; its apex is Jihad in God's cause.'[3] He continues, 'There are a hundred grades within Paradise, and between one to another there is a gap as wide as that between Heaven and Earth. God has destined these for those who struggle for the cause.'[4] Similarly, Ibn Taymiyya laid down how an Islamic state should be run. The Qur'an and the Sunna were the sole sources he turned to to produce rulings on such matters as finances, taxes, charity, justice and rules for the conduct of war.

Finally, Ibn Taymiyya endorsed the notion that the Qur'an is foremost among a whole hierarchy of religious texts, just ahead of the Christian Gospels. However, he stressed that, whatever hierarchy of texts might exist, God is sovereign and his commandments must be obeyed to the letter. For Ibn Taymiyya, it was in this context that God had chosen to reveal the Torah, the Bible and the Qur'an, and to send to earth such Prophets as Moses, Jesus and Muhammad.

ISLAMIC POWER ACCORDING TO IBN TAYMIYYA

Ibn Taymiyya clearly states his theory of power in his book entitled *The Politics of Theology*, in which he argues that politics should answer solely to the conscience of the divine law. He also develops in this book the idea that the good leader is he who puts his realm at the service of the faith. This principle, combined with recourse to the Jihad when need be, was to become the irresistible power that drove the expansion of Islam. On the personal level, Ibn Taymiyya supported individual intellectual research. However, he considered that affairs of state and of religion should be reserved to those leaders who could be described as 'servants of God'. Muslims should be ruled solely by the Islamic Shari'a and states which failed to heed revealed laws would inevitably become tyrannical.[5] In his view, the laws of the state and its political affairs were built on divine prophecy. In support of this view, he adduced the authority of the Prophet, who said, 'You are better acquainted than I with everything to do with this world below. But on the subject of religion, on the other hand, you should address yourself to me.' He made the further point that, though the Prophets are not immune from the commission of minor sins, they are infallible as concerns the transmission of the divine message. Ibn Taymiyya's fatwa expressed this as follows: 'The consensus of the *ulema* of Islam and every Muslim community confirms that the Prophets are immune from major sins, though they are susceptible to minor ones.'[6]

Ibn Taymiyya went on to define the nature of those laws devised by the authorities of the Islamic community, comprising the legislators, the *ulema* and the muftis. He makes it clear that, even when such laws are based on reason and show the evidence of divine wisdom, they cannot themselves be divine in nature, as divine power is absent from those who devise them.[7] Despite the absence of the divine essence, however, Ibn Taymiyya enjoined the Muslims strictly to obey the laws of Islamic states and those who legitimately represent them: the legislators, sultans, *ulema* and imams. In his view, legitimate rulers are virtually infallible, and deserve to be compared to the shadow of God on earth. This apotheosis of the religious authorities led him to go as far as to say, 'Sixty years under the authority of an unjust imam or ruler are worth more than a single night of anarchy.'[8]

Overall, Ibn Taymiyya's intellectual contribution in the field of methodology and the exegesis of the Shari'a was substantial. It had the virtue of simplifying and prioritising the principal Islamic precepts, which facilitated their assimilation by many generations of Islamists and enhanced the veneration in which they were held. He also left his mark on the Islamic educational system by proposing the establishment of Qur'anic schools (*madrasas*) down to the level of the smallest village. In this way, under the leadership of their Sheikhs, children learned to venerate the Qur'an and even to memorise it in its entirety, together with the commentaries of Ibn Taymiyya and his school.

However, the ubiquitous Ibn Taymiyya was also responsible for an excessive reliance on supposedly infallible fatwas. This was how he attacked his opponents, the Sufis, who practised a version of Islam too liberal for his liking. In many of his fatwas, he fiercely criticised the thinking of the most brilliant philosopher of the Sufi mystics, Muhy Al-Din Ibn Al-Arabi (1165–1240), whom he characterised as an 'innovator, who had strayed away from the Qur'an and the Sunna'.[9] Ibn Taymiyya also denounced the celebration of festivals, music, art, as well as the practice of visiting saints' tombs, to which not merely the Sufis but also the Muslim population as a whole were greatly attached. It should not be forgotten that Ibn Taymiyya had himself been briefly initiated into Sufi mysticism, from which he soon distanced himself.[10] Apparently his brief acquaintance with the liberal thinking of the Sufis was enough for Ibn Taymiyya to embark on a lifetime of hostility to anything other than the strictest interpretation of Islam.

Ibn Taymiyya also looked with disfavour on the social changes made in Egypt by the Mamluks, the 'slave-warriors' who dominated Syria and Egypt, in which they ruled from 1250 to 1517. The Mamluks were military slaves from the Ottoman Caucasus, a self-perpetuating dynasty whose original members had been purchased as promising young warriors under Saladin's Ayyubid dynasty. Their manners and customs were scarcely compatible with Ibn Taymiyya's ultra-puritan temperament. Socially and economically, however, the Mamluks had been hugely successful. They transformed the cities they ruled into centres of commerce, where opulent trading caravans met. The architecture of their palaces was extravagant and they led lives worthy of the fables of the 'Thousand and One Nights'. Artistic and cultural endeavour was at its height: poetry, music, dance, the decorative arts and literature flourished at the level of genius. There were periods when the prosperity of the towns trickled down to the peasants and craftsmen. Women often went unveiled and enjoyed personal freedom almost on a level with the men. It is also said that the sexual customs of the epoch were not as rigid as traditionally Islam would prescribe.[11]

This degree of licence was clearly not acceptable to Ibn Taymiyya. However, he was unable directly to influence the rationalist and liberal Egyptian and Syrian society of his day. He therefore attempted to exercise his influence instead through swaying the attitudes of political leaders. He energetically argued for the idea of a religion-based state for all the Muslim countries. This state, in which all temporal and spiritual power would be concentrated in the hands of a single leader, would be based on the Shari'a, which would serve as a unitary and unified system of law. Ibn Taymiyya also opposed any monopolisation of power by a single movement or ethnic group. Only personal worth and competence should be taken into account. On this issue, he said:

> God, the Prophet and the community of believers are betrayed by any person in authority who chooses any candidate for a public position, other than the most worthy and suited for the post, if the person chosen is his relative, his client or his friend. The same applies if the chosen individual comes from the same country, or belongs to the same school of law (*madhhab*), or to the same brotherhood (*tariqa*). The case is similar if such a person has the same ethnic origin, be it Arab, Persian or Greek; or if the person in authority has taken any bribe or accepted any service from the candidate of his choice. This also is the issue if the person in authority harbours any enmity or personal animosity towards the excluded candidate.[12]

The structure of the Mamluk state as it existed at the time of Ibn Taymiyya was hierarchical. At the top were the Sultans themselves, who governed with an iron fist; then came the religious *ulema*, and beneath them the peasants. Finally came the bedouin Arabs, who, though they enjoyed a certain level of freedom, were classed as pariahs within Mamluk society.

The Emirs

In Ibn Taymiyya's day, the Mamluk regime in theory venerated the Caliph as the supreme moral authority. In practice, however, the Mamluk dynasty was based from the outset on a military dictatorship that entrenched the Mamluk Emirs as the true pillars of the state and of society. There were some 24 Emirs, under the rule of a Sultan. Among them were Mongols, Turks and Kurds. Each had at his command one or more brigades (*halkas*) of 24,000 men.[13] The Emirs were in general uncultured men and had little interest in science, philosophy or the arts, in contrast to the Arab, Persian and Kurdish rulers of the day. The historian Henri Laoust says,

> They had a poor command of Arabic and had been perfunctorily converted to Islam. Their common language was Turkish, and all they knew of Islam was the rudiments taught them by the *fuqaha* they appointed themselves. There was often great personal rivalry between them: differences of origin and tribe set them against each other. Their political ambitions often led them into treasonable actions.[14]

They were on the whole rapacious, self-indulgent and not noted for their courage, though the men who served under them in the Mamluk armies were not seen as corrupt.[15] The Emirs had no scruples over claiming their actions were justified by the legitimacy of the Caliphate. The reality was that the Emirs held the real power, even if the Caliphate was credited with Islamic legitimacy. It should be said that the relative impotence of the Caliphate did not come to pass suddenly. Instead, the process of the usurpation of power by the Mamluk Emirs had happened over time. Ibn Taymiyya admonished the Emirs, reminding them that they should pay respect to the Caliphate and obey the Shari'a in all its detail.

A further issue was that the society in which Ibn Taymiyya lived was deeply feudal in nature and was constantly subjected to redistributions of land ownership that accompanied changes in power. Redistribution in general tended to the profit of the Emirs, who sought always to increase their wealth. In their own interests, they did take care to enhance the strength of their forces. However, even here they failed to grasp and develop the techniques and strategies of warfare.

The Religious Class (The *Ulema*)

The privileged class of religious functionaries, with some difficulty, maintained their independence from the Mamluk military leadership. In contrast to the Emirs, the *ulema* enjoyed the support of the people. They served a severe and monastic apprenticeship. They recruited through a system of the co-opting of intelligent and promising bright pupils into their ranks. Their scholarship was based on the memorisation of the Qur'an and the Hadith of the Prophet Muhammad. For the mass of the population, the wisdom of this learned clergy was seen as divine in nature, as it expressed the Word of God.

The Peasantry

The agricultural proletariat and the artisan class made up the third group within the structure of the Mamluk state. They were servile, crushed with taxes and intermittently ill-fed, as the crops they produced went to feed the Emirs and their armies.

The Bedouin

Finally, the fourth socio-cultural category within the Mamluk structure consisted of the bedouin. For the most part they in practice kept their own counsel and succeeded in evading state subjugation. The Arab nomads and the tribal federations were in fact renowned for their independence. Some of them were still pagans, and some lived as brigands, flagrantly pillaging caravans going on the pilgrimage. Their blood feuds were constant. The Mamluk central authorities sometimes relied on the bedouin when they needed a bulwark against external threats, especially from the Mongols. Whether in Ibn Taymiyya's time or in our own day, no political authority in the Arab world can afford to antagonise the bedouin. Their often crucial position in the balance of power in Muslim political societies and their capacity to survive the testing nature of life in desert areas have made them indispensable partners for the survival and security of successive Muslim states.

CONCLUSION

Ibn Taymiyya was congenitally disputatious and had little inclination to compromise, either with any member of the *ulema* who might oppose his positions, or with the Sufi mystics. He was fearless and provocative, and as a result was imprisoned on a number of occasions. His fatwas were an amalgam of piety and ruthlessness, and his discourses on religious issues were highly subjective and tendentious. It might be guessed that his turbulent trajectory through life was the result of his inability to master the fears and traumas of his youth. The disruption of his earliest childhood by the fearsome onslaughts of the Mongols led him to condemn them repeatedly in fatwas that described them as brutal and uncultured pagans. It was to promote resistance to the Mongols that he continued to emphasise and even idealise the concept of Jihad. In addition, Ibn Taymiyya lived at a time when the Mamluk state itself was rent by social and political tensions. The Mamluks faced bloody peasant revolts as well as bedouin rebelliousness, which threatened to plunge the Mamluk domains into an anarchy spreading from Syria by way of the territory of present-day Jordan into Egypt.

Ibn Taymiyya's conclusion from the evident decline of society was that it was incumbent upon him as a theologian to rethink how power might be exercised within the Islamic nation. He began with a reconsideration of the role of the *ulema*. In his view, the *ulema* should occupy a leading position in the structure of the Mamluk state. They alone had mastered the Shari'a, and they, therefore, were naturally qualified to govern a theocratic state, and should not be subordinate to the authority of the greedy and incompetent Emirs. As regards the peasants and the bedouin, Ibn Taymiyya's plan was that they should be subjected to intensive Islamisation. His reasoning was simple: the more advanced the level of religious belief among the peasants and the bedouin, the higher would be their level of morality and civic awareness. Ibn Taymiyya was also the first to advocate intensive proselytisation of the faith and the conversion of non-Muslims. Alluding to the ferocity and paganism displayed by the Mongols and the desirability of converting them, he declared that human beings imbued by faith and the divine law would no longer fall prey to destructive instincts and pagan ways.

Centuries later, the essence of Ibn Taymiyya's thinking was to influence the renowned Imam Muhammad Ibn Abd Al-Wahhab (1703–87), a follower of the strict Hanbali school, as was Ibn Taymiyya himself, who originated the fundamentalist Wahhabi movement in Saudi Arabia.

IBN ABD AL-WAHHAB AND WAHHABISM

Collaboration between Muhammad Ibn Abd Al-Wahhab and the tribal chieftain Ibn Saud brought the Saudi state into being in the eighteenth century. Abd Al-Wahhab was born in 1703 in Al-Uyayna in central Arabia, 30 kilometres north-west of modern-day Riyadh, into the Bani Tamim tribe. His father and grandfather were strict Hanbali jurists. As a child, Ibn Abd Al-Wahhab was described as prodigious and pious. He had memorised the 114 Suras of the Qur'an by the age of ten and soon went on the pilgrimage. As an adolescent, he was shocked by the resumption by the bedouin of pre-Islamic pagan practices. He found it impossible to ignore the decline in the level of Islamic observance in the Arabian Peninsula. During the eighteenth century, both bedouin and townsfolk blatantly relapsed into practices traditionally forbidden by Islam, such as the consumption of alcohol and the worship of idols. Yves Besson has made this comment:

> Islam was often no longer observed, except in the most rudimentary sense, both in the villages and towns and among the nomads. In practice ... all manner of alien rites developed, as well as superstitions often associated with the religion of the Sabeans, a pagan faith that still existed in Arabia and was undergoing a resurgence of popularity.[16]

In his struggle against this deviationism, Ibn Abd-Al Wahhab set himself up as the indispensable moral guide of these tribes of the Arabian desert who had strayed from the true path. To equip himself for this difficult task, he made an exhaustive study of the fundamentalist ideas of Ibn Taymiyya. For this reason, he placed great stress on the unity of God, condemning all forms of polytheism (*shirk*). Like Ibn Taymiyya, his wish was to see a return to the Islam proclaimed and established by the Prophet Muhammad in Medina and Mecca. In addition, he sought to lay the groundwork for the establishment of an Islamic state, with statements like the following:

> The will of God is entirely present in the Qur'an and the Sunna of the Prophet. This will is expressed in the Shari'a. Any community that is resolute in its determination to live by the Shari'a is a Muslim community. To achieve this, the Muslim community must establish certain institutions, of which the most important is the state.[17]

Like Ibn Taymiyya and Ibn Hanbal, his preference was to see a society organised collectively on Islamic principles, with little latitude for individual inclinations. In the interests of the promotion of social harmony and stamping out vice, he imposed the strictest discipline. He forbade alcohol, tobacco, music, gambling, magic, superstition, the invocation of spirits and visits to the tombs of saints. He also prohibited all proximity between men and women in public, and denounced the Sufis for introducing innovations into Islam. These social guidelines were to be the basis of the state that Ibn Abd Al-Wahhab sought to bring into being in the Arabian Peninsula. In order to realise his ambition, however, Ibn Abd Al-Wahhab needed power on the ground. He therefore allied himself with the Al Saud, a clan of Arab warriors. It was thanks to the support of Muhammad Ibn Saud, then a local ruler, that the first Wahhabi entity came into being in 1744. The object of the Wahhabis was the purification of the faith and a full application of the Shari'a, which went comfortably in tandem with the ambition of the Al Saud to put an end to the oppressive domination of the Turks. These two elements together formed the foundations of a Wahhabi fundamentalist state in Arabia.

The Wahhabi state went through a number of phases between 1750 and 1932, when the Kingdom of Saudi Arabia finally came into being. In 1912, Abdul Aziz Ibn Abdul Rahman Al Faisal Al Saud, known as Ibn Saud, set his stamp on the Kingdom when he gave his patronage to the redoubtable Wahhabi *ikhwan* (the Wahhabi brotherhood). These *ikhwan* were bedouin fighting men who had been attracted into the Wahhabi *madrasas*. It is easy to see a parallel with the Taliban model in Afghanistan from 1994 to 2001, except that the early *ikhwan* were able to deploy only cavalrymen while by the 1990s they had tank crews. Alongside this institution, there were also the *mutawa*. These were 'zealots selected by the *ulema* to preach among the bedouin and instruct them in the simplest elements of the Wahhabi law'. This was a police force whose remit was the propagation of the faith and the suppression of the 'unruly customs and manners of the desert'.[18] Mohamed-Chérif Ferjani has noted that the structure of the *ikhwan* movement was similar to that later utilised by the Muslim Brotherhood in Egypt under the leadership of Hassan Al-Banna. This he described as 'a combat organisation of a military nature, based on loyalty, ideological training, strict discipline and a "phalangist" command structure based on a charismatic leader who embodies the unity and the political, ideological, and organisational authority of the movement.'[19]

As the inspiration for their institutions, the Al Saud basically turned to the Qur'an. As King Faisal observed on many occasions: '. . . the Qur'an is the oldest and best constitution in the world'.[20] From their first appearance, Saudi institutions were consciously modelled on a perception of the state founded by the Prophet Muhammad in Medina in the seventh century. The Kingdom of Saudi Arabia has always strictly enforced the Shari'a, which it has installed as the supreme law. According to Wahhabi doctrine, the Prophet Muhammad and the pious *salaf* who followed him foresaw and provided for all aspects of political, social and economic life. Ghassan Salamé gives this account:

> The Kingdom of Saudi Arabia is a country where fasting and prayer are supervised by the police and where justice, teaching and

legislation are thoroughly permeated by Islam ... The Qur'anic *zakat* is the sole tax gathered by the government and the banking system continues to be underdeveloped, thanks to the traditional Muslim prohibition on interest. The hands of thieves are cut off, savage punishments are inflicted on those who smuggle alcohol and the female form is obfuscated in black. Everyday life in Saudi Arabia is that of a country where Islam is always the chosen standard, the infallible criterion of behaviour, the Rule, and the Way.[21]

It should be added, however, in defence of Saudi practices, that Islam prescribes that the rich should come to the aid of the weak, the poor and those in need. For this reason, every Muslim must give to the public treasury a part of his wealth in the form of alms (a tax known as *zakat*). Alms have always played and continue to play a crucial role in providing for social and humanitarian needs in Muslim lands. The duty of giving alms is one of the pillars of Islam. It has always been respected by the *umma*, even at the worst and most self-absorbed episodes of Muslim society. According to some sources, *zakat* in Saudi Arabia amounted in the early years of the twenty-first century to some us $10 billion each year, which is spent throughout the Muslim world for the construction of mosques and Qur'anic schools and for the maintenance of Muslim political organisations.

A further point is that the rigorous and 'unitarian'[22] Wahhabism of the Saudis has scarcely changed with the passage of time. In the past, as it is today, it has been the bulwark of regional stability in the face of the dynamic Shi'ism of Iraq, Oman and Iran, an adversary against which Saudi Arabia has traditionally defended itself. Despite the harsh criticism directed at Wahhabism after the events of September 11, 2001 in New York, it remains at bottom a faith that essentially addresses itself to the bedouin and their community, who are bound together by the unshakeable solidarity known as *asabiya*. Over time, it was this communitarian Islamism that gave rise to the Saudi nation, with the twin resources of the presence within its territory of the Holy Places of Islam and of vast reserves of oil. Close historical study of Saudi Arabia reveals that for the most part the Wahhabi version of the Islamic faith has been concerned with internal Saudi affairs. It has not sought identification with any political tendency, or sought to propagate itself in neighbouring countries. Saudi Arabia did not even wish to appropriate the prestigious title of Caliph, which Sherif Hussein, as the ruler of Hejaz, had claimed on 24 March 1924, after it had been renounced by the Turks, and which Hussein himself later relinquished.[23] The doctrine of Wahhabism has always presented itself as non-exportable. Anyone unused to Saudi bedouin tradition would in any case find it difficult to stomach the puritanism and rigour of the Wahhabis.

An amalgam of nomadism and a stern faith were what brought this exceptionally observant and Godly state into being in the heart of the sacred desert where Muhammad received his divine revelation. The relatively modest demography of the country, with only some 27 million inhabitants in 2007, and its vast oil income have had the consequence that the Saudi princes have been able to enjoy a luxurious way of life, while the majority of the Saudi monarch's subjects have a comfortable existence. The Saudis have always been a source of fascination for the world. In its private capacity, the royal family has taken on board various contemporary ideas, but does not rule alone. The Wahhabi *ulema* and the religious charitable organisations occupy a privileged place at the head of the Saudi state.

During the 1990s, the war in Afghanistan against Soviet occupation was a serious challenge for the Wahhabis, breaching their customary reserve and introversion. In the light of the suffering of the Afghan people, the obligations of international Islamic solidarity won the day. In their conflict with Russia's atheism, Saudi citizens and institutions were unstinting in their financial and military aid to the Afghan Jihad. At the same time, the spread of Wahhabi ideas throughout the Muslim world was intensified, through the agency of the World Islamic League, established in Jedda in 1962.[24] The Deobandi Islam of the Taliban was also a stern faith, based on the teachings of the *salaf*, so there was a natural confluence of ideas. In addition, the works of Ibn Taymiyya were systematically translated and disseminated in the Islamist strongholds in Central Asia, the Maghreb and the Middle East.

The Saudi *ulema* wield virtually unrestricted power. The institution of the *mutawa* puts at their disposal a formidable religious police. The *mutawa* are in a position even to challenge the royal family if its members transgress against Wahhabi prescriptions. For instance, we read that 'King Faisal, who ruled from 1964 to 1975, was obliged to keep secret the installation of television in his palace, as the Wahhabis had attacked the headquarters of the national television station in Riyadh.'[25] As to the telephone, the religious establishment in Mecca deemed it the tool of Satan and permitted the King to use it only when he demonstrated to them that it could be used to transmit the recitation of the Qur'an over long distances.

Despite strong pressure from Islamic civil society within the Kingdom, the Saudi authorities, under Wahhabi influence, have stood firm against the idea of a foreign policy that would extend the power of Saudi Arabia beyond its frontiers. Saudi Arabia has maintained its tradition of existence as an isolated Islamic entity. The idea of an intensification of the external Jihad against the infidels found support in certain provinces of the Kingdom and from the younger generation across the country.[26] Nevertheless, Wahhabism continued to be primarily preoccupied with the internal decline of Islam and the degeneration of morals (including the failure to pray, the consumption of alcoholic drinks, sexual latitude and the liberal behaviour of women), as well as with the tribal equilibrium of the Kingdom itself.

It should be said that Saudi Arabia has suffered less from the impact of colonialism and its resulting social injustices than have other Middle Eastern countries, especially Egypt. Napoleon's expedition, which landed in Alexandria in 1798, was the harbinger of waves of western intrusion that shook the Arab world and came to be seen as comparable to the 1258 invasion of the Abbasid Caliphate in Baghdad by the Mongols. The western invasion of Egypt, a country already exhausted by three and a half centuries of Mamluk exploitation, seemed to threaten the destruction of a Middle Eastern state in which intercultural dialogue had been possible. Its likely consequence appeared to be the elimination of influence of Egypt's civilisation, in which Arab and Islamic elements were mingled with Christianity and the Pharaonic heritage.

This first confrontation, one that was followed by many others, had profound consequences for relations between Muslims and westerners.[27] It was no accident that Egypt was the country in which two significant and opposed phenomena made their appearance. One of these was the emergence of Muslim reformers of Sufi affiliation, such as Sheikh Jamal Ad-Din Al-Afghani and Sheikh Muhammad Abduh, who took up the cudgels against popular ignorance and its exploitation by colonial imperialism. The other was the appearance of the leaders of the third generation of popular Islamists, such as Sayyid Qutb and Hassan Al-Banna, who built an international network of Jihad and rejected the values of the West. In the following chapter the spotlight will fall on these men, who are the authentic heirs of the Islamism of the second generation.

3

THE THIRD GENERATION OF ISLAM: THE FATHERS OF CONTEMPORARY ISLAMISM: AL-BANNA, QUTB, MAWDUDI

The third generation of Islamism arose, as did the generations that preceded it, as the result of a crisis. At its origin were the unfolding consequences of the arrival on Egypt's shores in 1798 of Napoleon Bonaparte's expeditionary forces, together with the pervasive intrusion into the Middle East of western cultural values that followed. In Egypt, as well as in Syria, the Maghreb, India and even in Europe itself, Muslim intellectuals reacted sharply against the new values that the West attempted to introduce, in every field, as part of its newly minted programme of colonialist domination in the economic, military and cultural spheres. These new and unwanted contacts were unwelcome to the majority of the Muslim population, who felt their dignity and their beliefs were under assault. In addition, those few Muslims who had engaged in dialogue with the West soon felt betrayed by the non-fulfilment of the fabulous prospects of emancipation, equality and the brotherhood of peoples advanced by the colonisers. In the nineteenth century, idealist Saint-Simonian notions of the intermingling of peoples to produce a new and vigorous synthesis were disappointed, giving way to exploitation and western contempt for the indigenous populations.

After the First World War, the Muslims also looked in vain for succour from the post-war settlements. Colonialism seemed if anything further entrenched, and post-war chaos underlined their helplessness. The Muslim community saw no way out of the exploitation and disempowerment to which colonialism subjected them. They were not consulted over the bargaining connected to the plan to create a Jewish National Home in Palestine, following the Balfour Declaration of November 1917. Still less were their views asked about the abolition of the Caliphate in 1924, which was swept away without any real discussion with the Arabs or other Muslims. This peremptory gesture looked all the more unjust to the Arabs as it was the responsibility of Kemal Ataturk, the new leader of Turkey, who was uncompromisingly secular and pro-western.

All these grievances, piled on top of underdevelopment, social poverty, ignorance, hunger, unemployment and disease, had devastating consequences for the Islamic world. The situation led to bitter disagreements among Muslim intellectuals. Broadly, two main positions emerged over time. One of these favoured an Islamic renewal open to dialogue with other civilisations and characterised by reformist modernism combined with non-violence. Its leading advocates were Jamal Ad-Din Al-Afghani, of Iranian origin, and the Egyptian thinker Muhammad Abduh. The other tendency, puritanical and anti-western, and also more political, advocated a radical return to the sources of Islam, in accordance with the teachings of the Shari'a. Its originators were the Egyptians Hassan Al-Banna and Sayyid Qutb, and, from the Indian subcontinent, Abul Ala Mawdudi. Today, certain ideas originated by Qutb and Mawdudi have re-emerged in the Islamism of Osama Bin Laden, from Saudi Arabia, Abdullah Azzam, from Palestine, and Ali Belhadj from Algeria. This school of thought is the true inheritor of the religious rigour of the great forebears of modern Islamism, Ibn Taymiyya and Ibn Hanbal.

HASSAN AL-BANNA (1906–49) AND HIS INFLUENCE ON THE CONTEMPORARY ISLAMISTS

THE LIFE OF HASSAN AL-BANNA

Hassan Al-Banna was born in 1906, and grew up in the particular social circumstances of a feudal Egypt of which the great landowners were the absolute masters. Society was rigidly stratified. In common with most of the Arab countries, the ordinary people of Egypt were stultified by their ignorance and superstition. In addition, the injustices of colonialism and exclusion afflicted particularly the most deprived classes of society. Hassan Al-Banna was a brilliant pupil and flirted briefly with Sufism. As a schoolteacher, he was regarded as a member of the middle class. His father was a watch repairer, as well as being a religious scholar of the Hanbali school. From the age of 22, Hassan Al-Banna was involved in political Islamism, and in 1928 he established the first branch of the Muslim Brotherhood, in Ismailiya, on the Suez Canal. Up to our own times, the organisation he founded remains the leading pan-Islamic religious movement in the Islamic world. It is the common ancestor of many other movements, for which it continues to set the standard. Because of its international membership and the intellectual ability of many of its adherents, it maintains its position at the heart of Islamism and is the key source of information on Islamist activities throughout the world.

HASSAN AL-BANNA'S POLITICAL PROGRAMME

From the outset, Hassan Al-Banna anathematised westernised Arab governments and agitated for their replacement by ruling bodies with social and political institutions based on the Qur'an and the Sunna. His ideas were in line with those of Ibn Taymiyya, for whom the Shari'a was the sole remedy for the distress of the oppressed Muslim peoples. In Al-Banna's words, 'Islam is ideology and faith, homeland and nationality, religion and state, book and sword.'[1]

As Al-Banna saw it, Islam was a comprehensive model for living, which would also, through its power of illumination, be strong enough to withstand the incursions of the West. Al-Banna's strategy for the attainment of the ideal Islamic government was twofold: first, he planned to implement a curriculum of Islamic education, and second, to elevate the political consciousness of the people. Social development, as he saw it, should express God's will through the establishment of a Muslim state under a strong leader. This leader should have been 'enlightened' by the Islamic faith and his power should come 'from the nation-community which he rules'.[2] It goes without saying that in Al-Banna's model of Islamic polity, alcohol, dancing, gambling, and interest-bearing loans, classified as usury, were all utterly forbidden.

ECONOMIC, ORGANISATIONAL AND MILITARY STRATEGIES

In his programme for the achievement of the Islamic state, Al-Banna did not content himself with drawing on the model of the Saudi *ikhwan* but also introduced novel forms of organisation. The structure of Al-Banna's Muslim Brotherhood was organised around a multiplicity of cells known as 'families', which in turn were grouped into larger formations that included both national and international wings.

Al-Banna's originality lay in his intention over the longer term to take political power, on the basis of his starting points of Islamic education and the transformation of the attitudes of individuals. With this in mind, the Muslim Brothers took over schools, universities, mosques, hospitals, government social service departments, professional organisations and trades unions. They also took control of organisations connected with physical education and culture. For example, in 1943 the Muslim Brotherhood maintained, '99 football teams in Egypt as a whole, . . . 32 handball teams, 26 table tennis teams, 19 teams of weight-lifters and so on'.[3] In addition, many small businesses and workshops were run by the Brothers. The Brotherhood has always favoured private property and what might be called 'capitalism with a human face'. Today, with its 450 branches, 6,000 affiliated mosques and two million members, the Gama'a Shari'a, the charitable organisation which represents the banned Muslim Brotherhood, is virtually a state within a state.[4]

In the sphere of direct action, Al-Banna set up units for espionage, special operations and self-defence. What motivated those who enrolled was basically the concept of Jihad, with the goal of imposing God's will in the world. They distinguished themselves in the war against Israel in 1948, and also took part in subsequent actions in Cairo, where the targets were the symbols of the pro-western orientation of the contemporary royalist regime, such as bars, dance-halls, cinemas, and luxury hotels for foreigners.

Whether fighting men or civilians, the Muslim Brothers were easily distinguishable by their sober dress, with fringe beards in imitation of the Prophet Muhammad. They led austere lives, eschewed gambling and visits to the cinema or theatre, and never frequented cafés or bars. Like the Wahhabis, they condemned the Sufi mystics for their music, dancing and spiritual practices. As the Brothers saw it, mysticism was primitive and pervaded by ignorance and superstition. Al-Banna often referred to the Islamist Rashid Rida, who was of Syrian origin but had been brought up in Cairo, who held that westernisation, Sufi mysticism and the secularisation of Muslims were the consequence of atheism. Rida was a former reformist who turned to radical Islam. He was in the habit of saying:

> The Muslim community will not succeed in revitalising the moral and cultural life of Islam, nor in building a new Islam founded on the principles of sovereignty and control, except through *ijtihad* [intellectual effort] and the reinterpretation of the law, whose nature it is to be flexible. It is because they have neglected *ijtihad* that some have relapsed into bedouinism or a state not far from it, and that others have drifted into Europeanisation, heresy and atheism . . .[5]

After 1948, the Muslim Brothers began to criticise more severely the westernised Arab regimes, and started to agitate for social and political reforms based on the application of the Shari'a. In Egypt, the Brotherhood was dissolved, accused of 'attempts to overthrow the established order, terrorism and murder'.[6] In 1949, Hassan Al-Banna was assassinated, almost certainly by King Farouk's agents. In 1951, the Brotherhood was relegalised, though under the leadership of Hassan Al-Hudaybi, a less charismatic supreme guide. In 1952, the Free Officers, led by Gamal Abdel Nasser, overthrew the Egyptian monarchy and installed a secular nationalist regime. This was at first supported by the Muslim Brothers. In 1954, however, a member of the Brotherhood made an attempt on the life of Nasser, which led to a period of brutal repression. 'There was chaos, with the execution of leaders, and the imprisonment of hundreds of activists in camps and jails.'[7] With the Muslim Brotherhood in the grip of grave internal dissent, radical dissidents such as Sayyid Qutb filled the ideological gap, drawing their inspiration from Abul Ala Mawdudi, the Pakistani Islamist thinker.

CONCLUSION

Hassan Al-Banna's Muslim Brotherhood represents the antithesis of progressive and secular Muslim society. Its methodology is both intellectual and educational, and it is rooted in the fundamental values of the Islam of the *salaf* (the pious ancestors). It takes its inspiration from the early Saudi *ikhwan*, from whom it took its name as well as its emblem of the Qur'an flanked by two swords.[8] Mohamed-Chérif Ferjani makes the following assessment of the doctrinal connection between the Muslim Brotherhood and the Saudi *ikhwan*:

> Each of the two movements bases itself on the literalist tradition of Ibn Taymiyya and Ibn Hanbal, who maintained that the role of reason in the strict and literal interpretation of the Qur'an and the Sunna must be circumscribed. Their shared doctrinal origins led both movements to condemn what they saw as innovation, both in the field of religious observance and in the political and juridical sphere. The two movements, therefore, in virtually identical terms, demanded the literal application of the Shari'a in its most fundamental form.[9]

After Nasser's dissolution of the Muslim Brotherhood in Egypt in 1954, a number of Brothers sought refuge in Saudi Arabia, whence the writings of their new intellectual leader, Sayyid Qutb, were mainly distributed. At this time, the Muslim Brotherhood succeeded in establishing itself as the ideological and organisational model for all Islamist parties throughout the world. In Algeria, for example, Sheikh Ben Badis, who established the 'Association of Ulema' in 1931, based his Algerian Islamism on the basis of the educational programme laid down by Hassan Al-Banna and his mentor Rashid Rida. As time passed, Ben Badis pressurised his Algerian followers more intensely to return to the puritanical principles of the pious ancestors.[10] He dismissed the liberalism of the Sufis and 'marabouts', setting up Qur'anic schools in which the curriculum resembled that developed by the Taliban in Afghanistan in the period from 1994 up to 2001. A small minority within the National Liberation Front (FLN), where the majority consisted of secular nationalists, maintained this tradition up to Algeria's independence in 1962. It was the Islamic Salvation Front (FIS), however, which truly took up the banner of Al-Banna and Ben Badis, together with the Algerian Hamas movement led by Sheikh Nahnah. Elsewhere in the Maghreb, Al-Banna served as the inspiration for the Tunisian Islamist party 'Ennahda', and the Justice and Charity Party (*Adl Wa l-Ihsan*) in Morocco.

The Muslim Brotherhood is today well entrenched on the international scene, with branches in over 70 western and eastern countries, and maintains, incidentally, a strong presence in Great Britain.[11] Its geographical spread underlies the Brotherhood's ability to act as the directing influence in international Islamism, and its principle remains to reject any action or concept that contradicts the Qur'an and the Sunna.[12] This is a goal clearly set out in the Brotherhood's official slogan:

> 'Allah is our objective; The messenger is our leader; Quran is our law; Jihad is our way; Dying in the way of Allah is our highest hope.'[13]

THE THEORETICIAN OF CONTEMPORARY ISLAMIC RADICALISM: SAYYID QUTB (1906–66)

More than 30 years after Al-Banna created the Muslim Brotherhood, the Islamist movement found in Sayyid Qutb a new Arab ideologue from whom to take its inspiration. Qutb was able to give a new impetus to the international dimension of Arab Islamist activism.

Sayyid Qutb was born in Assiut, in Upper Egypt, in 1906. After graduation in Egypt, he travelled to the United States, where he studied for a master's degree. He was appalled by what he saw in America, where he denounced what he saw as immorality and condemned the prejudice of the Americans against black people and Muslims. From the 1960s, he became the ideological point of reference of the Muslim Brotherhood and indeed of contemporary Islamism in virtually all its aspects. What is most striking in the moral ideas of Sayyid Qutb and his brother Muhammad is the extent to which they echo the views of Ibn Taymiyya. The Qutbs took their emulation of Ibn Taymiyya to the point of imitating his style of writing. For instance, in Sayyid Qutb's criticism of the derivation of western values from Greek and Roman philosophy, he largely reproduces the brilliant argument of Ibn Taymiyya in his pamphlet 'The Refutation of Logic' (*Al-Radd Ala Al-Mantiqiyyin*). In this tract, Ibn Taymiyya seeks to refute the Greek logicians and those Arab rationalists who drew their inspiration from them. For the most part, in his justification of the applicability of the Shari'a, Qutb leans on quotations from Ibn Taymiyya.[14]

What was new in Sayyid Qutb's thinking was his violent rejection of the West and its classical humanistic values, based on Greek and Roman thought. In his view, Arab philosophy, particularly that of Averroes (Ibn Rushd), Avicenna (Ibn Sina) and Ibn Al-Arabi was distorted by Greek thought. He also took issue with the westernised elites of the Muslim world, as well as with the Sufi mystics, whom he accused of drawing their inspiration from Christian and Hindu spirituality. On this subject, he was echoed by his brother Muhammad Qutb, who wrote:

> Parroting the ideas of their western teachers, these people betray their own ignorance. They know nothing about Islam or its mission in human existence ... It is a very pernicious spirit of Grecian culture that still pervades the sub-conscious of the modern West.[15]

In fact, in Sayyid Qutb's scheme of things, the idea of coexistence with non-Muslims or of any form of dialogue was totally lacking.

Islam, in his view, should be entirely self-contained and concerned solely with the welfare of the Muslim community.

Sayyid Qutb's strong intellectual dependence on Ibn Taymiyya was something he had in common with most Islamist thinkers of the third generation. In support of his absolutist theory, his point of origin was that 'there is no God but God'. He went on to explain that the immediate significance of this text was to 'reserve the divine nature to God alone and to refrain from attributing to any of God's creatures qualities properly appertaining to God himself'.[16] In Qutb's view, the crucial element of the deity's nature is 'the absolute prerogative over the prescription of laws for mankind, injunctions on their conduct, and the definition of the moral values to which they should adhere'.[17] Clearly, therefore, any human being arrogating to himself the ability to formulate juridical or social principles that would regulate the lives of any group of Muslims would be purporting to usurp one of the principal attributes of God. He also severely condemned any recognition by Muslims of the validity of laws devised by men, even constitutional laws relating to political democracy. In his view, any such legal system would trespass on God's domain. Therefore, any contemporary regime, governing a Muslim population, whose philosophical roots were nationalist rather than religious, would be illegitimate, as it would have presumed to usurp the prerogatives of God. He also had more to say about the inadequacies in practice of law of human origin: 'Human law, that is to say law laid down by an individual, family or group in a position of power, cannot by its nature be uninfluenced by the emotions and the interests of those by whom it is originated.'[18]

In a style reminiscent of that of Ibn Taymiyya,[19] he continues this theme, arguing that because of their partiality, men should leave control of the human world to God:

The way of God, who governs the lives of men, leads to the disappearance of this biased quality, so that true and global justice, unattainable by any human means, can come into being. Human law-makers are always susceptible, whether to human emotion, human weakness, or the search for personal profit.[20]

On the basis of the premise that God is the absolute ruler of the Islamic community, Sayyid Qutb takes issue with the secularism of the early twentieth century. He declares himself opposed to the notion of any separation of political and religious powers. In his well-known tract, *Islam, Religion of the Future*, he declared that Islam should not be, as he put it:

> ... hedged about by the evocative and the ritual, or hindered from playing its full part in life. Nor should there be any obstacle to its primacy over all secular activities, which it derives from its nature and its role.[21]

According to Sayyid Qutb's project, once Islamic institutions and laws had been installed in the Muslim polity the next task would be to build an Islamic moral order. Morality was the second string to Qutb's bow. As he himself put it:

> Humanity and human conceptions about mankind are in decline; man is degenerating in his spirit, his intelligence and his morality. Men engage in sexual relations at a level lower than the animals, and harm themselves stupidly with drugs and alcohol. They hurl themselves into futile philosophies of despair and avoidance, such as existentialism. One may therefore conclude that whatever material facilities may be afforded by technology to this luxury-loving civilisation, as a substitute for acknowledgement of the needs of the soul, they will in no way be sufficient to hold back the contemporary decline of humanity.[22]

Sayyid Qutb attacked western civilisation at its roots, holding it responsible for the ills and the decline of the Muslims and savagely attacking the decadence of modern society, which he compares unfavourably with the society of pre-Islamic times:

> The primacy of the white man, whether Russian, American, British, French, Swedish or any other nationality, is over. It has come to an end because of the appalling double standards of the Europeans, which are evident in all fields of ideas and in all western practice.[23]

Sayyid Qutb was not unaware that in the first instance this 'white man' essentially drew his strength from the heritage of Greek and Roman civilisations. This is why Qutb was so vehement against these twin sources of western civilisation. On the Romans, he commented:

> The Roman Empire reached the zenith of military and political power, but as its civilisation reached its apogee it underwent a strange reversal in its morality, its religious faith, and its social behaviour. The Romans became lascivious and licentious . . . Their tables glittered with gold and silver vessels studded with precious stones. Servants clustered around them in finely worked garments and half-naked girls excited their base desires.[24]

He also rejected the greater moderation of the Islamist thinkers who had preceded him, including notably Hassan Al-Banna. Though he paraphrases Ibn Taymiyya in these arguments, he does not acknowledge his influence. His constant theme is the Shari'a, as followed by the pious ancestors, the *salaf*: the first generation that followed the Prophet Muhammad. In many of his sermons, he asks rhetorical questions, in which a tone of gratification at the miracle represented by the Prophet mingles with surprise:

> How could a single individual, Muhammad Ibn Abdallah, alone, have faced the whole world, or even the entire Arabian Peninsula, or the tribe of the Quraysh, who were the masters of all the Arabs at the moment when he began his preaching? He scorned their beliefs and defied their powers in order to overcome them and to install his new order.[25]

Qutb's view, in which he was echoed by his brother Muhammad, was that Islam should resist all the incursions of modernism, holding fast instead to the traditions established by Muhammad and the *salaf*. This was the Qutbs' way of combating the moral lapses of Arab society in general, and that of Egypt in particular, invaded, as they saw it, by modernist ideas imported from the West, including western ideas about science. Science, they said, had become the Europeans' God, and the Muslims should beware of it. For these two Islamic thinkers, the fundamental problems of science admitted of no solution without faith in God. Islam would survive only by melding the spiritual with the temporal. In other words, only the path of fusion between religion and politics could be a harmonious pattern of faith for the Muslims, as well as a practical programme for living.[26]

As the Qutb brothers saw it, the Christian Orientalists and Islamologues were nothing other than modern crusaders, whose motivations were dubious in the extreme.[27] The Qutbs saw researches into Islam by westerners as no more than a means of coming to know the strengths and weaknesses of the faith, the better to overcome it. Their attitude to the West was aggressive, and their followers were highly critical of the activities of westerners in the Muslim world. According to Muhammad Qutb, colonialism and imperialism had been in conflict with the Muslim East for more than a century.[28] From the capture of Algiers in 1830, up to the final subjugation of Egypt in 1880, the forces of colonisation had not hesitated in their onslaught. What was at stake was substantial. The objective of the West was to ensure that the economic interests of the colonial powers remained unobstructed. The Islamist threat, therefore, needed to be extinguished or at least neutralised. According to the followers of the Qutbs, the British Prime Minister Gladstone, in Victorian times, had provided an illustration of the West's fear of Islam. Speaking to an audience of British Members of Parliament, Gladstone brandished a copy of the Qur'an while speaking as follows: 'While the Egyptians have this book in their hands, we shall never have peace or tranquillity in that country.'[29]

For Qutb and Islamist authors like him, what is today called the 'clash of civilisations' was a confrontation that was already well under way, though it had not yet found a name. In our own time, the Islamist analysis is that this conflict has taken the form of western aggression against Muslim countries, which continue the colonialist aggressions of yesteryear.

ABUL ALA MAWDUDI AND HIS
INFLUENCE ON THE ARABS

Similar ideas to those of the Qutb brothers are to be found in the writings of Abul Ala Mawdudi, who had begun in the 1920s to prepare the ground for Islamism in India and Pakistan. Mawdudi was the spiritual father of Islamism in South Asia. Today, his name is venerated by the pupils (*taliban*) of Qur'anic schools throughout the Indian subcontinent.

Mawdudi wrote more than 80 books on Islam, and originated the concept of a Pakistani Islamic community that would be distinct from Indian nationalist aspirations and religion, though he was not necessarily in favour of territorial separation. In that sense he was the antithesis of his compatriot, the brilliant lawyer and secularist Muhammed Ali Jinnah, the founder of the Muslim League, whose ideas held sway in 1948 and resulted in the creation of the modern Pakistani state. However, the Islamic influence of Mawdudi quickly gained ground in Pakistan, as elsewhere in South Asia, under the aegis of the well-known fundamentalist party, Jamaat-e-Islami. In his best-known work, *Risala-e-diniyat* ('Understanding Islam'), Mawdudi begins with a declaration that in the modern world in general, and particularly the Indian subcontinent, a new phase of Islamic resurgence was emerging, the signs of which were visible in many countries. The celebrated Pakistani Islamist Khurshid Ahmed, Mawdudi's translator and the editor of the 1990 English edition of 'Understanding Islam', has this to say in his preface about the book's context:

> The old order is disintegrating; the new one, however, is yet to come. And history tells us that such ages of restlessness have also been periods of birth for new movements and cultures. A significant feature of the present century is the new and widespread trend of Islamic revival. After a long period of stagnation the world of Islam is rising from its stupor. A new awakening has appeared on the horizon; a new life is being infused into the community

of Islam. This trend is visible in every country and at every place and has within it the possibilities of its becoming the harbinger of a new age.[30]

The reality, however, was not quite so simple. In the territory of the Indian subcontinent, and indeed throughout the Muslim countries, there had always been a variety of diverse spiritual concepts of Islam. Over the space of several decades, Muhammed Ali Jinnah's concept of a secular society had played a dominant role, and, together with Sufi ideas, had coexisted with the Salafi Islamism of Mawdudi across the region. Jinnah's motives came out of nationalism and the politics of identity, and his objective was the creation of a modern Pakistani state. Mawdudi, meanwhile, wanted a Pakistan that would be entirely religious and theocratic, and he 'denounced Jinnah and the Muslim League as blasphemers who were misusing Islam to promote a secular nationalism'.[31]

Jinnah's ideas initially had the upper hand, but in due course these two great social projects achieved coexistence but continued to compete. As the years went by, concessions were made to Islamism, enabling Mawdudi's followers to continue to promote a traditional Salafi Islam that would in the end exert its influence over all of South Asia, from Kashmir to Afghanistan.[32]

What, in detail, however, are the essential characteristics of Mawdudi's Islamic model, as expressed in *Risala-e-diniyat*? First of all, it should be noted that as with Al-Banna and Qutb, he drew heavily on Ibn Taymiyya, though he deployed his ideas with an Anglo-Saxon energy and prose style. In more practical terms, he expounded in prophetic tones the rights and duties of all faithful Muslims in general and of the Pakistanis in particular, enunciating four basic rules that the faithful are obliged to follow. These were:

1) A Muslim must obey only the commandments of God, which Mawdudi calls 'the rights of God', which every man is obliged to fulfil.[33] Among the rights of God, he says that Muslims must 'obey him honestly and unreservedly'. He goes on: 'We fulfil the needs of this right by following God's Law as prescribed in the Qur'an and the Sunna.'[34] He is careful to repeat the

inalienable commandments which Ibn Taymiyya had already laid down in the thirteenth century, namely, in addition to the profession of the faith, alms (*zakat*), prayer (*ibadat* and *salat*), pilgrimage (*hajj*) and Jihad, for which a Muslim should be willing to sacrifice his wealth, his goods and even his life.[35]

2) The Muslim enjoys rights over the disposal of his own person: 'the rights of one's own self'.[36] For Mawdudi, this arose from the necessity of mastering the physical needs and overweening appetites of man. It also included the struggle against the temptations of the flesh, alcohol, drugs, and the importance of not consuming forbidden foods: pork or blood. Mawdudi writes:

> The Shari'a forbids the use of all those things which are injurious to man's physical, mental or moral existence. It forbids the consumption of blood, intoxicating drugs, flesh of the pig, beasts of prey, poisonous and unclean animals and carcasses, for all these things have undesirable effects on the physical, moral, intellectual and spiritual life of man.[37]

Similarly, Mawdudi forbade Muslims to dispose of their own lives as they saw fit, or kill themselves. Life, he said, belongs not to man but to God. Death should come solely from God. Consequently the individual has no right to harm his own existence by committing suicide or placing himself in heedless danger.

3) A Muslim is obliged to respect 'the rights of other men' within the Muslim polity.[38] Thus, Mawdudi concludes that there is a constant necessity to find the true balance between the rights of the person and those of the Islamic society. He adds that if a conflict arises between the interest of the individual and that of the community, a decision between the two must be made on the basis of the Shari'a.[39] In practice, in order to safeguard the rights of other Muslims, Mawdudi forbade lying, theft, corruption, cheating, interest and usury, games of chance, lottery and profiteering. In addition, in a purely Salafi spirit,

he called for a high degree of morality in Muslim society. In particular, he forbade adultery, fornication and homosexuality. On this issue, he wrote as follows:

Adultery, fornication, and unnatural sexual indulgence have been strictly prohibited, for they not only vitiate the morality and impair the health of the perpetrator but also spread corruption and immorality in society, cause venereal disease, damage both public health and the morals of the coming generations, upset relations between man and man, and split the very fabric of the cultural and social structure of the community. Islam intends to eliminate root and branch such crimes.[40]

Finally, Mawdudi concludes that in order to avoid harm to individuals and the destruction of society, it is necessary to respect the restrictions imposed by Islamic law. In passing, he exhorts all Muslims to display kindness, nobility and humanity. Concluding that every Muslim should consider himself a representative by whose standards the faith will be judged, he writes:

He should win the hearts of people by his character and example. Then alone can he become a true ambassador of Islam.[41]

It should be recalled that Mawdudi wrote these words in 1932. At that time, many Europeans, Asians and Africans were fascinated by Islam. Muslims were seen as unaggressive, living within their faith in peace, spirituality and serenity.

4) The believer should respect what Mawdudi calls 'the rights of all creatures'.[42] Mawdudi's appeal for respect for animals relates to an Asian tradition. He states that it is forbidden to kill them for amusement or sport, and prescribes how beasts of burden are to be treated:

Regarding the beasts of burden, and animals used for riding or transport, Islam distinctly forbids man to keep them hungry, to put intolerable burdens on them and to beat them cruelly.[43]

In an indication of the ecological aspect of Islam, Mawdudi declares it is forbidden for Muslims to cut trees or burn off scrubland, adding that snaring birds and keeping them in cages is also abhorrent to Islam.[44]

THE ISLAMIC OPPOSITION: 1980–2001
(BELHADJ TO BIN LADEN)

In the 1980s, an Islamic movement of a new kind arose that posed a strong challenge to authority and to the Islamic establishment. This politicised faction made its first appearance in the mosques, and as time passed became more visible on the political scene of the majority of the Muslim countries. This rebellious tendency has appeared to affect most social groups, including students, workers, peasants, the unions, the army and the police. Henceforth, Islamism would set itself up in competition to both secular nationalism and the progressive left, which has lost ground both in the Middle East and the Maghreb. Among the reasons for this significant moment in the rise of Islamism, four factors seem to have been important. These are:

1) The impact of national and international events, including the Lebanese civil war (1975–90), the Iranian revolution (1978–9), the Afghan resistance to the Soviet invasion (1979–92) and the first Gulf War (1991–2), as well as the situation in Palestine ensuing from the Arab defeat of 1967. A further factor has been the extreme hostility towards Islam that followed the events of September 11, 2001 in New York.

2) The consequences of the resentment and frustration long felt by Islamists subjected to what they regarded as 'infidel' local governments. The Islamists rejected the westernisation and the Europeanisation (*tafarnuj*) of the ruling elites. They also reacted against what they saw as the religious innovation (*bid'a*) of the mystic Sufi brotherhoods, and the secularisation of some governments (notably in Turkey, Egypt, Tunisia and

71

Algeria). They believed the objective of the move towards secularisation and the alien values promoted by the Nasserist and Baathist nationalists was the dehumanisation of society and the obstruction of the emergence of Islamic power.

3) Corruption, as well as the misuse of the region's natural resources, including oil, minerals, phosphates and diamonds. There were significant distortions in the distribution of income derived from natural resources, particularly as these resources were controlled and largely used by governmental agencies, specifically by ministries linked to key activities of the state, such as defence, security and foreign affairs, to name the three most significant. In the status quo, once these greedy state sectors had been satisfied, other activities vital to the state, such as social services, health, transport and housing, were flung only the remaining crumbs.

4) The economic trough of the 1980s, which threw a significant section of the population of the Muslim countries into poverty. This applied especially to Turkey, Tunisia, Algeria, Egypt and Jordan.

The conjunction of all these factors had led, in varying degrees, to a state of unrest and to disturbances in a number of countries in the Middle East and the Maghreb. By the same token, the standing of the Islamists rose among frustrated and deprived populations, who had begun to demand dignity, social justice and a return to their ancestral values.

The Islamists of the third generation drew a comparison between the current state of deprivation of the Muslim world and that of the pre-Islamic period or *jahiliyya*, when ignorance, injustice, barbarism and materialism prevailed in the Arabian Peninsula. The Islamist writer Fathi Yakan, in a proselytising tract, suggested that Muslims should alter their attitudes, and ought to cease to elevate western materialism to the level of God. As he puts it:

I am aware that the path of the Du'at [preacher] in this age is strewn with temptations and pitfalls. Twentieth-century Jahiliyyah has destroyed all the concepts of virtue, goodness and nobility ... The materialism of this age has stuffed the noses of everyone until man can only think in terms of it, can only live by it and can only judge things from its point of view. It has blinded him physically and spiritually, and deadened his feeling and sensitivity.[45]

Fathi Yakan's position is that of the majority of neo-fundamentalist Islamists, who consider that only by faith and morality can a Muslim regain the nobility and virtue of his soul. In the view of these writers, only through re-Islamisation can a Muslim rise above materialism and the blandishments of modern industrial society. They believe, however, that their plans for re-Islamisation are deliberately frustrated by the secular nationalist governments of those Muslim countries whose interests are linked to those of the western Christian powers, hence the antipathy of the Islamists for current governments. Nevertheless, the Islamist movements do not fail to listen with great care to the people.

Two groups of contemporary radical Islamists can be distinguished, which have emerged in recent years. One of these, the radical wing, is made up of those groups that seek redemption (*tawba*) through violence and armed action. These include, for example, the GIA (Armed Islamic Group) and the GSPC (Salafi Group for Preaching and Combat) in Algeria; Gamaat Al-Islamiya and Islamic Jihad in Egypt; and As-Sirat Al-Mustaqim and Takfir Wal-Hijra in Morocco, in addition to Al-Qa'ida itself. Al-Qa'ida is the key organisation for the Islamists. It takes the form of an international secretariat, which serves as a base and an ideological and financial network for Salafi Islamist groups (the name Al-Qa'ida means literally 'the base'). Adherents of its ideology are found in Asia, in the Middle East, in the Maghreb, in Europe and elsewhere. They call themselves 'Salafists' or 'Islamic Groups', titles that conjure up overtones of group solidarity and historical legitimacy. This is the situation with groups in Egypt, Algeria, Morocco, Indonesia, and the Abu Saif organisation in the Philippines.

Meanwhile, the other wing, which is more moderate, consists of parties that prioritise political action and the peaceful acquisition of power. These include the Algerian FIS (Islamic Salvation Front), Ennahda in Tunisia, and Adl Wal-Ihsan (Justice and Charity Party) in Morocco.

REDEMPTION THROUGH VIOLENCE AND JIHAD

In the 1980s, formations began to appear in the Muslim countries which sought to obtain redemption (*tawba*) for the Muslim countries through Jihad, or holy war. They are commanded by young self-styled 'Emirs', often veterans of the Afghan war, whose goal is to overthrow established governments and attack sections of the population who refuse to submit to the Islamic model and accept its values in their entirety. Such authoritarian groups benefit from contacts and logistic assistance from like-minded colleagues around the world. This global solidarity is based on the idea of Jihad, within the framework of a classic hierarchy of cells. An article by the Algerian journalist Bedreddine Manaa on Al-Qa'ida explains their simplistic philosophy:

> They believe the only means to set up an Islamic state is armed violence, and to reject elections as a means of gaining power. Is not democracy itself contrary to religion (*kufr*)?[46]

A statement made by Hassan Hattab, later the Emir of the Algerian GIA, confirmed that he was fighting 'neither for the return of impious democracy, nor to win parliamentary seats, but for the supremacy of the word of God'.[47] The slogan of the movement was, 'No dialogue, no reconciliation, no truce'. Hassan Hattab replaced Antar Zouabri, who was killed on 8 February 2002 by the Algerian security forces. Both men were renowned for their fatwas relating to perceived lapses from the faith (*takfir*). They were both responsible for the killing of Algerians who refused to rebel against the government, who sent their children to the secular government schools, or whose behaviour offended against Islamic rules, including neglect of obligatory covering by women. Hassan Hattab never denied his links with Al-Qa'ida.

Groups that seek redemption by force of arms, referred to by some western writers as 'apocalyptic',[48] are structured and organised in a very pragmatic fashion, with their Emirs at the head of their restricted hierarchies. They have little centralised structure and the cells of which they are made up comprise small groups of only a few dozen fighters who disperse at the slightest sign of danger. They are able quickly to reform, and individual fighters can transfer from one group to another. Their logistic needs are provided for by active or dormant networks of autonomous cells set up to supply the operational Jihadists.[49] Some groups launched attacks on the civilian population, especially in the countryside, and on representatives of the state. Others, such as Gamaat Al-Islamiya in Egypt, also targeted the Coptic Christian minority, as well as Jews and western tourists. The notorious fatwa of their mentor, Bin Laden, is explicit on the choice of targets.[50]

On the eve of the attack by the United States on Afghanistan in 2001, the human resources of Al-Qa'ida reportedly consisted of 2,830 men. These seemingly too precise figures were given by an Arab intelligence source at the time, repeated by the James Martin Center for Nonproliferation Studies in Monterey, California, and cited in a report to the French National Assembly. According to the information given, of the 2,830, 594 were Egyptians, 410 Jordanians, 291 Yemenis, 255 Iraqis, 162 Syrians, 177 Algerians, 11 Sudanese, 63 Tunisians, 53 Moroccans, 32 Palestinians and a few dozen Saudis.[51] In the same report, it was said that, 'Between 5,000 and 20,000 fighting men were said to have passed through the dozen or so training camps which Al-Qa'ida maintained in Afghanistan before the attacks.' In the light of the internal changes within Al-Qa'ida in recent years, all these figures relating to the membership of the organisation and their national origins have had to be been totally revised.[52]

The international connections of groups seeking redemption by violence were basically with Islamic groups in other countries, and all were to some extent, and through a variety of channels, in contact with Al-Qa'ida, the cornerstone of the network. Material support and reliable intelligence also came from sleeper organisations in place in western countries, particularly the United Kingdom, Belgium, Austria, Italy and Germany. Nothing less than a globalised co-ordination of operational cells committed to Islamic action was taking shape. The attack on Al-Qa'ida in Afghanistan by the western allies in 2001 in fact had few consequences for the organisation other than to disperse its fighting men. Scattered throughout the world, they easily regrouped into dormant cells, needing only a signal from their Emirs to reactivate. Other militants linked up as individuals with established international cells of sympathisers of the Algerian GIA and GSPC, as well as the Islamic Group for Jihad in Morocco, which had already established cells in the Balkans, Britain, Italy, Belgium and Pakistan. In other words, Al-Qa'ida became a virtual 'state', of an anomalous kind, balancing according to the daily fluctuation of circumstances its resources, its alliances and its internal ordinances, decentralised in its structure as were its territories.

If the underlying international and national issues that exercise the Jihadists are not equitably solved, the possibility remains that they may carry out further attacks as spectacular as those of September 11, 2001 on New York and Washington. Anniversary dates are particularly susceptible, and it should not be forgotten, incidentally, that anniversaries under the Islamic calendar, which the Islamists observe, are not the same as those by the Christian reckoning.

THE ALTERNATIVE ISLAMISTS: PEACEFUL POLITICAL ACTION

The religious extremism of the redemption groups, and the outbreaks of violence they perpetrate, create a strong impression in the West and cause much anxiety. In reality, however, they represent only a tiny minority of Muslims. It is of course true that the radicals have a very high profile at the present time in comparison with the moderates whom they have apparently vanquished. However, it is important not to leap to the wrong conclusion. The great majority of Muslims practise an Islam that is tolerant and liberal, and neither identify themselves with those who resort to violence to impose their religious and individual rights, nor share their dogmatic interpretation of Islam.

However, it should not be forgotten that even within Islamism itself there are political organisations that reject violence. Such parties are those that have taken their inspiration directly from the thinkers of the 1920s, such as Hassan Al-Banna, Mawdudi, Rashid Rida, Ben Badis and Sayyid Qutb, and have not been influenced by the violence of the new extremists. Their rise was the result of their perception of the deterioration of the social and political situation in the Arab and Muslim world. These parties appeared on the political scene, resolved to use the machinery of democracy to achieve their aims and to eschew violence. As John Esposito rightly comments, a 'quiet revolution' took place in the Muslim countries between 1980 and 1990:

> Islamic activity was seen to be an effective political and social force, working within the system in the framework of institutions and of social life in general. Islam-based organisations set up schools, clinics, hospitals, banks and publishing houses. They also made available to the public a whole range of social services. In this way, a new elite generation has taken its place within the professions, educated in the modern way but motivated by Islamic rather than secular values. They include doctors, lawyers, engineers, teachers and social workers, and they seek to introduce into society policies and attitudes derived from Islam.[53]

Such Islamist movements mainly appeared in the Maghreb and in the Middle East. Two leading figures will serve as an illustration of the thinking of these political formations. These are Sheikh Rachid Ghannouchi, the ideologue of the Tunisian Ennahda Party, and Sheikh Ali Belhadj of the Algerian Islamic Salvation Front. Before embarking on an analysis of these two, however, it should be said that in general terms what is striking about Islamic leaders across the Maghreb, including Sheikh Abdessalam Yacine of the Justice and Charity Party in Morocco, is the similarity of their ideological and organisational positions. Each takes the view that the crisis that affects his country is related to the concept of 'civilisation', and that the solution is to be found in social justice and the 'revalorisation of Arab Muslim identity'.[54] Similarly, all take as their starting point the organisation and ideology of Hassan Al-Banna's Muslim Brotherhood, as well as making reference to the fatwas of Ibn Taymiyya. They also agree that a return to the institution of the Caliphate will be a prerequisite for the establishment of the rule of the Qur'an and the Shari'a in the lands of Islam. Sheikh Yacine, for instance, has called for the creation in Morocco of a 'national Islamic state, until the time is ripe for the construction of a federal Caliphate'.[55]

Lastly, the leaders of the moderate parties, in contrast to the heads of the radical Islamist groups, are careful to maintain their contacts with politically inclined intellectuals and academics, and benefit from a wide social base rooted especially in the less privileged classes and members of the liberal professions. The leadership of such parties is often twofold. On the one hand there will be a well-educated and moderate leader whose role is to reassure and to promise respect for individual liberties. This role is played by Rachid Ghannouchi in Tunisia and Abassi Madani in Algeria. Meanwhile, there will also be a preacher who will galvanise the militants with his virulent and uncompromising sermons and even tackle taboo subjects connected with the Jews and the Christians. Two such preachers are Salah Karkar, Ghannouchi's right-hand man, and Ali Belhadj, Madani's associate.[56] The philosophy of these groups is to apply pressure through democratic means, though the transformation of democracy may be their goal.

In the case of the Ennahda Party, Rachid Ghannouchi, who lives in exile in Britain, is regarded by Islamologues as the most accomplished theorist of 'modern' Islamism.[57] He is a professor of philosophy who differs from the majority of contemporary Islamists through his espousal of the principles of action through democracy, pluralism and religious non-violence.[58] His ideas relate to those of the Iranian left-wing Islamist Ali Shariati, and to the liberal reformist school of Al-Afghani and Muhammad Abduh. His philosophy is nuanced, and takes into account the modern principles of human rights, tolerance and humanity. He is one of the very few Islamists to pay any heed to the western thought of the Enlightenment. However, in the last resort, his goal is to further the interests of the Salafi Islamic movement in Tunisia. His long-term goal is to establish new institutions for Tunisia, and a framework of law that will sustain them, on the broad principles of the Shari'a.

For him, Islam takes priority over all. He therefore believes the state must be completely restructured so that it can be adapted to the needs of an Islamic politics freely chosen by the people. The avowed objective is to arrive at 'a complete transformation of the Tunisian reality through Islam'.[59] However, the current president of Tunisia, Zine el-Abidine Ben Ali, who inherited a purely secular state from his predecessor Habib Bourguiba, has sworn that in Tunisia, 'there will never be a place for a religious political party'.[60]

On the Algerian side, a similarly intransigent stand against certain religious political parties has been taken by the existing authorities. The FIS was banned in 1991 by the Algerian government, and its leaders, Abassi Madani and Ali Belhadj, were imprisoned. Ali Belhadj has always rejected the idea that Algeria should be run on the secular principles it has espoused since its independence in 1962. In his view, the Islamists have a duty to take political power in Algeria in order to impose the Shari'a. Without this, as he has said:

Islam is reduced to the level of sermonising and worship without practical effect: a situation that is unacceptable to Muslims who understand the true faith. Government and the Qur'an are like twins: they are inseparable.[61]

Belhadj then locates the problem in an international context, as follows:

It is essential for the Muslims of the whole world to involve themselves in the advent of the pure dominion of Islam, and of government based on the Shari'a, faithful to the model of the orthodox Caliphs.[62]

Belhadj's ideas relate directly to those of Ibn Taymiyya, Qutb and Mawdudi, all of whom he takes as models. He writes, for instance:

> Islam has established laws, collected in the Shari'a, which represent divine commandments. Did not Muhammad say, 'Obey no one who fails to obey the Creator'?[63]

And he goes on:

> Verily, Islam is *din*, *dunya* and *dawla*: religion, world and state. To ignore this is to subvert Islam.

On the issue of democracy, he adds:

> We find no trace of the word democracy either in the dictionary of the Arab language, or in God's Book, or in the Sunna, or in any of our great writers.[64]

For Ali Belhadj, consultation of the religious notables by the ruler (the concept of *shura*) is the only acceptable limitation on the exercise of power within Islam. In relation to the issues of Jihad, of the position of women, the veil and the problem of apostasy, he differs virtually not at all from the Islamists of the second generation.

4

THE THREE GENERATIONS
OF ISLAMISTS IN THEIR
SOCIAL DIMENSION:
THE ISSUE OF APOSTASY

Islam, in common with the monotheistic religions that preceded it, is essentially concerned with human beings, their actions, their value and their fate. Muslims believe that man is a creature singled out by God, who has deliberately endowed humanity with particular capacities based on pity, mercy, dignity and liberty, which all derive their force from divine authority. On this issue, the Qur'an is unambiguous, declaring: 'We have privileged man and bestowed dignity upon him.' According to the theologians, and especially Ibn Taymiyya, a good Muslim acquires his liberty and dignity solely by virtue of his obedience to the Shari'a. In other words, Islam does not endorse the primacy of fundamental liberties as conceived in the West, such as the freedom of expression, belief and thought. In Islam, such freedoms are not absolute, but limited, and they may even be annulled where they conflict with the Shari'a.[1] There are absolute prohibitions, such as those on the consumption of alcohol and pork; the exercise of certain professions such as that of banker, because of the problem of usury; and sexual misbehaviour, identified as fornication. According to Ibn Taymiyya, these are transgressions reprehensible in the eyes of Islam, since God privileges the ordinances he proclaims and requires human-kind to conform to them.[2]

Another prohibition is that on apostasy. What consequences would there be, were an individual to repudiate his membership of the *umma* and declare himself to be an apostate? In principle, there is a contract (*mithaq*) between the individual and God that binds them together, in which no other person is involved. Even

Ibn Taymiyya accepts that no third party can claim the right to interfere in the relationship between God and the faithful Muslim, provided the latter respects the principles of the *mithaq*. Only if the Muslim abrogates his relationship with God can denial of Islam or 'apostasy' be spoken of.[3] Nevertheless, any such apostasy remains a private matter between God and the Muslim who has broken his contract of fidelity with his creator. Consequently, the privilege of punishing the apostate belongs to God, and not to any individual or religious authority. In Islam, forgiveness flows from God, and is not conferred by any intermediary, whatever position that individual might occupy in any religious hierarchy. It should be noted here that certain contemporary theologians of the third generation have challenged the principle that punishment belongs to God alone, by taking upon themselves the right to condemn an apostate to death.[4]

The theologians of the first two generations did not regard apostasy as one of the five most serious infractions against Islam.[5] To some degree, this is why the sentence of death was not in general pronounced on apostates. Instead, they were banished from the community of the believers, while their goods were disposed of by the authorities. Specifically, on the basis of the Hadith which rules that 'a Muslim may not inherit from an unbeliever, nor an unbeliever from a Muslim', the theologians concluded that the worldly goods of a renegade should devolve to the public purse, rather than to his legitimate heirs.[6] This ruling requires some qualification, since if the apostate had made during his lifetime a will (*wassiya*) in favour of his heirs, they would, notwithstanding his condemnation, receive at his death a third of the goods he had to leave. The Basra school of Shi'ite Islam, which bases its teaching on doctrines laid down by the Imam Ali, goes as far as to permit the apostate to leave his entire estate to his inheritors. The views of this school are based on the common-sense notion that the estate should benefit the family of the apostate, who depended on him, rather than the loosely defined 'public purse' which would undeservedly inherit the fruits of the labour of another person.

In any event, it seems clear that the first two generations, the founding generation of Islam and the generation of political

Islamism, took a much more liberal line over the issue of apostasy than does the contemporary neo-fundamentalist generation. This was an issue over which the rulings of the earlier theologians were more forthright. In their view, a person who has renounced Islam must forfeit some of his worldly wealth but his life is secure. The most draconian punishment to which he might be liable was that of ostracism and banishment from the *umma*, pending the judgement to be passed upon him by God. The third generation of Islamists appears to have taken up a more uncompromising stance, in relation both to apostates and to infidels. This position has hardened in response to the successive foreign incursions into the Muslim world and with attempts by missionaries from certain Christian sects to effect conversions, with the acquiescence of the colonial powers. It should be said that the Sufis have yet another view on the issue of apostasy, which will come under examination in the second part of the present study.

WOMEN IN ISLAMIC SOCIETY AND THE WEARING OF THE VEIL

Among the central issues in the Muslim world, the status of women has especially preoccupied the fantasies of westerners. In general, westerners view Muslim women through a distorting mirror. The image they have of women is of a fleeting shadow, enveloped inside a dark covering, servile, and subservient to any masculine whim. The imagination of the West has been moulded by the conviction that women's rights have been systematically frustrated by a despotic masculine power, which has arrogated to itself the right to confine females to the roles of household labour and reproduction of the species. This image has been reinforced by the images of women presented by the Orientalists. As the *Encyclopedia of Islam* puts it:

> Hierarchically, women were relegated to the level of children and the weak, who need protection . . . Women were kept for centuries

in a position of virtually total subjection, thanks to the paternalism of the Qur'anic tradition.[7]

Some western observers, meanwhile, quote out of context the following verse from the Qur'an:

Your women are a tillage for you, so go to your tillage when you wish.[8]

Others again, Louis Milliot, for example, contend that the specificities of Arab society are responsible for all the ills which beset women. As he writes:

The predicament of women could perhaps be said to be primarily caused by the 'sacralisation' of women's inferior status. Thus, woman has been relegated to the ethical status of a second-rank human being, below men in the hierarchy of God's creation, with a particular burden of duties, restricted in her powers, and the mistress of neither her fate nor her body. The status of women is regarded as not open to argument. Thus, issues related to relations between men and women are beyond logic and lie in the same region of discourse as the application of reason to truth.[9]

Moving away from these western stereotypes, however, what does Islam actually have to say about the rights of women? One basic fact is that under the Shari'a, sexual relations outside marriage between a Muslim woman and a non-Muslim are forbidden and may be punished by death. Within Islam, however, the Hadith recognised by orthodox Islam include exact prescriptions governing the position of women, including the crucial dictum, 'The best of you is he who treats his wife best.'[10] In addition, at the time of his last pilgrimage to Mecca, Muhammad is reported to have made a declaration as follows to his disciples: 'Fear God in what concerns your wives, whom I command you to treat well.'[11]

On the basis of such injunctions coming from the Prophet, the status of women palpably improved in the course of the first two generations of Islam from that of the pre-Islamic period. Women gained their freedom and became economically independent. The Prophet's wife, Khadija, the owner of a flourishing business, was there to serve as an example. A number of accounts testify that 'women sometimes occupied important positions, for example as priestesses'.[12] Indeed, in the time of the Caliph Omar it is known that a woman occupied the important position of director of the prestigious market in Medina. In addition, legal scholars (the *fuqaha*) ruled that women could sit as judges.[13] The rights of women appear to have been enhanced in other ways after the advent of Islam. Henceforth, women were able to ply trades that had been hitherto regarded as limited to men. More precisely, in contrast to the myth disseminated by some westerners, Muslim women were not slaves, silent and pliant to the whim of the Arab male. In regard to the legal status of women, it was also evident that women enjoyed rights within marriage, just as men did. On this point, the Qur'an's ruling is as follows:

> If a woman fears maltreatment or aversion from her husband, they would commit no offence if they are reconciled amicably, reconciliation is best . . . And if they separate, God will give each one plenty of His abundance.[14]

In other words, if a woman suffers from her husband's neglect, the couple should try to reconcile. In the last resort, however, the implication is that a woman should not suffer as the result of a separation. Non-Muslim women also enjoyed inalienable rights in the matter of marriage and divorce. When they marry Muslims, they have 'the full right to maintain their faith and to practise it'.[15] In the field of property rights, Islam accepts that a woman has the absolute right to dispose of her goods, completely denying the husband any rights in the matter.[16] The Qur'an also swept away the pre-Islamic convention that a woman was a possession to be disposed of by the husband in his will. In practise this custom assigned to a brother or a cousin the right to inherit the wife of the deceased by the same token as his disposable goods. The Qur'an strictly forbade this practice in the verse:

> O believers, It is not lawful for you to inherit the women against their will; nor to restrain them in order to take away part of what you had given them . . .[17]

It must be conceded, however, that the practice still exists in certain Muslim countries that a family member inherits not merely the personal possessions of a deceased person but also his wife. Some exponents of contemporary neo-fundamentalism give their endorsement to this custom, provided that the wife consents to become the wife of the heir of her late husband.

THE PHYSICAL SECURITY OF WOMEN: ASSAULT AND RAPE

In the event that a woman becomes the victim of assault during a tribal conflict, a fight or a raid, she receives a recompense for blood spilled (*diya*) twice as large as that granted to a man. Islamic custom prescribes that the price of a woman's blood is set at twice or three times the amount given to a man who is the victim of an attack of the same kind.[18] The crime of rape is also taken very seriously in Islam. If a woman loses her life in the course of a rape, or as its consequence, the *diya* is between three and four times more than that accorded to male victims. The issue is aggravated further if the woman is pregnant. In this case, the compensation set is equivalent to that of two non-pregnant women.

On the basis of the examples quoted above, it is evidently wise to set aside preconceptions and to avoid hasty conclusions on the issue of the status of Muslim women. As Abu Al-Faraj Al-Isfahani said in his renowned tenth-century Kitab Al-Aghani ('Book of Songs'):

> For some decades, it appears that the obligation on women to keep themselves apart and to wear the veil has been in abeyance. Female riders, displaying their legs, have taken part in horse races at Medina. Women with uncovered faces meet strangers, go out visiting at night, and talk about poetry in the mosques.[19]

In addition, certain chroniclers recount that 'there are women who emulate the literary myth of the female hero: they help the warriors in the struggle against the crusaders and take part in the maintenance of social order.'[20] According to further reliable sources, women had the right to divorce men in matriarchal Muslim society. For instance, in certain parts of Yemen, men were wholly dominated by their wives:

> When a woman is angry with her husband, she places a scrap of red cloth at the opening of the tent. The man understands from this that he is in disgrace and dare not cross the threshold of his home until the wife removes the signal with her own hand.[21]

Similar customs were observed in other Muslim countries, especially in the Algerian Kabylie region and among the Berbers of Morocco and the Sahara. The Muslim woman, as several of the ancient chroniclers say, was 'the mistress of her fate, since she might at her own discretion leave her man whenever he has displeased her'.[22] This custom was also widespread in antiquity among the wealthier social classes of Arabia. In addition, it was much mentioned at the time that the women of that region would agree to wed only on condition that they would retain the right to leave their husbands if they so wished. Finally, counter to the stereotype of a submissive woman, it may be noted that old tales often portray the Muslim woman as 'sharp, malicious, defying supervision, and enjoying despite everything sufficient liberty to embark on adventures of the heart'.[23]

In this connection, it is impossible not to query whether, in early times, women were in reality as sequestered as has been supposed, and it must certainly be asked whether they were obliged to cover themselves as has been thought. In the first place, it should be noted that early Islam did not insist that all women should be veiled, which was no more than a recommendation. On the basis of the Qur'an, it seems that only the wives of the Prophet and the women of his family were instructed to cover themselves, in order to keep themselves from public scrutiny. Nevertheless, all Muslim women were faced by the choice of deciding whether to wear the veil or not. This was a real instance of individual liberty. According to Professor Muhammad Hamidullah, a representative of the academic Sunni clergy, 'The veil in no way signified the seclusion of women: its function was to prevent strangers from being attracted to them.'[24] This author adds in passing that there are no legal penalties if a woman fails to observe the advice to cover her face with a veil.

It should also be noted that it may be learned from ancient historians that the veil was not by origin an Arab custom. On this issue, Will Durant asserts that the practice of the veil was a borrowing from the Greeks and the Persians. In the words of this author: 'after the time of the Persian Emperor Darius, the situation of women declined, especially among the wealthy classes ... In ancient Persian frescos, not a single woman's face appears, and apparently no allusion to women is made.'[25] Ayatollah Mortada Motahari, an Iranian cleric and intellectual, explains in his pamphlet on the veil (hijab) that 'strict and severe veiling prevailed in ancient Persia, to the point where a married woman became a stranger even to her father and brothers'.[26]

A further comment on the importation of the veil into the Arab world from neighbouring regions in the early days of Islam comes from Jawaharlal Nehru, the founder of the Indian state, in his book on the history and development of Asia:

> There was also a significant and unfortunate change in the status of women. The use of the veil was unknown among Arab women. They did not live apart, nor were they hidden: quite to the contrary they appeared in public places, going to the mosque and to public gatherings ... After their great victories, however, the Arabs increasingly adopted a tradition that prevailed in the two neighbouring empires, that of Persia and that of Rome ... They took up the regrettable customs of these two empires and installed among the Arabs the practice of keeping women in seclusion and of separating them from men.[27]

It must be conceded, on the other hand, that too great an emphasis on the non-compulsory aspect of the veil may be misleading in view of the evident occurrence of veiling in practice. The wearing of the veil may not have been the subject of strict rules in Arabia, but it is true that women already veiled themselves on specified occasions, including mourning periods and public ceremonies of various kinds. In addition, the conquering Muslims who overcame Persia and the Greco-Roman Empire in the eastern Mediterranean were not merely following the customs of the conquered people, but were also following the injunctions of the Qur'an. Though these were, as has been pointed out above, principally directed at the Prophet's wives, it needs to be acknowledged that the Qur'anic verse in question explicitly extends the injunction to other women:

> O Prophet! Tell your wives and daughters and the wives of the believers to draw their outer garments closer.[28]

Nevertheless, it remains true that what is striking in the documentation relating to the lives of women in the time of the Prophet Muhammad and the *salaf* is the evidence of the existence of a liberal system. Women appeared to have more rights than they do in Islam today. As has been seen, women were free to attend the mosques, to occupy senior positions and to be priestesses; the veil was not rigidly required and was not obligatory in all circumstances. Women were also empowered to participate in referendums or oaths of allegiance (*bai'a*), which were in terms of the recognition of social rights the contemporary equivalent of the right to vote. Meanwhile, men could be required to be monogamous, with the condition that the first contract of marriage could be dissolved if a man were to marry a second time; while in certain circumstances, a woman could divorce a man.

Today, however, it must be admitted that the status of women has considerably declined in the Muslim world. Codes of family law based on Islam, with the exception of those developed by Ataturk in Turkey and Bourguiba in Tunisia, subject women to the dominance of their male relatives until marriage, after which they fall under the legal authority of their husbands. A husband may prevent his wife from travelling and forbid her to work, as well as being able to divorce her at any moment he might choose. In this way, most Muslim systems of family law reduce women to a condition of unreasonable deprivation, offering them nothing but the choice between submission and quitting Muslim society. The exclusion of women is one of the reasons for the failures and distorted development of the countries of the South, and such states will only progress if, among other reforms they may implement, they confer equal status on their women.

SPECIFIC ISSUES: WOMEN'S EVIDENCE; ADULTERY; STONING

It is often stated in connection with the right to be a witness that women are regarded as inferior to men, to the extent that according to Islam the evidence of a man is equivalent to that of two women. In reality, Islamic law distinguishes between two kinds of evidence. One of these concerns only accusations of adultery, while the other applies to civil and criminal cases.

In the first of these two types, it is the emotional and personal nature of the transgression under investigation which leads to the requirement that the evidence of one woman should be confirmed by another. The point is the elimination of the subjective element and the need to reach a secure consensus on the veracity of an accusation of adultery. It is accepted that a single woman may be a witness if her personality, her reputation and her dignity furnish sufficient justification. In providing for the reinforcement of one woman's testimony by another, Islam intends to avoid the occurrence of any vindictive misrepresentation of the facts that could lead to the unjust imposition of the death penalty on an accused person. It should not be forgotten that the crime of adultery comes into the category of 'grave offences' whose perpetrators are subject to the penalty of death. This is a penalty, however, that is never invoked by moderate Muslim judges, who consider that in the matter of adultery those culpable are obliged to give an account of themselves only to God, in the hereafter. This is in fact the opinion of the majority of Sufi Muslims. Despite the legal situation in some countries, the stoning of women is contrary to custom and is seen as shocking by most Muslims.[29]

SHI'ITE POSITIONS ON CERTAIN ISSUES RELATING TO WOMEN

Two such questions are temporary marriage and inheritance. In relation to the Shi'ite practice of temporary marriage, all marriages must be subject to the rules of the Shari'a. A particular quirk of Shi'ism, however, is that the ancient institution of temporary marriage, known as *nikah al-muta'*, has been preserved. The defining characteristic of this relationship is that it is for a specified period. It is entered into before witnesses, and is performed by a religious dignitary. The temporary spouses may consummate the marriage, afterwards parting from their temporary husband or wife. Temporary marriage was prevalent among the bedouin in the pre-Islamic period, and continued to be tolerated in the early days of Islam. However, the Caliph Omar forbade it for Sunni Muslims. The Shi'ites, on the other hand, who did not accept the legitimacy of Omar's Caliphate, have continued up to modern times to accept the practice, which is regarded within the Shi'ite sect as legitimate according to the Shari'a.

Turning to inheritance, the difference lies in the greater favour shown to women under Shi'ism than is the case under the Sunni faith. Sunni law accords a daughter a portion of an inheritance half the size of that given to a son.[30] Shi'ites, on the other hand, place male and female heirs on a footing of equality. In other words, the Shi'ites do not accept the ruling of the Qur'an that a daughter, even an only daughter, should not receive more than half a total inheritance. The Shi'ites take their justification from their contention that Fatima, the daughter of the Prophet Muhammad, had the right to inherit in its entirety her father's legacy, and especially the oasis of Fadak.[31] In practice, however, the Caliph Abu Bakr never agreed to confer the legacy in its entirety upon Fatima. In reaction to this perceived injustice, the Shi'ites turned to interpretations of the Qur'an that favoured women and their descendants. To be more exact, the Shi'ite jurisprudential tradition, as well as the Shi'ite Hadith, tend to refer to the 'gift' made by Muhammad to Fatima, avoiding the expression 'inheritance'. The intention here is not to contradict the literal interpretation of Verses 7–12 of Sura 4 of the Qur'an which insists that part of every inheritance must be received by men.[32] The so-called 'gift' is justified on the basis of another verse of the Qur'an, which says: 'Give the kinsman his due.'[33] The Shi'ite Hadith is as follows:

> God sent word to his Prophet, saying: 'Give to your kinsman that which is due.' The Messenger of God did not know who the kinsman in question might be, and therefore returned to Jibril, who went to God to get the answer. Then God sent him the revelation that he must give the land of Fadak to Fatima. Then the Messenger of God called Fatima, and said to her, 'O Fatima, God has instructed me to give you the land of Fadak.' And she replied, 'O messenger of God, I accept this gift from God and from you.'[34]

To sum up, even if the Shari'a appears in principle to discriminate against women in matters of inheritance, the Shi'ite view is that there is no reason why family members should not compensate for such inequity by making gifts, in accordance with the Qur'anic concepts examined above. The situation relating to discrimination between men and women in the matter of inheritance has become much less clear cut in modern Shi'ite doctrine since the ancient controversy over Fadak. Nevertheless, it can still be observed that Sunnis whose objective is to confer an inheritance upon their female offspring sometimes convert to Shi'ism solely for this reason.

THE MUSLIM COMMUNITY AND SEXUALITY

Problems concerning relationships between men and women in Muslim society have been studied extensively by Arab researchers.[35] It should be said that the issue of sexuality is one of the most delicate questions faced by Muslim society. The subject is never broached directly in public. The taboo is reinforced by the way

Muslims are conditioned to approach it. Without turning their backs on the natural relationship between the sexes, Muslims learn from childhood to treat the subject with discretion and delicacy. Islam accepts and encourages the coupling of male and female. In fact, the importance of the issue has led to its being hedged about with injunctions and detailed prescriptions that are on occasion somewhat surprising. For instance, Bokhari gives a Hadith which may be cited here:

> According to Aisha, a man had definitively set aside his wife. The Prophet, when asked if the woman in the case could remarry her first husband, said 'No, not until her second husband has consummated the marriage as the first one did.'[36]

More directly, Muslims take their lead from the behaviour of the Prophet, who set an example of how to pay proper attention to his wives, and especially to Aisha. According to Aflaki, the biographer of Rumi:

> Aisha, lacking the Prophet's company, was missing the delights of the flesh. One day, happening to see an amorous encounter between some sparrows, she drew the sight to the attention of the Prophet. That very night, Aisha's desires were more than satisfied.[37]

The history of the Arab conquests, particularly in Spain and Portugal, teaches us that Islam was in its earlier days more tolerant and understanding of individual wishes in the field of sexuality than in the Christian communities confronted by the Muslims. For example, there were laws in effect in Christian countries at the period that condemned homosexuals to castration, flogging and the humiliation of having their heads shaved. Those who breached the rules of chastity were often excluded from Christian society. The Muslims, however, were more tolerant and liberal towards marginal sexualities, which were the object of serious medical scrutiny. The most subtle student of the psychology of sexual deviation was Qusta Ibn Luqa (820–912), a doctor, philosopher, musician and translator of Greek texts.[38] Ibn Luqa advocated an understanding of the psychological and emotional differences between individuals, cautioning them against value judgements in regard to individuals whose destiny had been determined by nature. He made a systematic study of some two dozen types of sexual variations among women as well as men.

Qusta Ibn Luqa saw the differences between those he studied as natural and lying for the most part within the field of sexual choice. He explains, for example, that some men are predisposed to be attracted by women, while others are drawn to other men, and others again are attracted to both sexes.[39] He adds that such sexual tendencies are also found among Muslim women, especially among the educated classes. The Muslim community was thus acquainted with ideas seen in modern times as related to psychoanalysis, long before such theories were developed by Sigmund Freud. Unfortunately, for dogmatic reasons, Ibn Luqa's ideas were never followed up.

Freud, for his part, seems never to have taken into account specific aspects raised by Muslim sexual life. He claimed universal status for his theory of the Oedipus complex, where the relationship of a son with his mother, and the supposed accompanying desire to kill his father, is seen in an erotic light. This psychoanalytic phenomenon seems, however, to be in fact specific to western society, or even to Freud's Vienna, and is unknown to Muslim society. In the Muslim community, there is no triangular relationship between the child, the mother and the father, in which the father is the object of the son's jealousy. In Islamic society, the father tends to be excluded, while the mystical relationship between the son and his mother is placed in the foreground. A Muslim's love and devotion to his mother is unrelated to anything known in the West. In Islam, the love of the son for the mother is simply an extension of the commandments of God. The young Muslim learns from childhood that it is his mother who will be waiting for him at the gates of the afterlife, to admit or refuse him to Paradise. It is for these reasons that in Islamic society Oedipus has no place and the father stands aside as God places his son under his wife's authority.

Other aspects of Muslim society merit more intensive study by psychoanalysts. This has prompted A. Reza Arasteh to observe: 'If Freud had been more aware of other cultures, he would have made fewer mistakes.'[40] As will emerge below in the second part of the present work, the concept of sexuality developed by the rationalists and mystics is not radically different from the ideas of the early generations of Islam, though it is equally complex.

THE STATUS OF MINORITIES (THE *DHIMMIS*)

The *dhimmis* are protected minorities of non-Muslims within Islamic society. The expression refers particularly to the Christian and Jewish minorities. For the Islamists of the first and second generations, the *dhimmis*, who enjoyed the contractual status of protected minorities paying a specific tax, the *jizya*, to the Islamic state, enjoyed the privilege of permission to practise their religion. They were subject to specific legal provisions relating to marriage, divorce and inheritance, and were allowed to worship according to their faith and to engage in social activities appropriate to their customs and their religion. In Medina, in the Prophet's time, 'the Jews of the various tribes living in Yathrib [Medina] constituted together with the Muslims a single national entity. . . . Their freedom to worship was recognised in a special provision.'[41]

Later, protection was granted to two types of person exiled within the Muslim community – those whose presence was permanent, and those who were temporary. In the first of these cases, a non-Muslim foreigner who lived in an Islamic land was entitled to a status of temporary protection known as '*aman*.[42] Such persons were often Christians or Jews, who were known as *musta'min* and were fleeing persecution, war or famine. Their temporary immunity was unassailable, and ceased only when they were able to regain a place of safety.[43] On this subject, the Qur'an says, 'if one of the idolaters should seek refuge with you, give him protection so that he may hear the word of God; then convey him to his place of security.'[44] The length of time over which a temporary sojourn might extend was in principle one year. At the end of this period, the stranger was obliged either to leave the country, or seek to transfer to another basis, the status of permanency, the other form of protection granted under Islam to those known as *dhimmis*.

In contrast to the status of the *musta'min*, a *dhimmi* who was resident on a permanent basis was subject to the *jizya* tax. On the other hand, he had the privilege of worshipping openly according to his own faith, and enjoyed the right to receive, if appropriate, charity from the public purse that was otherwise reserved for Muslims. The imposition of *jizya* was intended to compensate the authorities for the non-Muslim's exemption from military service, and under Islamic law should be calculated proportionately to the *dhimmi's* social and financial standing. The amount of tax paid was not the same for a rich merchant as for a farm worker or a labourer, while the poor, the blind, children, women and clerics were exempt. *Jizya* levied on foreigners was used to finance the Islamic armies that were carrying their conquests to wide swathes of the world, and one of the principles underlying the exemption was that non-Muslims who did not share the Islamic faith should not be called on to participate actively in its propagation. At the time of the crusades, non-Muslims were also thus protected from the risk of being constrained to fight against their co-religionists.

A further aspect of the treatment of *dhimmis* was that in time of war against Christians and Jews, no restrictions were placed on the freedom of the religious minorities. As the commentator Marcel Boisard puts it:

> The rights and guarantees collectively extended to minorities living in Islamic societies are inalienable and permanent, whatever the state of relations between the Islamic world and the co-religionists abroad of the minority populations.[45]

Under the Fatimids in Egypt, the religious minorities were so well treated that Ibn Taymiyya went as far as to claim that their status constituted a form of discrimination against the Sunnis. He agitated against this situation, writing a resentful commentary on the Fatimid position:

[The Fatimids] have harassed the Sunnis, giving preference to the Jews and even more so to the Christians. The community has been in disarray ever since the Christians entered the service of the state. Since that moment, they have evaded taxation, claiming to be simply part of the population as a whole, at the same time as flaunting their wealth. They have wheedled their way into posts of responsibility in the Sultan's service and the financial administration, and have used their experience and their position to accumulate excessive riches, at the expense of the Muslims. Their greed is infamous; they play games of chance inside their churches; and the Jews sell alcohol to the Muslims. Their worship is an affront to neighbouring Muslim places of prayer, and their places of prayer become increasingly numerous and dangerously intrusive.[46]

Whatever their motivation, Ibn Taymiyya's hostile observations do indicate that the religious minorities enjoyed much latitude in Fatimid Egypt. In reality, their treatment by the Muslims was no more than respectful and fair, reflecting the view that the diversity they represented was an unmixed benefit to Islam. Ibn Taymiyya's severity was not shared by the Muslim community as a whole, whose custom, according to extensive historical evidence, was to welcome and offer protection to Christians and Jews living among them. Despite this, however, some western commentators have been critical of the principle behind the concept of *dhimmi* status, regarding the *jizya* as a form of punishment and humiliation to which Christians and Jews were subjected. In reality, if contemporary legislation on minorities were to be compared with the status of *dhimmi* devised by the Prophet Muhammad in the first century of Islam, the modern situation would be in some respects deficient.

In historical times, it is clear that Muslim treatment of minorities provided them with an undeniable level of security, by comparison with the status of Muslims at the same era living in Christian lands. These latter, for example, were not allowed openly to practise their faith. On this subject, Hélène Vandevelde makes the following remark:

Discriminatory attitudes towards the *dhimmis* may today be found shocking, but are seen to be in fact moderate and tolerant when it is considered that in Europe a non-Christian had no right to exist. The sole alternatives on offer were execution or expulsion.[47]

This was certainly the fate undergone by the 'Moriscos', Spanish Muslims who ostensibly converted to Christianity after the reconquest of Spain by the Catholic kings. The Moriscos were driven out into North Africa, reaching Oran in small and perilous craft at considerable personal danger, in an episode which, according to Rodrigo de Zayas, was perhaps the first modern instance of ethnic cleansing. The stated reason for this persecution was that despite the ostensible conversion of the Moriscos to Christianity, Catholic Spain saw evidence of hypocrisy in their continued refusal to eat pork or drink alcohol.[48]

The qualification should be made, however, that the status of *dhimmi* underwent modifications according to circumstances. For example, in the ninth century, at the time of the second generation of Islamism, hostility towards the Christians and the Jews had begun to be more pronounced, especially at times of economic crisis. Thus, 'in the event of famine or military setbacks, the people of the towns quickly turn against those they have hitherto protected, overrunning the quarters where they live, and looting and burning their places of trade and commerce'.[49] By the eleventh century, thanks to the widespread influence of the altruistic position of Al-Ghazali, there were for a time no further pogroms against the minorities. Al-Ghazali put forward the argument that any Christian or Jew of good faith was a person obliged to remain outside Islam for reasons not of his own volition, who should therefore enjoy a status comparable to that of the Muslims. He therefore enjoined Muslims to respect their property, their faith and their persons.[50]

Today's Islamists of the third generation, however, refrain from any allusion to *jizya* in what they have to say regarding the treatment of those outside Islam. They see the erstwhile existence of *jizya* as of historical interest only, particularly as it was repeatedly abolished under the Caliphs Omar and Mu'awiya.[51] The contemporary Islamists prefer to speak only of the generalisation of *zakat* together with respect for foreigners living within the Islamic lands. In general, they follow Al-Ghazali's advice to be tolerant and behave with civility to the Christians and Jews who live in the Muslim world.[52] It remains evident, however, that the Islamists insist that the government of the state should be confided only in leaders who profess the faith and have the will to put the Shari'a into practice. Such leaders, they contend, should be capable of defending the Islamic state against proselytisation and influences contrary to the values of Islamic education. They should also possess the ability to organise the Islamic state on an economic model based on social co-operation.

THE SOCIAL AND COMMUNITARIAN ISLAMIC MODEL

The Islamists appear to be more adept in the field of small-scale social activism than in devising viable large-scale economic policies. In the social domain, Islamic principles are unambiguous. Primarily, the family stands unchallenged as the basis of society. For example, every Muslim is exhorted to fulfil the sacred duty of assisting his or her family, as well as other believers, to achieve an education, to care for themselves and to feed themselves adequately. Such assistance is not to be extended only to those nearest to oneself, but also to all Muslims within the *umma* (Islamic nation), whatever the ethnicity or creed of the Muslims concerned.

On the basis of this inter-Islamic solidarity, and thanks to the *zakat*, or *sadaqa* (additional and voluntary alms), the Islamists have been able to mitigate the deficiencies of states that are corrupt and inefficient. They have made use of the channels of finance available to the Islamic NGOs, which have been able to call on reserves of foreign exchange sometimes more substantial than those at the disposal of many states, which have in any case been little concerned with issues of social welfare. Help for children in scholastic difficulties, the sick and the poor have always been the most effective investment the Islamists could make in their campaign to recruit faithful supporters devoted to their cause.[53]

As regards their parties' positions on broader economic policy, however, the Islamists tend to avoid the question. The principal reason for their reticence is their tacit reluctance to embark on western-style economic programmes, which they deem inappropriate to Muslim society. They are more comfortable basing their ideas on policies promoting the kind of commerce that was practised in the seventh century by the Prophet Muhammad and his wife Khadija, who engaged in profitable ventures throughout the Arabian Peninsula. Though they favour profit, and a model not unlike that of capitalism 'with a human face', the Islamists do however also advocate the social ownership of certain goods such as water, pasturage and the resources of the forest, as well as mineral and energy supplies. This principle is based on a Hadith, where the Prophet is reported as having said, 'Three elements – water, fodder and fire – make all men brothers.'

5

THE ISLAMIC CONCEPT OF
THE LAW OF ARMED CONFLICT:
MUSLIM LAW IN TIME OF WAR

By long custom, Islam places great stress on humanitarian law. Its approach to humanitarian values is, in the words of Hamed Sultan, 'deliberate, thoughtful, determining and deeply significant, emanating as it does from a strong, sincere and heartfelt philosophy'.[1] The Islamic concept of humanitarian law forms part of the Islamic juridical system in general, which is of divine origin, and is independent of any secular dispensation. Humanitarian law is therefore from the Shari'a, a global and universally applicable system, based on the Qur'an and the Sunna, which reports the actions and reported sayings of the Prophet Muhammad. Within the system, the various juridical principles form a hierarchy according to their importance. The divine injunctions known as *hadd* take precedence. The word *hadd* signifies 'barrier' or 'frontier', with reference to the barriers of the divine laws which must never be breached, or even approached.[2] The barriers of *hadd* are broken through the following five transgressions: rebellion against a just authority; banditry; slander, in particular accusing a person of fornication; theft; and the consumption of alcohol. These are followed by lesser sanctions for serious offences under the Shari'a imposed by a judge (a *qadi*) under the system of rules known as *taazir*.

Humanitarian law within Islam distinguishes between different types of war, such as civil strife and international conflict. Its rules, as they apply to various types of conflict, are mediated by the human emotions of pity, mercy and compassion, but draw their force from divine authority. The humanitarian aspects of Islamic law were in advance of their time. Islam has always demanded

101

that combatants who are believers should conform to three principles. The first of these is the general principle, which might even be called the 'Islamic clause', namely not to overstep or exceed the bounds of justice and equity, or commit tyranny and oppression. This may be derived from Sura 2, Verses 190–4 of the Qur'an. The second principle is expressed in the Qur'an as follows: 'Whoever kills a soul, not in retaliation for a soul, or for corruption in the land, is like one who has killed all mankind; and whoever saves a life is like one who saves the lives of all mankind' (Sura 5, Verse 32). Thirdly, it is prescribed that 'the blood of women, children and old men shall not sully the victory of the believers'.[3]

In the event of any violation of the laws of combat, as with the violation of other laws, there is provision for retribution against the offender. The severest punishments provided for in Islamic law are those for the *hadd* offences which are explicitly mentioned in the Qur'an and the Sunna.[4] Lesser transgressions are not provided for in divine law but are left to the discretion of the *qadi*, or dealt with under the *taazir*. It should be pointed out that the level of retribution for misdemeanours for which the divine law does not provide specific punishments fluctuates over time, and may actually be very severe. For example, in the Ummayyad period, those who plundered corpses, whether in time of peace or war, were buried alive.

THE APPLICATION OF *HADD* PENALTIES FOR INSURRECTION OR AGGRESSION (OTHER THAN IN INTERNATIONAL CONFLICTS)

INTERNAL INSURRECTION

In the case of rebellions against local or regional Muslim rulers, Islam provides for two distinct situations. If the ruler has deviated into heresy, or has been tyrannical or has behaved unjustly, it is legitimate for the Muslim community to refuse to accept his authority and rise up against him. However, if the accusation against him is unjust, or if he returns to the proper path of Islam and makes amends, then he may fight against a rebellion, in accordance with the prescribed rules.[5] The ruler may employ against rebels only sufficient means to overcome them on the field of battle and oblige them to surrender. It is forbidden to pursue them from the battlefield and slaughter them. It is forbidden to kill the women and children of rebels, or seize their possessions. In addition, their wounded must not be killed, and prisoners or those who flee the battle should not be killed. Once an insurrection has been quelled, nothing further is to be exacted from those who provoked it. On this subject, the Qur'an says: 'If two parties of the believers should fight one another, bring them peacefully together; but if one of them seeks to oppress the other, then fight the oppressors until they revert to God's command. If they revert, then bring them together in justice and be equitable, for God loves the equitable' (Sura 49, Verse 9). In any case of flagrant violation of the laws of war by rulers or their representatives, a judge is empowered to apply legal sanctions against them based on the *hadd* penalties.

INTERNECINE STRIFE

From the earliest days of Islam, aggression between factions has been condemned. As we see above, the Qur'an says: 'Fight the oppressors until they revert to God's command.' If an aggressor is defeated and captured, the judge will apply *hadd* penalties to him, which may be death, exile or some other sanction.[6] In practice, the penalties will vary according to the gravity of the insurrection. *Hadd* penalties apply to infractions of the laws of war and serious misconduct in the course of hostilities. Aggression against another party within Islam is regarded as a grave crime, which may also attract *hadd* penalties. This is to be compared with the situation in current western law where there is relatively weak pressure to adhere to defined rules of conduct in internal conflicts, including insurrections. This was a subject of considerable concern to a number of states at the diplomatic conference on the reaffirmation and development of international humanitarian law held in Geneva from 1974 to 1977.

INTERNATIONAL CONFLICT

The conduct of hostilities in wars between nations and in Jihad does not attract *hadd* punishments. In this type of conflict, there nevertheless exist clearly defined rules of war, violation of which attracts the application of the *taazir* and is applied by a judge, or *qadi*. It should be recalled that in the hierarchy of legal norms, *taazir* occupied second place, after *hadd*. In international wars of conquest, there are various kinds of infractions which may be seen as falling into the category of crimes demanding the intervention of the *qadi*. A list of the main types of such infractions is as follows:

INHUMAN TREATMENT

Muslim doctrine is agreed that it is forbidden to inflict inhuman or degrading treatment on enemy combatants. The same doctrine, based on Sura 16, Verses 126–8 of the Qur'an, condemns the mutilation, torture or killing of soldiers captured in combat. However, though Verse 126 authorises proportionate reprisals in time of war, it places restrictions on them by recommending that pardons should be granted. More precisely, the Qur'an says: 'If you punish, let your punishment be proportionate to the wrong done to you. Yet should you forbear, for it is truly better to forbear.'[7]

PRISONERS OF WAR

It is forbidden to threaten the lives of prisoners of war. The Shari'a prescribes that they should be well treated. The Qur'an has the following to say on the subject: 'And they give food, despite their love of it, to the destitute, the orphan and the captive' (Sura 76, Verse 8). In addition, the Prophet is reported to have said, when prisoners were being divided up among his companions, 'Always care for prisoners.'[8] Ibn Taymiyya always respected the principles of the Prophet Muhammad and the *salaf* relating to the good treatment of prisoners. For instance, he personally sent a message to the Mongols during the invasion of Syria in 1299–1300 asking for the freedom of Muslim, Jewish and Christian prisoners.[9] Ibn

Taymiyya also acknowledged the commonality of human values between Christianity and Islam. In this intellectual context, he wrote his 'Letter to a Crusader King' in Cyprus to ask for the 'liberation of his Muslim prisoners, or at the very least to treat them well and not oblige them to undergo baptism'.[10]

RESPECT FOR MONASTERIES AND MONKS

The slaughter of men of religion such as monks is also forbidden, according to the pronouncements of Abu Bakr, the first Caliph and Muhammad's early companion. At the time of the conquest of Syria and Iraq, Abu Bakr said to his fighting men, 'As you advance, you will encounter men of religion who inhabit the monasteries and who serve God in seclusion from the world. Leave them be. Do not take their lives and do not destroy their monasteries.' [11]

It should be pointed out that in addition to the humanitarian reason for this injunction, the Christian monks had been of service to Islam, playing a major role in the translation of Greek and Syriac texts into Arabic.[12] Similarly, as Henri Galland points out, from the days of the Emperor Justinian, Greek works had been translated into Syriac in order to disseminate the Greek cultural heritage in the East:

> Translations of Greek works were made mainly by Syrian or Chaldean Christians, and especially by the Nestorians. Many of the doctors at the court of the Caliphs were Christians and were able, due to their familiarity with Greek literature, to point out to the Arabs the books which would be of the greatest interest to them. It should also be noted that there already existed a body of indigenous Syriac literature which was strongly influenced by Greece and which to some extent contributed to the development of Kalam.[13]

In general, as the Arabs took power, the translations undertaken by the Christians seem to have been welcomed in a Muslim social context that was dynamic, tolerant and in general open to science and culture.

RESPECT FOR VULNERABLE PERSONS

In Muslim law, it is forbidden to take the lives of old men, women and children. The Prophet Muhammad repeatedly said, 'Do not kill children, do not take their lives ...' and the second Caliph, Omar, repeated this injunction: 'Do not kill old men, women or children, and take care they do not lose their lives in fighting or under the hooves of horses.'[14]

TREACHERY AND STRATAGEMS OF WAR

Treachery and treason are strictly forbidden in fighting. According to the Qur'an, 'God does not like the treacherous' (Sura 8, Verse 58). Within Islam, tradition forbids the deception of an enemy by perfidious means. Muslim jurists unanimously condemn all forms of deception. In the conventional view, stratagems are permitted, but deception is anathema. The Prophet Muhammad said, 'Good faith in return for treachery is better than treachery for treachery.'[15] The ban on treachery is customary, rather than absolute. The rule is in principle to be obeyed not only in relation to non-Muslims but also in relations between Muslims.[16] On the other hand, a simple trick whose intention is to deceive the enemy into making mistakes or to be rash is not forbidden under Islamic law. The Prophet is reported to have said that 'the art of war is deception', so the use of camouflage, false manoeuvres or misleading information is not forbidden. The line between deception and treachery may be hard to draw.

LOOTING

The rules covering the conduct of hostilities forbid the destruction of civilian goods, such as orchards, crops and houses, or the theft of possessions. The Sunna forbids the malicious looting of the enemy's livestock, though it is permitted in the case of hunger. Inspecting his troops after a victorious battle, the Prophet observed that the combatants were celebrating the end of hostilities by eating the vanquished enemy's cattle. He immediately called a halt, declaring, 'The consumption of stolen livestock is no more permitted than that of animals that have not been properly killed.' The Prophet's basic teaching was unambiguous on the issue of booty. According to the principle stated above, Muslim law has always banned soldiers from pillage or theft of goods abandoned by the enemy. Pillage (*ghulul*) is a variety of war crime that is severely punished.[17] Further sanctions may apply under the *taazir* to a range of acts including the destruction of the houses of civilians not involved in fighting, the tools of their trades and their other possessions. Penalties imposed by the *qadi* may range from capital punishment, for extreme offences, to flogging, banishment and various forms of humiliation.

GENERAL PRINCIPLES

From all this it can be seen that the humanitarian rules of war in the early days of Islam were precise and detailed. They were to be applied in clearly defined circumstances and only by the administrative hierarchy. The general principles, sometimes known as Abu Bakr's 'Ten Commandments', are customarily stated as follows:

> Do not act treacherously; do not act disloyally; do not act neglectfully. Do not mutilate; do not kill little children or old men; do not cut off the heads of the palm trees and burn them; do not cut down the fruit trees; do not slaughter a sheep or a cow or a camel except for food. You will pass by people who devote their lives in cloisters; leave them and their devotions alone. You will come upon people who bring you platters in which there are various sorts of food; if you eat any of it, mention the name of God over it.[18]

These 'commandments' are a humanitarian heritage which is well in line with the values of modern humanitarian law.

THE THIRD GENERATION OF ISLAMISTS AND THEIR VIEW OF ARMED CONFLICT

A question mark remains, however, over what stance the third generation of Islamists adopts in modern times on these issues. The third generation of Islamists in theory bases its ideas on the teachings of the Prophet, as did earlier Muslims. They also claim to rely on the classic authority of Ibn Taymiyya regarding the conduct of hostilities. In practice, however, they diverge from these principles. Declarations made by Sayyid Qutb or Bin Laden, and by Hassan Hattab, the former leader of the GIA in Algeria, often draw no distinction between civilians and combatants. According to Sayyid Qutb, echoed by the ideologues of the GIA, war should be waged against 'all heretics, whether moderate Muslims, leaders of the faithful who traffic with the Americans, other heretics, Christians or Jews'. The position taken by Qutb is developed in his published works, particularly *Islam, religion of the future*,[19] and the posthumous *Islam par le Martyr*.[20] The aggressive declarations of Bin Laden, as well as those of Hattab and the GIA, have been widely publicised in the press and elsewhere. Pamphlets, communiqués and reports they have allowed to be published have gained wide credence, having not been denied.[21] Hassan Al-Banna, the founder of the Muslim Brotherhood in Egypt, was, however, an exception to the general spirit of hostility. It should not be forgotten, however, that early in his career Al-Banna himself declared a Jihad against foreign occupation at the time of the Israeli–Arab war of 1948.[22] The Egyptian group Gamaat Al-Islamiya has also recently adopted a more moderate stance, distancing itself from the strategy of Al-Qa'ida and advocating instead a return to the humanitarian values of the humanists of the earlier Islamic generations.[23]

It is possible to infer from the manuals of instruction for Islamic combatants written by such Islamist leaders as Abdullah Azzam[24] and Hassan Hattab[25] that today's rules of Jihadist combat have departed from the humanitarian spirit of the regulations prescribed by the first generation. These traditional rulings prescribe the sparing of prisoners and civilians, and consideration for vulnerable persons such as women, children and old men. Such leaders as Azzam and Hattab, it is true, laid down in the orders they gave to their militants that civilians should be spared. Nevertheless, they made the proviso that if these civilians are found near key sites related to political or economic sovereignty that are legitimate targets for attack, it is apparently not imperative to avoid taking their lives. This was the justification that legitimised the attacks on the World Trade Center in September 2001.[26] In May 2003, Bin Laden's deputy, Ayman Al-Zawahiri, also called for 'attacks on interests, companies and personnel that represent the presence of the Americans and the English . . . in the Muslim world'.[27] None of these Jihadist manuals has any legal standing, since they have never been properly scrutinised in fatwas with legal status issued by the qualified and recognised muftis of Al-Azhar or any other generally recognised Islamic authority.

The unavoidable question is why so much barbarism exists in practice in Muslim theatres of war, despite the existence of such high-minded principles as those examined above. This is a very serious question, and is difficult to answer. First, it should not be forgotten that Islam has no monopoly of violence. Human beings, no matter what their level of civilisation, may be carried away by their baser instincts. In a violent world, Muslims, like other men, are led into violence in response to the violence of others and in imitation of them. Violence breeds violence. In the modern world, rivalry for natural resources and greed for political power create situations of conflict in which principles often go by the board. This applies to Muslims as much as to other communities. More specific to the issue of violence by Muslims, however, is the phenomenon that might be called sacralisation.[28] Sacralisation, if it comes into play, leads to the intensification of conflicts when they take place in a religious context. The phenomenon of vengeance or reprisal for violence suffered intensifies when such a conflict has been sacralised by a spiritual leader or through an appeal to God. Such behaviour may have been observed in the past in traditional Muslim society but also exists in the contemporary Muslim world.

In the context of violence between religious communities, human beings may in the end entirely lose sight of the original object of the dispute. The phenomenon of the expression of hatred as a response to becoming the object of hatred quickly develops into an emotion so powerful that it overcomes pain and the fear of death. Anthropologists are unanimous in the conclusion that the fear of the other leads human beings to commit the worst atrocities. Hopefully, after such episodes of irrational violence and brutality come to an end, the Islamic world may at last, as other religions and civilisations have done, return to reason and moral order. Islam may succeed in finding a satisfactory resolution to its dilemma through the renunciation of violence and the restoration of its own proper code of conduct, in the shape of the Muslim 'humanitarian commandments'. Humanity learns and profits from its experience. The human instinct for survival, together with the intelligence of mankind, is what will enable the Muslim community to evolve and come to terms with the future.

6

THE THREE GENERATIONS
OF ISLAMISM

After its initial expansion, Islam was at once exposed to the challenge of the existing 'animist' religions of the newly conquered peoples. With the passage of the centuries, the reaction of conservative clerics to the mixture of cultures within Islam was to radicalise them, so that they made ever-more strenuous attempts to end the importation of alien practices. This was why many jurists had agreed by the twelfth century that the doors of *ijtihad* (the intellectual attempt to widen the available interpretations of the Shari'a to cover new circumstances) should be closed. According to such experts as Louis Gardet, there was in existence as early as the ninth century a process that could be described as the resurgence of the Sunni faith, which was especially strong in the eleventh century.[1] The conservative *ulema* thereafter entrenched themselves in a defensive position, accepting only the interpretations of the four classic Sunni schools of law, without taking the risk of devising novel interpretations of the law based on the Qur'an and Sunna. As Gardet puts it, the conservative *ulema* 'protected themselves, fearing that any acceptance of change could lead only to their destruction'.[2] Up to the present day, traditionalists continue to advocate a return in due course to the origins of Islam. They have been the first to express the fear that a globalisation predominantly driven by westernisation will lead the Muslim community towards the destruction of their ancestral cultural heritage.

Throughout its history, Islam has always closed ranks in the face of challenges both from progressive ideologies and from the mystic Sufi institutions. The reasons for this retreat into conservatism are not traceable to any economic deprivation in the

111

Muslim world. Poverty alone is neither a necessary nor sufficient condition for the expansion of Islamism. There are extremely poor Muslim communities in Africa and Asia that have not adopted religious radicalism. Islamism does not require a reductive explanation, but has its own coherence and cultural motivations, based on the Shari'a. This has, throughout history, been supervised by a Caliph, acting in turn through the agency of Muslim rulers and the religious hierarchy. The goal of the system is to permit the Muslim sovereign to 'rule his peoples through a system of nations in which the individual is subject to laws and regulations according to their religious affiliations and not to their geographical locations'.[3]

In other words, in the name of Islam, a Turkish or Arab sovereign may be the ruler, at arm's length, of a West African, a Pakistani or an Afghan. No other terrestrial power, even that of the Pope, has ever exercised absolute power to reign in the name of God over such varied cultural communities. The governing idea of the Islamist fundamentalists is that the religious and secular powers are both of a divine nature, and that they should be entirely fused into one. Above all, it is the interest of the *umma* (the Islamic community) that must prevail. Individuals are a factor only to the extent that they serve as intermediaries for the articulation and exercise of the power of God. William Zartmann offers the following analysis:

> There is no concept of the state in Islam, since some of the functions of the state lie in the hands of God, withheld eternally from the hands of the faithful on earth. There is one sole community of believers (the *umma*), bound together by the contract of submission (*islam*) which they have made between themselves and, as individuals, with God.[4]

It is salutary to recall that Islam came into being in very particular historical circumstances. At various epochs of its history, it has taken action as a *deus ex machina*, coming out of nothing to rescue peoples sinking into the slough of vice, chaos, injustice and the degradation of moral standards. Islam effectively put an end to the barbarism that prevailed throughout the East. It also served as the point of departure for a humanist conception of political, cultural and social life, to the benefit of millions of human beings. It should never be forgotten that before the advent of Islam in Arabia, the population consisted of a multitude of bedouin tribes who murdered each other without compunction and lived on the proceeds of pillage, raids and slavery. On the positive side, some of the special qualities of these scattered tribesmen should also be acknowledged. They cultivated the virtues of courage, and of endurance in the face of the severest desert climate, while maintaining their innate gift for poetry and songs of love. The coming of Islam completely overturned the way of life of the tribes, suppressing their vices and cultivating their virtues, as they themselves would be the first to recognise. The revelation of Muhammad, handed down to them unchanged by the earliest of the faithful, the *salaf*, and by their successors, the *khalaf*, has been followed to the letter by every Islamist. Even in our own times, none would dare amend the rules laid down by divine law, among the ancients. Within Islam, innovation is a sin, as the divine law is complete. To quote Zartmann again:

> For fourteen centuries, Islam has done duty as a religious authority, accounting completely, in other words, for every event and story, explaining the reasons for both successes and failures, and offering a Way to be followed, for the achievement of fulfilment both in this world and in the eternal life to come. There is no separation between church and state, as neither one nor the other can properly be said to exist within Islam.[5]

All, therefore, should be content to obey God's rules, as elaborated by the masters of the two most recent of the generations of Islamism that this book has discussed.

Before moving on to examine the Sufis and the rationalists of Islam, it should be clear that the intention of the argument as it has been presented so far has not been to minimise or deprecate *salafi* Islamic fundamentalism. This interpretation of Islam has from the start been at the origin of the progress Islam has made in the fields of justice, peace, solidarity and the brotherhood of man. It has also preserved the basic rituals and has promoted respect for the practices of orthodox Islam as they were laid down by Muhammad and continued by the Caliphs, with the assistance of the religious clergy. The clergy, and especially the *ulema* recognised by the great Islamic universities, have maintained the tradition and preserved the Shari'a by protecting them from distortion and radical interpretation. In this respect, they deserve obeisance and respect. The orthodox *ulema*, as well as the Islamists of a moderate, tolerant and legalist tendency, represent a threat neither to society nor to the fundamental liberties of either Muslim or western nations. On the contrary, they may well be a factor militating in the direction of stabilisation and equilibrium in countries where extremism and the decline in political and social values, together with confusion in the sphere of national identity, have been the outcome of poverty, illiteracy, violence and injustice.

Moderate Islamism has in fact always been tolerant of free thinkers and has been able to coexist with Sufism. It has never attempted to extinguish Sufi mystic currents of thought, even if history has from time to time thrown them violently into opposition with each other. Neither can moderate Islamism hope to dominate in every redoubt of society and politics in the Muslim world. It is obliged to accept the idea of living side by side with the secular nationalists and the proponents of Sufi spiritualism whose ideas are beginning increasingly to win acceptance throughout the Muslim countries and in the West.

It remains only to express the hope that the present study will not be interpreted in a partisan and subjective manner, and that it will not be seen as systematically hostile criticism of those who adopt the fundamentalist theories advocated by Ibn Taymiyya and his successors. The intention has been no more than to contrast the positions of the fundamentalist schools of Ibn Taymiyya, of Hassan Al-Banna, of Ben Badis and of others with the free-thinking followers of Ibn Rushd and Ibn Sina, and with the hope represented by the mysticism of Rumi and Al-Hallaj. It has not been to set up a scale of values against which these schools of thought are to be measured, nor to distribute medals for good conduct to theologians and thinkers whose ability lies beyond that of the present author.

Each of the schools of thought examined in this study has its own specific virtues, its own access to truth, and is beset with doubts of which both their adherents and their antagonists are well aware. Overall, the goal is not to sway the reader in favour of support for any particular school, or tendency, as distinct from others, but to introduce him to, and guide him through, the esoterica of a Muslim world that has become ever more complex and diverse. Finally, the author of this work, on the basis of his own experience and his awareness of the socio-political developments that have faced most of the Muslim countries, remains convinced that over the space of some years to come, the leading figures of the moderate Islamic tendencies have a role to play. Together with their secular supporters, and the Sufi orders, they will emerge as a vital factor on the political scene in the majority of the Muslim countries, beginning with the states of the Maghreb, and with Palestine.

PART TWO

INTRODUCTION

As the first part of this book has indicated, a philosophical and mystical trend has always been strongly present in Islam, making its presence felt alongside the influence of the fundamentalist ideas that have come from the three generations of Islamists. In addition, from the eighth century onwards, in addition to the Sufi mystics, a group of philosophers known as the Mu'tazilites broke with the dominant school of thought of the traditionalist Salafist theologians who were ultimately represented by Ibn Taymiyya. These alternative philosophical thinkers reinterpreted and adapted for the Muslim world the major Greek, Indian, Hebrew and Persian works, and even texts that had come down from ancient Egypt. Their inclination towards freedom of thought and mystical reflection (*fikr*) led inevitably to original and liberal interpretations of the Qur'an and of Islam in general. This brought down upon them the opprobrium of the stalwarts of the official orthodox faith, upheld by the serried ranks of the conservative Caliphs and the muftis, imams and cadis who represented the Muslim establishment.

Both the rationalist philosophers, including the Mu'tazilites, and the Sufis, such as Al-Hallaj, paid heavily for their independence of mind. Al-Hallaj lost his life as a result of his opposition to orthodox dogma, and the philosopher Ibn Rushd was ostracised from society. The *ulema*, orthodox theologians and clerics whose expertise lay in the Shari'a, appointed themselves Ibn Rushd's inquisitors and decreed that his books should be burned. In the eyes of the Sufis, and of the rational philosophers, however, the *ulema* were in reality nothing more than blind imitators unquestioningly following tradition, and were not qualified to be true religious scholars. Sufis and rationalists insisted that the knowledge of the *ulema* was limited to a body of doctrine which they uncritically accepted together with their capacity to remember it. As the great Sufi Nasafi put it, 'they listened and absorbed, and their acceptance was not based on reason and logic'.[1] Though the Sufis chose at times not to draw themselves to public attention, owing to the persecution they faced and the vindictive attitude of the Islamic courts, they never disappeared entirely and through the course of some 12 centuries continued to uphold the values that have always sustained their beliefs. They often worked in secret, seeking divine inspiration and developing their meditative faculties as they sought to achieve interior freedom in a world of despotic legal repression.

It should never be supposed, however, that these philosophers and mystics at any time rejected the broad rules of the Muslim faith. Phoenix-like, they have always been able to rise from the ashes to continue the dissemination of their ideas throughout the Muslim world. In modern times, since the abolition of the Caliphate in 1924, they have again come under attack from the fundamentalist *ulema*, who are sometimes, though quite wrongly, described as 'reformist' despite their desire to return Islam to the state in which it existed in the time of Muhammad and the *salaf*.[2] In the course of the twentieth century, Sufi reformers and philosophers also faced official hostility from the governments of a number of countries, including Turkey, Egypt, Tunisia and Algeria. It should be observed that in these countries the principal result of attempts to discredit and eliminate Sufism was to create a vacuum in popular sympathies which Islamic fundamentalism was not slow to fill. In other countries, such as Morocco, Senegal and Tanzania, and in fact in most of Africa, where the Sufi orders are well integrated into the social and political scene, the influence of fundamentalism has been markedly less.

The second section of this book will be devoted to these alternative Islamic thinkers, beginning with a discussion of the innovatory philosophers, including the Mu'tazilites, who brought freedom of thought to the Muslim world. There will also be an examination of Sufi issues, with a discussion of two selected philosophers, Ibn Sina and Ibn Rushd. This will indicate how they inaugurated a process of invigoration of Muslim minds over a period of centuries, until the renewed relapse of the Islamic world into conformism and lethargy. Though detailed discussion will be restricted to these two, the significant contributions to rationalism made by other key figures in the spheres of Arabic poetry and literature will also be touched on. For instance, Abdullah Ibn Al-Muqaffa denounced religious obscurantism, drawing attention to the ways in which he believed values were being traduced.[3] Other thinkers and men of letters, such as Hunayn Ibn Ishaq, Al-Warraq, Ibn Al-Riwandi, Hayawayh Al-Balhi, Abu Bakr Al-Razi, Al-Ma'arri and Ibn Kammuna, also spoke out in support of the right of the individual to exercise independent reason, in ways that implied a degree of anti-clericalism that earned them in return the opprobrium of the religious establishment. For a detailed analysis of all these Islamic thinkers, the excellent studies by Dominique Urvoy[4] and Sarah Stroumsa[5] can scarcely be bettered. Finally, it will be indicated that there is a new generation of Islamic thinkers carrying on the work of their illustrious predecessors.

7

THE FIRST GENERATION OF
RATIONALISM AND MYSTICISM
IN THE MUSLIM WORLD

THE MU'TAZILITES

Islam's earliest rationalists were the Mu'tazilites, from the Arabic word *mu'tazila*, who emerged in the eighth century, in the closing years of the Ummayad dynasty. The first recognisable Mu'tazilite was a redoubtable Sufi philosopher named Wasil Ibn Ata, who lived and worked in around 750. Wasil Ibn Ata took his inspiration to a considerable extent from Greek philosophy and challenged a number of traditional Islamic teachings. For instance, in contradiction to the commonly accepted view, he contended, on the basis of rational deduction, that a Muslim who has committed a serious sin does not by that very fact become an unbeliever.[1] In our own times, this question is still asked, and different answers are forthcoming from traditional clerics on the one hand and modernisers on the other.

The rationalist Mu'tazilite school reached its zenith under the Abbasid dynasty. The first translations into Arabic of Greek works on medicine, science and philosophy appeared in the reign of the second Abbasid Caliph, Al-Mansur. Later, in the reigns of Al-Mansur's successors, and especially under the enlightened Caliph Al-Ma'mun, the son of Harun Al-Rashid, many scholars became involved in the translation of Greek and Latin classics, as well as works in Persian, Indian languages and even ancient Egyptian. Under Ma'mun, an institution known as the House of Wisdom (*beit al-hikma*) was founded to facilitate the work, which was widely disseminated throughout the Muslim East. According to the study by Baron Carra de Vaux, the Caliph Ma'mun, decreed that ancient books should be sought out, and encouraged translators to work on them. He established an official translation bureau, and it was thanks to him that literature and Greek science became known in the Islamic world, either directly or through the intermediary of the ancient Persians and Syriac authors.[2]

With the support of the highest authority of the state behind them, rationalist Mu'tazilite philosophers began to claim their activities were a proper complement to the teaching of the Qur'an. They were the first to turn to the power of reason (*aql*), as opposed to scripture (*sam'*),[3] and did not shrink from an open breach with the strict theologians, such as Ibn Hanbal, for whom all innovation was seen as wicked. The support of the Abbasid court encouraged them to intensify their struggle against the traditionalist *ulema*. For the first time in the history of the Islamic world, if only for a short time, they brought into the *madrasas* a style of teaching based on rationalist philosophy and embodying a spirit of freedom of inquiry, and tolerance between cultures and faiths.

A number of doctrinal innovations distinguished the Mu'tazilites. Central among these was the thesis that the Qur'an, though a sacred text, was nevertheless a created entity, and their argument that the Prophet drew his inspiration from the inquiring spirit of the human intellect. This, of course, completely contradicted the teaching of traditional Islamic theology that the Qur'an was uncreated, and that the Prophet's inspiration was entirely divine.[4] Trusting in their spirit of free inquiry, the Mu'tazilites also repudiated the official doctrine upheld by the *ulema* according to which human beings were predestined either to be saved or condemned. The Mu'tazilites were also well aware that they were outraging the preconceived ideas of the majority of Muslims when they asserted that 'each person bears full responsibility for his acts, which are not the work of God'. In the same way, they rejected the conventional idea accepted by the great religions in general, and in particular by Islam, that there exists a real Hell that is an eternity of torment for sinners. Finally, they carried their reliance on reason to the lengths of claiming that God 'is obliged always to act with justice and that in this respect he is bound by the same rules as men'.[5]

The upholders of Islamic orthodoxy never faltered in their opposition to the Mu'tazilites, however, and finally gained their satisfaction after the death of Al-Ma'mun, when the Mu'tazilites were collectively found guilty of heresy. Some traces of the Mu'tazilite world-view lingered on, however, and in the tenth century, according to the historian Henri Terrasse, adherents of the liberal Mu'tazilite school were still to be found in Spain, where such adepts as Ibn Massara continued to profess Mu'tazilite doctrines. In the end, they too attracted the opprobrium of the conservatives, and their books were burned as those of their predecessors had been. From the tenth century onwards, the Malikite *ulema* instituted a 'thorough-going inquisition'[6] against the Mu'tazilites. According to Terrasse, the antagonism of the official guardians of the strict religious law towards any manifestation of liberal tendencies was unrelenting. From that day to this, official Islam has anathematised the ideas of the Mu'tazilites, which have as far as possible been obliterated, with their teachings systematically ignored by the theological colleges. Despite the persecution and ostracism to which they have been subjected by the orthodox theologians, however, the Mu'tazilites succeeded in leaving upon Islam the indelible imprint of Hellenised freedom of thought.

After the Mu'tazilites, Muslim philosophy continued to flourish in the hands of such exceptional personalities as Al-Kindi in the ninth century and Al-Farabi in the tenth, who kept alight the torch of rationalism. Ibn Sina, Ibn Al-Arabi and Ibn Rushd took Muslim thought to what is widely regarded as its highest perfection. These were thinkers who had the gift of blending mysticism, faith and reason in the cause of setting the individual free from the shackles of social, political and religious conformism. As true humanists, they inaugurated a century of enlightened thought in the Muslim world, in which the forces of intelligence and scholarship carried the day against emotion and obscurantism.

The philosophers of this enlightened generation divided the subject matter of the differing fields of endeavour in which they were interested into three distinct areas, between which they nevertheless maintained a degree of linkage. One area was that of faith and the religious sciences of *fiqh* and the Shari'a. Another sphere was that of Hellenistic rational philosophy and the mystical tradition of the Persian and Hindu East; and a third was that of mathematics and the exact and observational sciences, including medicine. In their schools, for which, in common with the traditionalists, they used the word *madrasa*, pupils were expected to master topics from all these areas and to move easily from one subject to another to support their arguments. Once in possession of his final certificate, authenticated by a master, the student, or *talib*, would be regarded as an *alim*, or member of the *ulema*.

From the fourteenth century, however – and it is not coincidental that this is the date from which Muslim civilisation might be said to have begun its decline – the *madrasas* concentrated more and more on faith and religious knowledge. As Louis Gardet notes:

> Virtually every village would have its Qur'anic school, where children would learn long passages from the Qur'an, or even memorise the sacred text in its entirety, though often without understanding its meaning.[7]

Today, a painful fact that must be faced is that philosophy and science are completely ignored in the curricula of the *madrasas* and by virtually all the Islamic universities. From this flows the difficulty experienced by many Muslims educated in a traditional way in adapting to a modern world that is highly competitive, especially in the field of intellectual innovation and in scientific and social progress. The contemporary situation stands in contrast to the period of Islamic civilisation's finest flowering, from the eighth to the fourteenth centuries, when the schools were models of scholarship, founded on the study of a wide range of theological, philosophical and scientific sources. It was on the foundation of this breadth of learning that such masters of erudition as Ibn Sina, Al-Kindi, Al-Farabi, Ibn Al-Arabi and Ibn Rushd were able to emerge.

The Muslim passion for pure science is not alien to Islam. It can be traced back to the Sunna, where we find a Hadith that recounts that the Prophet said, 'Seek knowledge, even from as far off as China.'[8] According to another Hadith, the Prophet said, 'For him who treads the path of knowledge, God will ease his path to Paradise.'[9] For a Muslim, therefore, the search for knowledge (*'ilm*) is one of the ways to Paradise. The quest for scientific knowledge was in general in the past a matter for individuals, working co-operatively or alone, and was not organised by the Islamic state. From the earliest days of Islam, the search for scientific knowledge was nonetheless seen as a way for a Muslim to express his belief and his faith in God. In other words, science was an integral part of the faith (*iman*) of a good Muslim.[10] It is scarcely surprising today to see sections of the intellectual elite seeking to renew a tradition that was well established among Muslim intellectuals up to the Middle Ages. As a demonstration of the superiority of Islamic science in the past over that of the West, Muslims like to tell the story of how Harun Al-Rashid made a gift of an astrolabe to the Holy Roman Emperor Charlemagne. Charlemagne, however, was unacquainted with such novel technology and warily refused to accept it until the Caliph's ambassador had repeatedly explained its function. Similarly, Muslim technologists had made huge strides in civil engineering:

> They developed a sophisticated system of watercourses to remove used water from Baghdad, which was the cleanest city in the world at a time when Europe was ankle deep in its privies.[11]

The key idea to be derived from this excursion into history is that a 'good Muslim' seeks knowledge, or *'ilm*, not solely for financial reasons, or for celebrity or glory, but also because it will bring him the supreme recompense, that of the royal road to Paradise. Nevertheless, the progressive abandonment of intellectual effort and rationalist teachings by the Muslim community from the fourteenth century onwards plunged the *umma* into disarray and immersed it in ignorance. On the other hand, it can also be said that the knowledge gained by Muslims and their humanistic attitudes were incontrovertibly the spark that ignited the renaissance in Europe.

IBN SINA AND EASTERN MYSTICISM

Abu Ali Al Husayn Ibn Sina was a Persian, of Arab culture. He was born in 980 in Bukhara, in present-day Uzbekistan, and died in Hamadan in Persia in 1037. He was a towering intellect, both in the field of rationalist thought and of Muslim mysticism. By the age of 16, he was renowned for his writings on medicine and on pharmacy, where he was the first to offer a systematic account of the effects of certain types of remedies, including the medicinal use of chicory and balsam, the use of leeches and even the effects of alcohol.[12] Ibn Sina's medical researches were original and undertaken at his own initiative. In his philosophical studies, on the other hand, he was guided by the works of the brilliant philosopher and mystic Al-Farabi (872–950). It was Al-Farabi who first introduced Ibn Sina to the Hellenic culture of Aristotle and Plato, and in particular to the idea of adapting Plato's concept of the ideal or perfect city to the specificities of Islam. On this topic, Al-Farabi's view was that 'only an elite of enlightened philosophers . . . , capable of asceticism and of distancing themselves from the material world, would be able to attain the "ideal city"'.[13] Al-Farabi's great achievement was to detach philosophical rationalism from its subordination to religion, a process that even the Mu'tazilite master Abu Yusuf Yaqub Ibn Ishaq Al-Kindi (800–870) had not carried through to its conclusion.[14]

Inspired by the teaching of these Hellenised Muslim philosophers, Ibn Sina also espoused the supremacy of reason and philosophy, adding that Islam could not be adequately understood except in philosophical terms. In other words, in Ibn Sina's view, neither mysticism nor the science of religion could be understood except when illuminated by rationality. Ibn Sina's rationalism led inevitably to conclusions that shocked the traditionalist *ulema*, confident in their certainties. For example, he contradicted them with his declaration that the universe could not have been created out of nothing by the will of God. For him, the existence of the universe remained independent of the existence of God, though he accepted that God was in a position of dominance over it. Another way in which Ibn Sina affronted the orthodox Islamic view was with his denial that resurrection of the body could take place after death, which was an idea he was prepared to accept only in a symbolic sense.[15] In contrast to Al-Farabi, however, he agreed with the consensus of the *ulema* that the human soul was immortal, would survive after death, and that each soul had its individual fate in the world to come.[16]

A further achievement of Ibn Sina was his successful integration of the Sufi mystical dimension into his philosophical account of the rational world. He consistently took care to avoid any direct confrontation between Islamic law and rationalist philosophy. Despite this, the doyen of Sunni theological doctrine, Abu Hamid Muhammad Al-Ghazali, did not exempt him from attack in his tract, 'The Incoherence of the Philosophers' (*Tahafut al-falasifa*).[17] Al-Ghazali, who was born in 1058 at Tus in Persia, where he died in 1111, was one of the most charismatic and impressive personalities in the history of Islam. At the age of 36, after a brilliant career, he underwent a spiritual crisis which led him to abandon his family and his position, spending the rest of his life in search of Sufi enlightenment. In *Tahafut al-falasifa*, he accused Ibn Sina and the Greek-influenced philosophers of abandoning the Muslim faith and of immersing themselves in heresy (*bid'a*) and unbelief (*kufr*). Al-Ghazali developed the thesis, later disputed by Ibn Rushd, that no true Muslim could subscribe to Greek philosophy. Ibn Rushd replied to Al-Ghazali in a brilliant counter-tract entitled *Tahafut al-tahafut* ('The Incoherence of the Incoherence'), in which he argues that it is perfectly possible to be a good Muslim and a rationalist philosopher. Behind these mutual criticisms lies a profound division, which persists to the present day, between the conservative Sunni *ulema* on the one hand and on the other hand the mystical, Persian-influenced ideas of Ibn Sina, allied to those of Muslim free thinkers such as Ibn Rushd.

IBN RUSHD: THE END OF INCOHERENCE

Abu Al-Walid Ibn Rushd was the most distinguished philosopher and medical doctor of the twelfth century. This exceptional thinker, a member of an important family of Spanish Malikite jurists, was born in Cordova in 1126 and died in Marrakesh in 1198.[18] With his rationalist approach, he shook the foundations of the established frameworks of ideas of both Muslims and Christians. He was at the same time a philosopher, a student of medicine and a jurist who exercised the responsibilities of a judge, or *qadi*. When he was a young man, the Almohad ruler Abu Yaqub Yusuf instructed the great scholar Ibn Tufayl to commission Ibn Rushd to write a commentary on the works of Aristotle. Ibn Rushd prepared a masterly summary of Aristotle and was even able to develop some of his ideas further.

In due course, Ibn Rushd's inclination towards freedom of thought, together with the challenges he posed to received ideas on religious issues, predictably earned him the enmity both of orthodox Islamists and of some traditional Christian thinkers. Nevertheless, it must be stressed that Ibn Rushd never professed himself to be an unbeliever, or expressed hostility towards either Islam or Christianity. The problem was simply that his novel ideas were too much for certain traditional clerics to accept. A particular reason why the *ulema* accused him of impiety was that he claimed to have defined the precise relationship between rational philosophy and faith. It should be recalled that the argument regarding whether reason has primacy over faith, or vice-versa, is not peculiar to Islam. In Christian circles, the issue was already hotly disputed between the disciples of Tertullian, who believed in the total priority of faith over reason, and those who followed St Augustine, whose starting point was divine revelation but who developed this into a structure based on pure reason. Tertullian, who was born in Carthage in 160, condemned Greek philosophy and rationalism as heretical. Augustine, of Berber stock, was born in Thagaste (modern Souk-Ahras) in 354 and died at Hippo (the Algerian city of Annaba) in 430, where he became a bishop.[19] From his isolated bishopric in Annaba, St Augustine had initiated a revolution within Christianity, by reconciling the faith with rational thought and expunging its obscurantist tendencies.

It was left to Ibn Rushd, however, much later, to complete the triumph of pure reason, when the new directions taken by his thought in many fields of philosophy and religion brought him the opprobrium of the conservative clerics. Among their grievances, three appear to be the most grave. First and foremost, he laid the conceptual groundwork for later confrontations between knowledge and faith, and between philosophy and religion. A more specific charge was that he abandoned the Qur'anic conception of the creation of the universe. Third, he cast doubt upon the accepted religious notion of the survival of the soul after death.

THE SPLIT BETWEEN RELIGION AND PHILOSOPHY

In Islamic theology there is a single source of truth, namely God, who rules the universe and humankind through the Qur'anic texts revealed to Muhammad. Believers should be guided by the Qur'an and the Sunna alone, and should refrain from seeking guidance from any philosophy of human origin. For Ibn Rushd, however, there were two sources of truth: religion, which produced a vision of truth appropriate for the mass of the people; and philosophy, whose conceptual framework of truth was available only to the elite of philosophical scholars. Nevertheless, Ibn Rushd saw no contradiction between philosophy and faith: philosophy and religion could subsist side by side without clashing with each other, since, as they addressed intellects at different levels, their domains remained entirely separate.[20]

Ibn Rushd based his theory on two observations. First, in his day, there were violent sectarian and doctrinal splits within Islam; and second, those unable fully to comprehend religion were observably given to making inappropriate use of it for their own ends. As a result, as one commentator put it, 'he attributed these ills to the access to philosophical ideas enjoyed by those unable to understand them; and saw the remedy in defining closely the level of intelligence required for the comprehension of Qur'anic texts, forbidding individuals to go beyond the level appropriate for them.'[21] He in no way disputed that the Qur'an represented divine truth, but contended that since it was destined for all human beings, it should contain something to satisfy each person, whatever his abilities. He divided humanity into three types. First are the 'men of proof', who require rigorous demonstration of propositions they have been asked to accept and aim to attain knowledge by proceeding from one necessary truth to another by way of watertight arguments. Second are the 'men of dialectic', who are content with rhetorical arguments, demonstrating truth on the basis of plausibility rather than necessity. The third and final group are the 'men of exhortation', who are satisfied with mere oratory, appealing to the imagination and the passions. What showed the miraculous character of the Qur'an was that it was able to address these three audiences simultaneously, with an interior significance for scholars and an exterior meaning for the unlearned.[22]

In the view of Ibn Rushd, each person has the opportunity to understand the Qur'an according to his own ability. His preference, however, was that the interpretation of sacred texts should be the preserve of the elite, since they alone would be able to comprehend the 'true meaning' of what is revealed in them. He goes as far as to propose that complex exegeses of the Qur'an should not even be disclosed to those without the training and background necessary to understand their meaning. This has contemporary resonance, especially when it is observed that so-called fatwas purportedly based on the Qur'an are today pronounced on a daily basis by all who seek for whatever reason to condemn their fellow men. Even those whose literacy is open to question, let alone their scholarship, claim this privilege. In his day, Ibn Rushd described such unauthorised fatwas as heretical, as they were not validated by the 'sages'.

Ibn Rushd rounds off his reflections on the relationship between religion and philosophy by drawing a distinction between three levels of conceptualisation, parallel to his three levels of understanding. At the apex of the hierarchy stands philosophy, the source of real knowledge and absolute truth; then comes theology, the realm of dialectic and the probable; finally there are religion and faith, a resource that must be available for those who find them necessary. These constitute three separate levels of intellectual apprehension of one and the same truth.[23] Of course, the fact that religion is relegated to the bottom of the list infuriated the traditional *ulema*. This is one of the reasons why Ibn Rushd is never mentioned in traditional Islamic educational establishments, for fear of the corruption that might infect the minds of students who come into contact with freedom of thought and rational deduction.

IBN RUSHD AND THE CREATION OF THE UNIVERSE

Another specific problem for the *ulema* was the difficulty of Ibn Rushd's alternative approach to the creation of the universe, which appears to contradict the Qur'an. Islam conventionally asserts that the world was created by God out of nothing. Sura 6, verse 14 of the Qur'an has this to say:

> Say: Shall I take as guardian any one other than God, Who created the heavens and the earth, and who feeds and is not fed?

Ibn Rushd, on the other hand, claims to show that the world was not created. According to him, the existence of the world defies comprehension. As Roger Arnaldez puts it, Ibn Rushd says that 'nothing' cannot be understood as an entity capable of being the only thing that has ever existed, since the meaning of 'nothing' can only be comprehended as the absence of something. Therefore the existence of 'nothing' cannot have preceded the existence of the world. In a logically distinct argument, Ibn Rushd also asserts that 'something' cannot come out of 'nothing', since it is not possible for 'nothing' to change into something that exists (*al-mutakawinin*). This is so, because within 'nothing', which is by definition undifferentiated, there is no reason why change should occur and therefore no possibility that it can.[24]

THE SURVIVAL OF THE IMMORTAL SOUL

The traditional clergy never forgave Ibn Rushd for his rational examination of the origins of the universe. However, there is another misdemeanour for which he could not be pardoned, which was the doubt he introduced regarding the doctrine crucial to Islam that the soul survives after the death of the individual. The Qur'an declares the end of the world to be imminent, and that it will be followed by the resurrection of the bodies and souls of men. Sura 75, The Resurrection, says the following in its first verses:

> No! I swear by the Day of Resurrection; No! I swear by the reproachful soul. Does man think that We will not put his bones back together? Yes indeed; We are able to straighten his fingertips. Rather, man wishes to continue his profligacy in front of Him. He asks: 'When is the Day of Resurrection coming?' Then, when the sight is dazzled; and the moon is eclipsed; and the sun and moon are joined together; Man will say on that day: 'Where is the escape?'

Ibn Rushd appears always to have had doubts regarding the religious conception of the survival of the soul and the body after death. He gave the impression that he could find no philosophical grounds to believe in personal immortality. He was also convinced that it could not be demonstrated that the body could be resurrected.[25] However, the issue of resurrection is central for all religions, and critical to the question of the Last Judgement and the existence of Heaven and Hell. To query any of these basic doctrines could have dire consequences for any who expressed such ideas. As was only to be expected, therefore, this was another reason for Ibn Rushd to come under attack from the traditionalist theologians. In the end, the result was that he fell out of favour with the Almohad court, which ordered his books to be burned, though some copies of his works survived to be translated by his Jewish disciples who smuggled the manuscripts into France and to the Middle East. Later, Ibn Rushd's Christian disciples in Europe were to continue his struggle for the freedom of thought in the face of dogmatism and 'the spurious speculations of theology'. In 1240, this earned them the condemnation of the Catholic Church.

The most distinguished follower of Ibn Rushd in France was Siger de Brabant. In 1277, Siger was called before the Inquisition, which arraigned him for heresy. He was falsely accused of inciting revolution among the students of France by means of his doctrines.

He was alleged to have argued, among other things, that 'theology teaches nothing; adherence to Christianity is an obstacle to science; Christian law contains the same mistakes and misapprehensions as other systems; death is the end of everything; fornication is not a sin.'[26] The Christian response was comparable to that directed at Ibn Rushd by the Muslim traditionalists. Siger de Brabant was accused of 'the denial of divine providence, the immortality of the soul, and human freedom, leading to religious apathy and the abandonment of moral standards'.[27]

An apparently irreconcilable confrontation developed between free thinkers and traditionalists, under the Almohad rulers of North Africa, as much as within the Christian community. Free thinkers such as Ibn Rushd or Ibn Al-Arabi, the mystical philosopher, were no longer welcome in the lands of the Maghreb, which had long been a breeding ground for unorthodox thinkers. As time went on, North African intellectuals had a choice only between exile and death under torture. In the end, Ibn Rushd died in obscurity in Marrakesh. Ibn al-Arabi, who attended Ibn Rushd's obsequies when his body was brought back to Cordova, gives us a touching account:

> They had placed on the back of a beast of burden the catafalque of the master on one side, and his works on the other. How I would have liked to know if his prayers had been answered.[28]

These books, loaded onto a common ass, were the remnants of the scientific works and religious texts that had escaped the destructive fires of the inquisitors.

While expressing admiration for this Arab genius, the Orientalist scholar Ernest Renan appears hardly able to suppress his satisfaction when he contemplates the plight of Arab philosophy after Ibn Rushd:

> Arab philosophy presents a virtually unique example of a high culture instantly suppressed without trace, and almost forgotten by the people who created it. Islam here reveals the irremediably straitjacketed nature of its mentality.[29]

In reality, after the death of Ibn Rushd intellectual activity did not cease in the Muslim world, though it laboured under serious disadvantages. It is sometimes forgotten that Ibn Rushd inspired others such as the Sufis, who specialised in the decipherment of the hidden meaning of texts (al-batin), and his rationalist heirs, such as Jamal Ad-Din Al-Afghani and the Egyptian, Muhammad Abduh. In more recent times, Abd Al-Rahman Badawi, Mohammed Al-Jabri, Muhammad Arkoun, Muhammad Talbi, Samir Amin, Nawal El-Saadawi and others have also served as reinterpreters of Islamic ideas.

SUFI MYSTICISM: THE REFUGE OF MUSLIM THOUGHT

Sufism is not a heresy, despite what the Wahhabis and other fundamentalist *ulema* such as Algeria's Sheikh Ben Badis might say. In fact, the nature of the attack on Sufism mounted by Ben Badis is instructive. Born in 1889, Ben Badis was a learned and respectable figure who played an important part in the reconstruction of the Algerian national identity in the years from 1920 until his death in 1940. However, he used the power of his organisation, the 'Association of Ulema', to dismantle the Sufi brotherhoods, which represented serious competition to his spiritual authority. For example, the Algerian Sufi Sheikh Ahmad Al-Alawi (1869–1934), a leading figure of the Darqawiyya brotherhood, who was a target of Ben Badis's strictures, in no way resembled the stereotype promoted by Ben Badis. Ben Badis represented Al-Alawi as a bogus, pseudo-ascetic charlatan. In fact, Al-Alawi was an authentic theological scholar, a rationalist philosopher and a student of science, in precisely the style recommended by Ibn Rushd. None of this, however, was enough to mitigate Ben Badis's hostility.[30]

Sufism is, in reality, rather than a heresy, a discipline that advocates detachment of thought, achieved through an apprenticeship in asceticism and the appreciation of the purest Islamic faith. The Sufi way turns its back on conformity, dogmatism and religious fanaticism. Instead, it prefers meditation, intuition, reflection, the non-violent struggle against injustice and the protection of minorities and ordinary people. The Sufis vaunt their attachment to the Qur'an, though they choose to read it in an esoteric spirit. Shi'ite tradition claims that such esoteric knowledge was passed down by the Prophet Muhammad himself to his son-in-law and cousin Ali, 'from whom it passed in turn to the successive Shi'ite Imams'.[31] Sufism has been present across the ages. The spirit of Sufism is even recognised by the Qur'an itself, which refers to 'those whose hearts, upon mention of God, quiver with fear'. Ibn Khaldun (1332–1406), the celebrated medieval Tunisian sociologist, recognised the spiritual power of the Sufis and the efficacy of their practices, and complained only about the esoteric nature of their conception of truth.[32] The Sufis, it must be said, do not recognise a single truth, but multiple truths: religious truth, mystical truth and others. Only mystics of the stamp of Ibn al-Arabi,[33] Ibn Sina, Al-Hallaj or Rumi were able to grasp such truths, including the inaccessible mystery of God himself. However, their wide-ranging glosses on Islamic issues made them constant targets for the antagonism of the traditionalist *ulema* and the *fuqaha* (the legal scholars). Another reason for hostility to the Sufis was their acceptance of poetry, art, music and dance. Freedom and the enjoyment of life were their principal goals. Sufism, it has been said, was the 'science of the beautiful'.

The discipline of Sufism has not only brought innovations in the spiritual domain, but has also helped confer upon Islam the image of a religion of peace, compassion and tolerance. Undoubtedly, it re-established the humanist vision that properly belongs to Islam, and has thrown into relief the serenity and tolerance that is the dominant element in the practice of the majority of the world's Muslims.

THE MEANING, ORIGINALITY AND ORGANISATION OF SUFISM

Sufism is an ascetic movement inspired by spirit of generosity and charity comparable to that of St John the Baptist or St Francis of

Assisi in the Christian tradition. It emerged in the eighth century as a response to the wealth accrued by the victorious Muslim armies. The Sufis regarded as hypocritical the lives of luxury that certain of the Caliphs led in their harems. They also deprecated the wealth the clergy derived from their religious endowments while at the same time they presided over the austere doctrines taught in the *madrasas*.

The Abbasid era was a period in which Sufism particularly flourished. It was the product of a spectrum of diverse influences: Islamic, Hellenistic, Hindu and Jewish. The present author's investigations, however, have tended to indicate a hitherto less recognised influence on the Sufi tradition, namely that of the Coptic monastic tradition in Egypt, which was established as long ago as the fourth century. The monasteries of the Egyptian desert appear to have been an ideal place of refuge for those who wished to escape from the world and its temptations. It was in Egypt, therefore, that the concept of ascetic monasticism was developed for the first time, notably with Anba Antunius (known to the West as St Antony).[34] From its origins in Alexandria, asceticism then spread to Europe and finally, with the Sufis, to the Muslim world. The Egyptian monastic life was later to have a substantial influence on such thinkers as Ibn Al-Arabi, regarded as the 'pole' (*qutb*) of Arab mysticism, who said:

> My heart can take all forms: a meadow for gazelles, a convent for monks, a temple for idols, the Ka'aba for a pilgrim, the tablets of the Tora, the holy book of the Qur'an. My religion is Love, and wherever it may lead, Love is my faith.[35]

It is noteworthy that, after Ibn al-Arabi, leading Sufis have been inclined to make contact with Christian mystics, taking the view that Jesus Christ (in Arabic, 'Sayyidna Isa', or 'Our Lord Jesus') was, among God's messengers, the most perfect of the contemplative saints.

As regards the significance of the word 'Sufi', a number of interpretations have been offered. The most common supposition is that it is derived from the Arabic word *suf*, which means 'wool', and that the adjective *sufi* refers to the woollen robes that Sufi ascetics wore to signify their rejection of the worldly luxury of their contemporaries. Others, who include many Western Islamologues, believe it is derived from the Arabic word *sufiya*, whose origin is the Greek *sophia*, meaning wisdom, from which the word 'philosophy' is derived. Another theory links the word with *safa'*, an Arabic word meaning purity. In reality the etymology of the word 'Sufi' remains as mysterious and difficult to grasp as the discipline for which it stands. There is infinite variety within Sufism, and though the great Sufi orders (*turuq*, singular *tariqa*) dominate the institutional scene, there remains the potential for as many individual ways of practising Sufism as there are Sufi seekers in the world.

Beyond these difficulties of definition, however, there are constant elements that characterise the adepts of Sufism. All reject violence, all deplore religious conformism, and all repudiate injustice on the part of the authorities. Sufis seek to develop moral purity through the performance of rituals, including singing or chanting, and sometimes dancing or other ritual movements, and the invocation (*dhikr*) of the name of God. All Sufis practise asceticism and humility, and examine their consciences as a matter of duty. To achieve enlightenment, the Sufi ascetic in general follows an initiation ritual which takes the form of a pact (*bay'a*) between himself and a Sufi Sheikh. The Sheikh will in general be a spiritual master (the *murshid*) within a Sufi order (*tariqa*). With the assistance of the Sheikh, the Sufi postulant seeks to achieve the union of his soul with God. He never relents in his struggle to ascend to the highest level: namely to achieve a relationship with God and bring about the absorption of his soul into the divine essence. The goal of the pupil's spiritual journey is to open his mind to knowledge and truth (*haqiqa*). This mystical voyage is virtually identical in all the *turuq*. Its objective is progressively to transform the psyche, the physicality and the spirituality of the individual so that he can put them to the service of human values.

A grand master of Sufism described this process of apprenticeship in the following way:

When a neophyte approaches the Sheikhs because he wishes to renounce the world, he is subjected to a process of spiritual discipline lasting three years. If he achieves what is expected of him, all is well. If not ... he cannot be admitted into the *tariqa*. The first year of the three is devoted to learning to serve others, on the basis that the candidate is the worst of all men and should serve all others equally. The second year is devoted to the service of God, given that he can serve God only when he has renounced his selfish interests. The candidate should worship God for His own sake and not for any other reason. The third year is devoted to the scrutiny of the candidate's own spirit, which can only be done by gathering his thoughts and driving out all care, in order to preserve his spirit, with God's help, from the ravages of neglect. Only after these trials can the candidate don the *muraqaba*, the robe of patchwork or wool (*suf*) worn by the true mystic dervishes.[36]

In North Africa, the monastic establishment in which this training takes place is known as a *zawiya* or *ribat*, in Egypt and other Arabic-speaking countries a *khanaqah* (a word used also in Iran and as far as India), and in Turkish-speaking lands a *tekke*. In the Maghreb and in Africa, the Sheikh is known as a 'marabout' (*murabit*) who stands at the apex of the hierarchical structure of the branch of the *tariqa* he directs. This status is acquired only by right of birth. A marabout is in general descended from some personage recognised as having the status of a Muslim saint, and may lead one or more 'zawiyas' (Arabic pl: *zawaya*). These are not unlike medieval universities, with professors who occupy themselves with the mystical education of the students (*tullab* or *talaba*, singular *talib*: it should be noted that the plural of *talib* when it appears as a loan word in Persian or other eastern languages is *taliban*). The disciples study the Qur'an, Arabic grammar, Sufi sciences relative to astronomy and alchemy, as well as the meditative rituals of chanting (the *dhikr*) and sometimes of dancing. Such zawiyas are often in direct confrontation with the conservative 'madrasas' (*madrasa*, plural *madaris*), in which the Shari'a and its associated religious sciences are the focus, where science is neglected and Sufi rituals are strictly forbidden.

Sufi education is in fact entirely at variance with that prescribed by the *ulema* and *fuqaha*, who cling to the orthodoxy of the pious ancestors of the first generation of Islam, the *salaf*. First of all, it places a different slant on the interpretation of the Qur'an from the textual explication practised by traditionalist teachers. The Sufis are concerned more with the hidden meaning of the sacred texts (*'ilm al-batin*) than with the overt sense (*al-zahir*). The aim of the Sufis is to elucidate all the mysteries of the Qur'an and to interpret them in a humanistic fashion, socially as well as spiritually. Two examples will serve to illustrate this point. Traditional Islam exhorts men to love God, but God is under no obligation to return this love. The Sufis, on the other hand, base their position on an interpretation of Sura 5, verse 54 of the Qur'an, which says: 'God will certainly bring forth a people whom He loves and they love Him', which shows, they claim, that there is a mutual love between God and his servants. Similarly, in response to those who repudiate the Sufis for their supposedly non-Muslim beliefs, they point to Sura 18, verse 28, which asks Muhammad to be patient and compassionate with those who devote themselves wholeheartedly to God – 'those who call upon their Lord, morning and evening, desiring His face'.

The Sufis insist on the principles of equality between men and women and of tolerance between all men and among all races. Sufism forbids its adepts to be jealous or covet other men's goods. A Sufi born into poverty should accept his position, while trying to better himself through work and effort. His deeds should never be motivated by greed for his neighbour's possessions, and he may only rise up against injustice if it is flagrant in nature. Sufis deplore the use of violence and the instrumentalisation of religion for political ends. In the same spirit, they emphasise the importance of independence of mind and a refusal to bow to corrupt and unjust political leaders. This was the tradition of the great Sufi Sheikh Abd Al-Qadir Al-Jilani (1077–1166), the eponymous founder of the Qadiriyya *tariqa*, which is today found everywhere in the world. Abd Al-Qadir Al-Jilani was known for his refusal to meet Caliphs whom he regarded as despotic. His lesson to his disciples was that people get the leaders they deserve: as he put it, 'if a leader is thus, then his people are so'.[37]

AL-HALLAJ: THE MARTYR OF ISLAM

It was with an exceptional mystic of the tenth century, Al-Husayn Ibn Mansur Al-Hallaj (858–922), that the Sufi dissent from the political and religious domination exercised by orthodox Islam reached its peak. In the course of history, the Sufis have often been the target of fatwas issued by members of the *ulema* and Islamic jurists who have accused them of turning their backs on the universal rulings of the Shari'a. The mystics have always replied that they do not share the views of the official representatives of Islam and do not recognise what they regard as unjustifiable sentences pronounced upon them. In their view, the mysteries of Islam can only be unravelled by intellectual effort, complemented by meditation and mystical illumination. This stage of development could only be reached, according to Al-Hallaj and Ibn Al-Arabi, when an individual's love for God was so powerful and he was so far possessed by the divine spirit that he was subsumed into the divinity. This was, in other terms, a state of sublimity that permitted the human soul to lose its individuality and be absorbed by God. This Sufi thesis, which appeared to place a human being, created out of clay, on the same level as the One God, unchangeable, uncreated and to whom none was equal, was excoriated by the *ulema* of the day as a blasphemous invention.

Al-Hallaj was one of the first Sufis upon whom the Muslim jurists exacted an extreme penalty for his independence of mind and his efforts to interpret the Qur'an in a novel way. He was also one of those rare figures who evoked profound sympathy and a powerful interest among the Muslim population at large. Even today, all Arabs and most Muslims have stories to tell about Al-Hallaj. Some say he was an enlightened Sufi saint. Others say with an ironic smile that he was no more than a dervish who mistook himself for God. Others again will explain that he used to walk about Mecca telling all who would listen that he had God in person in his pocket: a terrible blasphemy. In fact, this legendary mystic was a personality whose depth was intensified by a spiritual power that seemed almost beyond human understanding.[38]

Al-Hallaj was born in 858 in Persia, in the eastern provinces of the Abbasid Caliphate. Like most well-born Persians, he claimed descent from the Quraysh, the tribe to which the Prophet Muhammad belonged. After his pilgrimage to Mecca, he travelled in the Middle East, the Caucasus and in Asia, preaching his doctrine of the union of God and man, 'to the point where the Lover and the Loved become one'.[39] This was not calculated to meet with the approval of the jurists (fuqaha), the guardians of the official religion of Islam, who could not accept the notion of equality of God with man, an entity of base origin, still less of fusion between them. In the words of the Qur'an (Sura 15, verse 26), 'And We have created man from potter's clay, moulded out of slime'.

Nevertheless, Al-Hallaj persevered, defying the jurists and the *ulema* with his claims to be mystically united with God. The unforgivable moment came when, during a debate at the Abbasid Mosque of Al-Mansur in Baghdad, in dispute with an adversary named Al-Shibli, he pronounced the words 'Ana al-Haqq': 'I am the truth.' For Muslims, 'Al-Haqq' (the Truth) could mean only one thing: God himself. Al-Hallaj made matters worse by adding that there was 'no I but God'.[40] Al-Hallaj then began to challenge the validity of the pilgrimage to Mecca, the Hajj. He declared that a Muslim should be content with a symbolic pilgrimage, submitting himself to a ritual that would take the place of the travails of a lengthy journey. He proposed that such a virtual pilgrim, rather than travelling to Mecca, should 'proceed seven times around the Ka'aba of his heart'. By this time, two powerful Abbasid ministers, Ibn Al-Furat and Muhammad Ibn Abd Al-Hamid, had joined their antagonism to that of the theologians. They saw in Al-Hallaj's activities a plot involving Al-Hallaj's contacts among the Qaramites (*qaramita*, singular *qarmati*), a bizarre Ismaili schism that preached egalitarian ideas and apparently wished to destroy Mecca and the Ka'aba, which they regarded as an object of superstition.[41] This was not a groundless fear, it should be said: in 930 the Qaramites actually seized control of Mecca and made off with the Ka'aba, which was not returned for 22 years.[42] In any case, Al-Hallaj was arrested on flimsy charges and was sentenced to be burned alive. His sole crime was to have felt himself to be possessed by the spirit of God, and to have attained the pinnacle of the Sufi experience. His martyrdom was in reality the result of the political and religious intrigues of his day.

His trial in Baghdad was conducted in circumstances of great formality. According to one account:

> Baghdad was then probably the most civilised capital in the civilised world. There, in a setting of heightened theatricality, the trial of Divine Love was enacted, amid the sumptuous luxury of the Abbasid court.[43]

Once condemned to death, Al-Hallaj was placed ignominiously on a mule and escorted by grooms to be, according to the testimony of his son, hoisted onto a cross where he was given 500 lashes, after which his hands and feet were cut off.[44] He was subjected to further barbaric cruelties that need not be described. At the end, his ashes were thrown into the Tigris. The authorities in Baghdad 'forbade his works to be further copied, in order to expunge all memory of him. With the originals destroyed this task had evidently been accomplished, though perhaps a few pages were retained by Ibn Isa.'[45]

JALAL AL-DIN AL RUMI: THE WHIRLING DERVISH

Mawlana Rumi was certainly the most stellar mystical poet of Islamic literature, and perhaps in the literature of the world. Of Persian origin, he was a humanist who was preoccupied by art, beauty, music and dance. Between 1318 and 1353, he wrote more than 5,000 rhyming couplets, the *Mathnawi*, which epitomised the Sufism of the so-called whirling dervishes of the Turkish city of Konia.

Rumi was an authority on Islamic law, which he studied with his father, an eminent theologian, until he became himself a jurist. He was at the same time swayed by the ideas of the great mystic Ibn Al-Arabi, whom he would later meet in Damascus. But what in fact set Rumi's feet on the path he was to follow was his meeting with Shams Tabrizi, an eccentric dervish who became his true master. The two became inseparable companions after an episode described thus by Rumi's biographers:

> Mawlana was reading, while sitting on a bench next to a fountain. Piles of manuscripts lay beside him. Suddenly, there appeared a strange man, dressed in a long black cloak. Without a word, he seized the books and threw them into the fountain. Mawlana stood up, astonished by this act. 'Why did you do that?' he asked, in furious tones. 'Those books belonged to my father. They were more precious to me than I can say, and now you have destroyed them.' Without a word, the man plunged his hands in the fountain and one by one brought out the books, which he returned to Mawlana, each one perfectly dry. 'Who taught you to do that?' asked Mawlana. Looking deeply into Mawlana's eyes, the man replied, 'The love of God.' At that moment in their gaze there appeared the light of an indescribable understanding, and the two left together.'[46]

In due course, however, the friendship between Rumi and Shams Tabrizi aroused the jealousy of Rumi's disciples, and of Rumi's son, Sultan Walid, who successfully plotted to get rid of Tabrizi in Damascus. Rumi never got over the loss of Tabrizi and never forgave his son, with whom he was angry for the rest of his life.

Nevertheless, Rumi continued to make his contribution to the enrichment of the philosophical thinking of the order of the whirling dervishes. His mystical devotions enabled him to complete the rhyming couplets that make up the *Mathnawi*, which he dictated to his disciples in the form of mystical poems that expressed an expansive vision of Sufi Islam. Today, this mystical and philosophical work is still the most read Muslim work after the Qur'an itself. This is a source of great irritation to the traditional clergy. Conservatives find Rumi unacceptable, in part because of the musical and artistic aspects of his interests, and in part for his philosophical ideas. 'Rumi's comportment put him in a different world from the rigour of strict Islamism, with his insistence that "many ways lead to God, of which I have chosen the way of music and dancing".'[47] It is beyond doubt that Rumi was an important innovator in the fields of art, poetry, music and dance, enhancing the joys of life in the Muslim world. His skill in arranging the dances of the dervishes was incomparable. His visions and ideas have never ceased to attract the attention of contemporary artists and performers.

His ideas about human society were also highly original and unorthodox, from the conventional Islamic point of view. For example, he has this to say about the evolution of the human spirit:

> From the moment you arrive in the world, a ladder is presented to you that you can use to make your escape. First, you were inanimate substance; then you became vegetative – how could you not know this? Then you were made man, endowed with knowledge, reason and faith. Think about the body, made from dust: what perfection it has achieved. When you have risen above the condition of man, you will no doubt become an angel: then you will have finished with the earth and your domain will be the sky.[48]

Rumi also believed in the equality of men and women. He often said, 'My wife should be my equal. It is like a pair of boots: if one is too tight, the pair is no use'.[49] Even prostitutes had the right to dignity in his view. He was vehement in his rejection of prejudice towards women, whatever their faults might be. In *Mathnawi* couplets 2233 and 2234, telling the story of how the Sufi Dalqak explained to Sayyid-i Ajall why he had married a prostitute, he says:

> One night, Sayyid-i Ajall said to Dalqak, you have hastened to marry a prostitute when you should have spoken to me so that we could have selected a chaste woman to be your spouse. Dalqak replied, 'I have married nine chaste and virtuous women who became prostitutes, racking me with grief. I have married this prostitute whom I did not know, in order to see how she will turn out. I have often resorted to intelligence; this time I seek refuge in folly'.[50]

By the time of Rumi's death, the Muslim world had been seduced by the influence of the innovations of the Sufi orders. On the other hand, the influence of the traditionalist *ulema*, for whom the Shari'a was the indisputable truth, was still strong. Nevertheless, the Muslim community's new-found experience of its spirituality continued undiminished. At that time, neither faction was able to impose itself above the other. It was only with the arrival of western imperialism in the Islamic lands in the nineteenth century that a third way, in the shape of the reformist school, made its appearance, initially in Egypt. This third way, between Sufism and traditionalist Islamism, was led principally by two former mystics, Jamal Ad-Din Al-Afghani (1837–97) and Muhammad Abduh (1849–1905).[51] These two intellectuals established a school of thought that was original but took its inspiration from the Muslim rationalists of the Middle Ages. Their originality lay in the wish to reform an Islam that had become antiquated, while attempting to resolve the crisis within Islam occasioned by its contact with western progress and culture.

8

THE SECOND AND THIRD GENERATIONS OF RATIONALISTS AND NEO-SUFISM: FROM JAMAL AD-DIN AL-AFGHANI AND MUHAMMAD ABDUH TO EDWARD SAID

THE SECOND GENERATION

JAMAL AD-DIN AL-AFGHANI

The new school of rationalist Muslim thought that first appeared in Egypt in the nineteenth century was in part a consequence of the intensifying confrontation with the West. Of its two leading exponents, one, Jamal Ad-Din Al-Afghani was of Afghan origin, from a good family. From his earliest days, he was keenly aware of the British imperialism of the era and agitated against it as best he could. As the result of his pro-Russian political activities, he was obliged in 1868 to leave Afghanistan, apparently at the behest of the British, and took refuge in India. From 1871 he lived in Egypt, but in 1879 he was expelled from the country by the Egyptian ruler Tawfiq, the successor to the Khedive Ismail who had been deposed after British and French pressure had been brought to bear against him. In exile, Al-Afghani lived for some time in France. Later he took up residence in Russia, where he seems once more to have engaged in anti-British activities at the behest of the Russians. Later he lived in Iran, before moving to London, and finally to Istanbul.

Al-Afghani was a man of high intelligence and was versed in many fields of scholarship in the human sciences and religion. All who met him were struck by his charisma and soon perceived his impressive powers of reason and his analytical facility. His insight, his wisdom and his ability to profit from circumstances rendered him one of the most striking Islamic personalities of his day. He struggled mightily to modernise Islam, which was in the grip of fanaticism and obscurantism. He stood out against injustice and the brutal incursions of the British, French and Russian imperialists into the Arab world, in both North Africa and the Middle East, and was particularly exercised over western interference in the Indian subcontinent, Egypt and Algeria. Al-Afghani was a leading spirit of Islamic renewal, and travelled widely both in the East and the West. While studying in France, he found a young Egyptian disciple, Muhammad Abduh, who was destined to become a leader of the movement for Islamic renewal in his own right. Al-Afghani had also chosen to become a freemason, which brought him even sharper criticism from the Islamists. To the end of his life, he continued to inveigh against imperialism, and also laboured in the cause of Islamic unity. As one commentator put it, 'He stressed the importance of a return to Islam's religious roots, and on the need for emulation of the earliest Muslims, the *salaf*, if the people were to be shaken out of their torpor. Religious reform, however, came second to another goal, namely to give the Muslim peoples the means to struggle against western colonialism.'[1]

Al-Afghani was thus an authentic precursor of universal Islamic militancy. He targeted principally the values brought by the civilisation of the colonialists, and his opposition to expansionism and the economic injustice it entailed were implacable. He had the gift of winning the attention and the trust of Muslim leaders, and succeeded in wielding influence over rulers in Islamic lands from Afghanistan to Egypt. He galvanised those who heard his fiery oratory against western infiltration, insisting on the message that the people needed to 'furnish themselves with the arms and other means to counter effectively the West's increasingly determined onslaught'.[2] He exhorted Muslims as a whole to unite behind a coalition of relatively well-endowed and modernised Muslim countries such as Egypt and the countries of the Maghreb in order to oppose the cultural invasion of the West and the iniquitous hegemony imposed by the industrialised countries. His struggle against the West never ceased to identify British imperialism and its hostility to the Ottoman Empire as a particular target. The Caliph in Istanbul was at that time seen as the legitimate representative of the Islamic community as a whole and therefore of pan-Islamism.

Despite his constant struggle against the West, Al-Afghani and his companion Muhammad Abduh, perhaps somewhat paradoxically, attempted to adapt Islam to the western ideas that were becoming inexorably more prevalent in the nineteenth century, but without abandoning the fundamental values of Islamic civilisation. The two took advantage of their stay in Paris to launch a prospectus for co-operation and partnership between the industrial nations and the Muslim world. Only in this way, they argued, could the Muslim peoples inaugurate what they saw as a necessary revolution in Islamic thought, with sweeping changes in political and social institutions and in the Islamic attitude to science. They set out an impressive programme of reform, which included the prioritisation of education for women, the abolition of slavery and social equality. Thus, they succeeded in setting in motion a movement for change in the Arab world that was without precedent. They were able to test certain aspects of their theories on the reawakening of the East in Egypt before disseminating them more widely through the Muslim countries. Their programme of enthusiastic reform began to take on the character of a true renaissance with the potential to give a new lease of life to an Islamic civilisation in which stagnation had by default become the order of the day. Muslim society seemed thus to become better able to withstand the intrusions of the West, which at the same time never hesitated to use its power and superior technology to cow a Muslim community weakened by internal dissent and its inability to adapt.

AL-AFGHANI'S REFORMIST PROGRAMME[3]

Jamal Ad-Din Al-Afghani's starting point was that religion should be liberal and tolerant. For this opinion, as he recounts, he was turned away from the doors of mosques where obscurantism held sway.[4] In Al-Afghani's view, reason and human intelligence should play the leading role in the application of the Islamic faith. Properly deployed, the faith should be a key that releases the passions of men and renders them 'able to set foot on the road to social development and progress'.[5] Al-Afghani also said: 'When religion speaks, it should address itself to the intelligence'.[6] He was a fervent advocate of philosophy, rational thought and criticism, all of which, he argued, are to be discovered in the sacred texts revealed to the Prophet Muhammad. Muhammad himself, Al-Afghani insisted, was unequivocal in his condemnation of ignorance, foolishness, blindness and obscurantism.[7]

Jamal Ad-Din Al-Afghani's central ideas are to be found in his major work, 'The Refutation of the Materialists' (*Risalat al-Radd ala al-Dahriin*), where he develops the new approach which he believed should be adopted by Islam in the light of the triumph of colonialism in the nineteenth century.[8] This was a time when the Muslim community was more than ever divided in the spheres of religion and politics. Some Muslim notables, like Seyyid Ahmed Khan in India (1817–98), were already convinced of the inexorable supremacy of western science over an Islam that was unable to progress and uncertain of its spirituality, and apparently in a state of inexorable decline. However, in Khan's somewhat pessimistic view, Islam could only flourish through accepting a secondary role and by submitting itself to a process of assimilation to the Christian West. Al-Afghani refused to accept such ideas. He was convinced that Islam could meet the West's challenge and would experience an unprecedented social and spiritual renaissance.[9]

What, then, are the ideas developed in 'The Refutation of the Materialists'? In his introduction, Al-Afghani pays homage to the sages of ancient Greece, or to be more precise, those whom he qualifies as 'deists', including Socrates, Plato, Aristotle and Pythagoras. For all of these, he expresses great respect.[10] In contrast, he does not show the same reverence for what he described as the Greek materialists of the 'hylozoist' school such as Thales, Anaximenes and Heraclitus, who argued that life is in some sense characteristic of all matter, as well as the Stoics and Epicureans. All these, whom he described as 'negators of divinity, who denied the existence of the Holy Creator',[11] he accused of having 'inflicted crimes upon the human race, leaving evil relics and unpleasant memories that persist to the present day'.[12] As he saw it, such 'materialists' had exercised their malign influence over certain Islamic reformists, who were to be found principally in India, who had deviated too far in their interpretations of God and could not be other than in thrall to the West. Al-Afghani said such materialists were unworthy of respect, adding:

> They present themselves as friends of the poor and protectors of the weak, who seek the welfare of the poor; often, they claim to be prophets . . . They do all this to gain credence to carry out their schemes and to gain acceptance for the corruption they spread . . . In whatever fashion the materialists present themselves, whatever guise they take, and in the midst of whatever people they arise, they deal a terrible blow to what their fellow citizens have constructed. They lay waste the fruits of their nation like a thunderbolt, opening a wide breach in its walls. Their insinuations poison the souls of men and their interference disturbs the social order.[13]

In addition to the Indian Muslim materialists, Al-Afghani added to his list of those deserving anathema a range of alleged miscreants including the so-called assassins of the fortress of Alamut,[14] the Mormon sect of Christianity founded in 1830 in the United States by Joseph Smith.[15] Perhaps unfortunately, he also included the proponents of Darwin's theory of the evolution of species.[16] He demanded the expurgation of all such confabulations, as he thought of them, and called for the religion of Islam to be elevated once more to the erstwhile pedestal it had occupied. He exhorted the Muslims to amend their ways of thinking and their behaviour, in accordance with Sura 13, verse 11 of the Qur'an: 'God does not change the condition of a people unless they change what is in their hearts'.

Al-Afghani was successful, as had been Ibn Sina, Ibn Al-Arabi and Ibn Rushd before him, in giving the Muslims back their pride and making them aware that the Prophet Muhammad's message is compatible with the scientific spirit, with tolerance and with progress. He was undaunted by the criticisms of western Orientalists, such as Ernest Renan, who in 1883 made the sweeping assertion that Islam was unable to cope with modernity, attributing 'intellectual nullity' to the Muslim peoples.[17] Al-Afghani's message was that an Islamic renaissance was still possible. According to him, to rise once more, as they had done in the past, the Muslim community should set its feet firmly on the path of modernity, aiming to assimilate the positive side of European culture.

MUHAMMAD ABDUH

Muhammad Abduh (1849–1905) could be said to have been the first native-born Egyptian creative genius in the field of Islam. He was the leading disciple and friend of Jamal Ad-Din Al-Afghani. Like Al-Afghani, he threw himself into the political struggle for progress in Egypt. He was exiled from Egypt between 1882 and 1888, during the reign of the Khedive Tawfiq (1879–1892), and as the result of his travels he became familiar with the national struggles of the Lebanese and the Tunisians. It was only with the advent of Tawfiq's successor Abbas Hilmi II (1892–1914) and the resurgence of the Egyptian nationalist movement that Muhammad Abduh enjoyed his moment of triumph. He had already become a judge in 1888, but in 1891 he was appointed Mufti of Egypt, a very senior position which effectively installed him as administrative head of the Islamic faith in the country. As a convinced moderniser, he seized the opportunity to dynamise Islam in Egypt, adapting it to the transformations of the modern world and endowing it with a human face. At the same time, he rejected servile imitation of western institutions, though he did counsel the Egyptian people to embrace much of Europe's civilisation.

The central plank of his programme was the gradual raising of consciousness among the mass of the people. The first step towards this goal was to be the intensive education of the Muslim population. As Henri Laoust observes, the issue nearest to Muhammad Abduh's heart was that of 'religious teaching and the need to put the moral education of the Muslim population on a sounder footing, while organising, as the Christians had done, a body of missionaries'.[18] Secondly, Muhammad Abduh encouraged Muslim educators around the Islamic world to take steps at once to purge Islam of all the accrued irrational beliefs and myths that prevailed at that time. Finally, as a third stage, he proposed that both civil society and the institutions of the state should be reorganised in conformity with the principles of Islam, but in a manner consistent with the exigencies of modern life. As he saw it, the salvation of the Muslim peoples lay in their ability to conduct their political and cultural struggles within the framework of religion, into which social innovations must be subsumed. As Mufti, he set an example with his liberal fatwas and the progressive reforms he introduced into the religious institutions. This irritated the traditionalist clergy, however, who were eventually able to remove him from office.

The aspect of Muhammad Abduh's thinking that most upset the conservative *ulema* was the inspiration he took from Ibn Al-Arabi's Sufism, together with his glancing acknowledgement of the Mu'tazilites. In detail, the traditionalists accused him of abusing his position by pronouncing fatwas and juridical rulings that were too liberal for their liking. For instance, he issued a fatwa that authorised Muslims in the South African Transvaal, if they were unable to obtain other food, to eat the meat of animals slaughtered by Jews or Christians that had not been killed by having their throats cut in the manner prescribed by Islam.[19] Another highly controversial fatwa he is alleged to have promulgated gave approval for Muslims to make interest-bearing loans, which was of course totally forbidden by the Shari'a. Henri Laoust, however, questions the authenticity of this report, which may have been circulated by Muhammad Abduh's enemies.[20] The strict Islamists also held it against Muhammad Abduh that he had attempted to reform Egypt's religious institutions, including Al-Azhar University, as well as the Islamic tribunal system in Egypt that dated from Ottoman times. Their fear was that his modernisation would undermine ancestral Islamic values. In any case, the Egyptian conservatives turned their backs on Muhammad Abduh's message, which sought the key to emancipation not in violence but in an internal struggle for self-improvement on the part of individual Muslims.[21]

Muhammad Abduh's book, *Risalat al-Tawhid*, is his principal work on the Muslim faith, which throws light on the role of Islam in history, underlining its tolerance and humanism. The book is intended for Muslims who already have an elementary knowledge of Islamic doctrine and practice.[22] Muhammad Abduh's goal was to encourage Muslims to improve their lives on the basis of knowledge and free will.[23] He often reiterated the dictum:

> Man is aware of what he does and uses his powers of reason to weigh the consequences of his deeds; he acts of his own will and accomplishes what he does by the power that resides within him. To deny this would be to fly in the face of the evidence and deny man's very existence.[24]

He also said:

> In the case of conflict between reason and tradition, decisions must be taken on the basis of reason. [25]

In purely spiritual terms, Abduh took a view opposed to that of Ibn Taymiyya and the Wahhabis when he paid homage to the Sufi saints, whose souls he considered to be on a higher plane and whose minds were superior, though they were not to be compared with the prophets. As he put it:

> Many of them are on a level close to prophethood, and in some of their states of awareness they achieve a partial knowledge of what lies beyond, with visions of the spiritual world whose authenticity cannot be denied.[26]

In regard to the interpretation of the Shari'a on certain issues concerning relations between Muslims and other peoples, Muhammad Abduh displayed a tolerance greater than that which would have been acceptable to Ibn Taymiyya and his ilk. For example, he took the view that Muslims could marry with the

'People of the Book' (an expression taken to mean Muslims and Jews) and share their food, while in moral terms he took the view that non-Muslims were subject to the same laws and shared the same duties as Muslims. On the subject of Jihad he said:

> The literal meaning of Jihad is a struggle, and this does not mean only the external struggle against those who do not believe but also the interior struggle against evil impulses, undertaken in order to achieve moral discipline and control over oneself.[27]

He added that Islam forbade all conversion of non-Muslims and excluded the exercise of any religious constraint over them by any means other than persuasion.[28] In other words, Jihad against the infidels was not to be seen as a religious duty, since such a struggle would in itself contradict the humanitarian vocation of Islam. He declared that 'Muslims should unsheathe their swords only to defend themselves against enemies and to repel attacks.'[29] As a general principle, Jihad should be undertaken only as a defensive war against the protagonists of other religions, when their armies were, as he put it, 'numerous and overbearing'.[30]

In conclusion, it could be said that from this major work by Muhammad Abduh there emerges a spirit of humanism and altruism founded on Sufi values, and that an understanding may be gained of the extent to which Muhammad Abduh's ideas represented the tradition of Islamic ethics and tolerance characteristic of the great days of the Muslim faith. He always held firm to his commitment to tolerance, freedom of thought and the moral and human values of an Islam determined to adapt to the modern world.

Like Ibn Rushd and Ibn Sina before them, both Al-Afghani and Muhammad Abduh were anathematised in the eyes of the official Muslim world by the time of their deaths, which appears to be the inevitable destiny of those who strive for reform. Their efforts, however, were not in vain, as they were able to sow the seeds of freedom of thought and tolerance among moderate pan-Islamists. They were the first to call explicitly for the modernisation of Muslim society and for the separation of religion from politics.[31] They also presented the Islamic faith afresh, making it more attractive to the people. This had the effect that an alternative form of spirituality became available to the Muslim majority, who were thus enabled to distance themselves from the strict doctrines of Ibn Taymiyya and Ibn Hanbal, and from the ideas of Wahhabism, which had come to dominate the Islam of the Islamic theocrats. In the light of such a programme, it can be seen that radicalism, fanaticism, terrorism and the negation of human values are far from representative of Islam. On the contrary, the Muslim faith embodies a noble civilisation whose standard bearers are the rationalists, the Sufis and the whole range of moderate Islam.

Between the end of the nineteenth century and the Second World War, Al-Afghani and Muhammad Abduh had therefore succeeded in launching an intellectual reformist movement that could not be halted. By this time, a phalanx of Muslim intellectuals too numerous to be individually enumerated had taken up the banner of anti-colonialism and the movement for the equality of peoples.[32] One exceptional Syrian reformer, however, Abd Al-Rahman Al-Kawakibi, merits detailed consideration.

ABD AL-RAHMAN AL-KAWAKIBI

Abd Al-Rahman Al-Kawakibi (1849–1903) was born in Syria into a notable family in which culture was cherished. He enjoyed the benefits of literacy in Turkish and Persian as well as Arabic. From his adolescence, he began to take a stand against the Ottoman domination of his country, which he regarded as riddled with corruption. As a result of his political activities and his involvement in a campaign to improve the lot of the poor, he was exiled to Egypt, where he wrote his book, *Taba'i Al-Istibdad* ('The Nature of Despotism'), a book in which he condemned Muslim political leaders for their exploitation and oppression, as well as their hostility towards intellectuals and culture.[33] Al-Kawakibi observed that the Muslim leadership showed no concern for the enlightenment of the population through knowledge, critical reason or philosophy.[34] He laid the blame for this on the linkage between the oppressive authorities and the financial establishment, whom he saw as the instigators of poverty and injustice and identified as the origin of all society's ills.[35]

Later, after travelling through the Arab world and Africa, Al-Kawakibi began to think about the reasons for the sclerosis of Islamic thought and the backwardness of the Arabs. Afterwards, he wrote a book entitled *Umm Al-Qura* (literally 'The Mother of Villages', an expression used to signify the city of Mecca), which was structured as a discussion among 22 scholars of the Islamic faith, depicted as gathered in Mecca to discuss the formation of a society to transform the Muslim world.[36] Al-Kawakibi's ambition was to stem what he saw as the decadence of Islamic society and, by countering fanaticism and the false interpretation of religion, to furnish Muslims with the means to embark on a fresh renaissance. In the book he sets out the principal reasons for the decline of Islamic civilisation and the steps required to redress the problem. Religious, political, economic and moral factors all play their part.

Addressing religious issues, Kawakibi writes that discord and futile polemics between various ethnic factions, and also against the Shi'ite sects of Islam, have been deleterious to the development of Islamic thought. He adds that in past eras, lack of freedom, subjection to authoritarian rule, exploitation and poverty had reduced the Muslim population to indigence and constrained them to abandon productive work.[37] Among the causes of contemporary Muslim decline, he points to the Muslim acquiescence in radicalisation and dogmatism, and to the arrogance of leaders who sought to legitimise their power with the support of corrupt religious authorities.[38] In economic and political terms, Al-Kawakibi singles out the deleterious tendency of Muslims to succumb to authoritarian rule and to allow themselves to be divided into rival factions.[39] He also laments the disregard of justice and freedom of expression characteristic of Arab governments. In the economic field, he points the finger at corruption and the absence of financial oversight. Finally, in the moral sphere, Al-Kawakibi denounces negligence in the field of religious education and the resultant lack of knowledge.[40] He also notes the deliberate oppression of Muslim women, which keeps them in a state of ignorance.[41] Last of all, Al-Kawakibi expresses his conclusion that the Islamic nation will awake from its torpor only through education, through the practice of consultative democracy (*shura*), and through the transfer of the Caliphate from the Ottoman Turks into the hands of Arabs of the tribe of Quraysh.[42] Al-Kawakibi was typical of a new generation of thinkers, disciples of Al-Afghani and Muhammad Abduh, who soon began to make their voices heard, taking up the cudgels in defence of freedom of thought in the Arab world.

THE THIRD GENERATION

This new generation has been represented in more recent times by a group of contemporary intellectuals who have become the standard bearers of a new wave of free-thinking reformers. These are men and women who have stood out against religious dogmatism, and are worthy heirs of the renaissance represented by Al-Afghani and Muhammad Abduh. Most of these contemporaries have personal experience of the injustices of colonialism and the misdeeds of imperialism, which have robbed their peoples of their identity. Some of them are especially notable for the influence they have had on the new school of emerging Muslim intellectuals at the beginning of the twenty-first century.[43]

The Egyptian philosopher and writer Abd Al-Rahman Badawi was one of the first to declare that the Muslim world would not be able to better itself in the absence of an engagement with freedom of thought and the recognition of the right of the individual to determine his own fate. Badawi, who died in 2003, was one of the most brilliant Muslim thinkers of recent times. He has written extensively on rationalism in Islam and the influence of the Greek heritage in Islamic civilisation.[44] Badawi was a scholar who sifted patiently through the ancient Greek writers and the liberal Arab thinkers of the Middle Ages, paying special attention to Ibn Rushd. He created a synthesis of points common to the two civilisations and pointed the way towards avenues for the future development of Arab and Muslim culture. Sadly, his innovative ideas fell on deaf ears and hostility to them led him eventually to seek exile in

France, where he found an intellectual home in Paris, at the University of the Sorbonne. His choice of voluntary expatriation was a conscious decision, enabling him to escape the suffocating cultural climate of the Arab countries, which he described as a 'vast prison'.[45]

Several other significant neo-reformists are based in Egypt, including Ali Abderraziq, whose key ideas are to be found in his book *L'islam et les fondements du pouvoir*.[46] Another is Samir Amin, the most influential theoretical economist of the third world and the author of a remarkable book which reveals the nature of the arrogance of Europe towards other civilisations.[47] An Egyptian woman thinker of great importance is Nawal Saadawi, a distinguished psychiatrist and the author of an exceptional work on the oppression of women, *The Hidden Face of Eve*.[48] From Morocco, the historian Abdallah Laroui, author of an incisive history of North Africa,[49] and Mohammed Al-Jabri are to be regarded as leading intellectuals.[50] The Tunisians Muhammad Talbi and Muhammad Charfi also deserve to be singled out.[51] Another noteworthy figure is the late Mahmoud Muhammad Taha of Sudan. Muhammad Arkoun, the well-known Paris-based scholar of Algerian origin, has been described as the father of 'applied Islamology', and has written books of key importance that have become indispensable benchmarks for Islamologists and have been reprinted and translated into many languages.[52] Finally, mention must be made of Edward Said, the Jerusalem-born American scholar, who was until his death one of the great figures of Arab intellectual commitment in the literary and political worlds in the United States. Edward Said is said to have described himself as a Christian 'wrapped in a Muslim culture'. His book, *Orientalism*, applies a severe critique to the western conception of the East.[53]

All these scholars have contributed to the process of giving a new intellectual impetus to Islam.[54] Their critical efforts have contributed to the emergence of the contemporary culture from which the present generation has drawn the benefit. Their influence in the Muslim world has been comparable to that exercised in its day over the younger generation in Europe by the ideas of Jean-Paul Sartre. While waiting for its own '1968', however, the Muslim younger generation of the twenty-first century still suffers in silence as it endures the yoke of the unimaginative and intolerant politics that prevail in the Muslim lands. As one commentator puts it, young Muslims 'yearn for a profound reform within Islam, on the basis of a new interpretation of the fundamental texts, with the goal of reconciling Muslim values with the exigencies of modernity'.[55] To attain this objective, a radical reform of the superannuated methods of education practised by the *madrasas* is required, together with the introduction of new subject matter drawn from the social sciences to be taught in parallel with religion. Some take the view that as long as the teachings of Ibn Rushd, Ibn Al-Arabi, Ibn Sina and the neo-reformists are excluded from Muslim schools, the Islamic world will remain under western hegemony. Whether this is so or not, the decline of Islam will be halted only if the tide of dogmatism is swept back and a halt is called to the internecine struggles that up to the present have been a serious obstacle to the true renaissance of the Muslim world.

It may well be, however, that even radical reform of Islamic education, a return to rationalism and the end of intra-Islamic strife will be insufficient to bring about such a renaissance and inaugurate a situation in which the East and the West are able to coexist peacefully and engage as equals. For a real resurgence within the Muslim world to come to pass, the status of Muslim women would need to be at the heart of the agenda for civil society. In addition, the mystic and artistic dimensions of Islam will need once more to be accorded the respect they deserve and there will need to be a guarantee of the freedom of artistic practitioners within the framework of democracy. Painters, sculptors, choreographers, musicians, dancers, actors and writers, as well as journalists, should be encouraged and should feel that their talents are valued. At present this is not the case in any Muslim country, where their rewards are most often opprobrium, mistrust and even exile.

9

THE MUSLIM MYSTICS AND RATIONALISTS: THE SOCIAL PROGRAMME

THE FREEDOM OF THE INDIVIDUAL

The Muslim mystics and rationalists have developed their own original ideas in relation to individual freedom. In contrast to the Islamists, they believe certain individual rights are absolute. In their view, only certain of the rules laid down by Islam are entirely sacrosanct and essential, for example the so-called five pillars of Islam, relating to prayer, fasting, the pilgrimage, the payment of zakat, and the shahada, or profession of faith. Beyond these sanctified rules, they interpret Islam in a way that privileges individual rights, such as freedom of expression and conscience, and recognises the existence of freedom of choice. The first Muslims to posit such restrictions on divine omnipotence were the Mu'tazilites, who proposed that God himself was subject to restrictions. The Mu'tazilite author Al-Nazzam put it thus:

> God is obliged to allow man his freedom and the ability to initiate voluntary acts, just as he is obliged to reward virtuous deeds, punish transgressions, and accept repentance (tawba) if it is sincere and sufficient.[1]

Such ideas were vigorously condemned by Ibn Hanbal, the father of Wahhabism, who saw them as derivative from the ideas of the Christians and the Zoroastrians.[2] It should be remembered, however, that at the height of Mu'tazilite influence, under the Abbasid Caliphate, it was Ibn Hanbal who was persecuted by the free thinkers, though the boot was soon once more on the other foot. Other Muslim rationalists such as the Qadiris also consider that man enjoys free will over his deeds and actions, and have always rejected the notion that human actions flow from the will of God.

Regarding the issue of voluntary change of religion, the rationalists and mystics have avoided the issue of excommunication (*takfir*) of the culprit and refuse to treat such an individual as a renegade or an infidel. In common with the view taken by most Muslims, they believe that the act of apostasy is not a matter for human punishment, and that only God is in a position to chastise or pardon the miscreant.[3] In contemporary Muslim countries individuals are not being executed for changing their religion as such, though in 2008 a draft law was under consideration in Iran which would have this effect if implemented. Nonetheless, judicial proceedings and sentences for blasphemy are frequent in countries that apply the Shari'a. In 1985, in Khartoum, Sudan, Mahmoud Muhammad Taha was executed for a crime of apostasy which was not connected to a change of religion. His fault was to have reinterpreted Qur'anic texts. As one comment on the case reported, Taha said that,

> the fundamental message of the Qur'an, which is spiritual and moral and addressed to the individual, must be distinguished from the contingent message, contained in the legislative verses that were addressed to the contemporary community. In his view, the legislative verses, those of Islam's second mission, are addressed to a community that no longer exists. However, this implies that the legislative verses as they have hitherto been understood require radical reinterpretation, and in consequence so also does the Shari'a.[4]

In the same sense, Ayatollah Khomeini's 1989 fatwa calling for Salman Rushdie to be killed was targeted not at a change of religion but at an act of alleged blasphemy contained in his book *The Satanic Verses*.[5] He was accused of insulting and denigrating the Prophet Muhammad and his family.[6] Ayatollah Khomeini's sentence was never carried out and though technically it cannot be rescinded after the decease of Khomeini, the government of Iran has formally committed itself not to do anything to bring about Rushdie's death. Other similar incidents have taken place. In Egypt, such free thinkers as Nasr Abu Zeid and Nawal Saadawi have been arraigned before Islamic tribunals, though without any mention of the death sentence. Similarly, in Pakistan, where the Shari'a is applied in religious matters, sentences of death for blasphemy have been passed but not carried out. For instance, in 1998 it was reported that a number of Pakistanis, including a young man of 25 named Ghulam Akbar Khan, had been condemned to death on the basis of a controversial Shari'a-based law passed in 1985, but that none of the sentences had been implemented.[7]

These examples indicate that even in those Muslim countries where the Shari'a is applied, the execution of individuals who are accused of actions injurious to Islam or of changing their religion is in general avoided. This significant movement towards the application of human rights has been progressively achieved largely thanks to those who advocate the modernisation of Islam.

TOLERANCE TOWARDS THE RELIGIOUS MINORITIES

As long ago as the tenth and eleventh centuries, the Mu'tazilites were concerning themselves with the fate of the Jewish and Christian minorities within Islamic society, those known as the dhimmis, and were already taking steps to improve their conditions. At the risk of clashing with the views of the majority of the Sunnis, they took their reasoning as far as the conclusion that those of the 'protected' minorities who were of good faith could expect eternal salvation.[8] Though the dhimmis were treated in very different ways by various Muslim rulers,[9] they have always been treated with respect by the Muslim free thinkers and by the Sufis. The Sufis take the view that the Christians, Jews, Hindus and others all form part of God's cosmos, and that the salvation of the world is to be achieved through equality and mutual respect between all faiths.

For the Sufi religious brotherhoods (the turuq, singular tariqa), all religions are in some sense gathered within a single monastery, divided into a multitude of corners set aside for prayer (zawaya, singular *zawia*), to which each person may resort according to his own way of expressing his faith. In practice, history shows many instances where Sufis have courageously protected Christians and Jews from the threat of massacre. In both Egypt and Syria, there are well-known instances where Sufis have intervened to protect Christians from mortal threats, in particular the incident in Damascus in 1860 when the Algerian Sufi and former Emir of Algeria, Abd Al-Qadir (Abd el-Kader), a leader of the Qadiriyya *tariqa*, saved the lives of thousands of Christians.[10] Sufis even offer protected Christians and Jews their spiritual blessing, or *karamat*, which God reserves for the saints.[11]

In the opinion of such rationalist mystics as Al-Afghani and Muhammad Abduh, Islam had been tolerant in the past and should be so once more. They point to the Arab conquests of the seventh century, in the course of which, though there were confrontations between Muslims and non-Muslims, the Muslims acknowledged the religions of the conquered territories. They respected the religions of those minorities who were accorded the status of *dhimmis*, protecting their religious and civil rights and safeguarding their worldly goods against unjust sequestration. Al-Afghani cites the well-known saying, 'Whoever becomes a *dhimmi* has the right to demand that we fulfil our obligations towards them.' Al-Afghani and Muhammad Abduh observe that Muslims have always accepted the obligation to treat non-Muslim outsiders with dignity, and suggest that Christians and Jews should be allowed to occupy responsible political positions.

In the early twentieth century, as part of his modernisation of the Turkish state, Kemal Ataturk abolished the status of *dhimmi*. The secular institutions he established have since been adopted by all the nationalist Muslim states of the Middle East and North Africa. Over time, legal systems based on European practice have replaced Islamic law. At the instigation of Arab nationalist parties such as the Baath, a more expansive conception of Arab nationality was substituted for the *dhimmi* status of Christian Arabs.[12] Arabism began to take precedence over distinctions appertaining to religious confession, and the rights of nationality and citizenship were distinguished from affiliation to the Muslim faith. Thus Muslims,

Christians and Jews became entirely equal before the law. Today, the status of *dhimmi* has disappeared in virtually all Muslim states. Some 40 years ago, in the high era of Arab nationalism, Robert Mantran concluded that 'in the Arab and Muslim countries, virtually no discrimination between non-Muslims and Muslims exists at the level of legal terminology, other than a widespread provision that the Head of State should be a Muslim'.[13]

The case of Sudan demands particular attention. Between 1983 and 1985 Sudan attempted to apply Shari'a law to the animists and Christians of the southern part of the country in the fields of both civil and criminal law. The minorities were consequently subjected to the provisions of the Shari'a without the corresponding status of *dhimmi* provided for in Muslim law. However, the agreement concluded in October 2002 between the government in Khartoum and the Sudan People's Liberation Army led by the late John Garang went some way towards the recognition of something not unlike *dhimmi* status. This pact provided for the autonomy of the people of southern Sudan and recognised their religious and ethnic specificity. Such a federalist approach could be the salvation not only of Christian minorities but also of other religious minorities around the world, including Muslims.

WOMEN AND THE VEIL

The Muslim mystics and rationalists have always taken a clear stance on the issue of the status of women. For Ibn Rushd, any state that fails to respect the principle of equality between men and women condemns itself to impoverishment. In such discriminatory states, where the role of women is restricted to procreation, their potential is not realised. In Ibn Rushd's own words:

> They are placed at the service of their husbands ... and are relegated to the business of procreation, rearing and breast feeding. But this undoes their other activities. Because women in these States are not fitted for any of the human virtues, it often happens

167

that they resemble plants. That they are a burden on the men in these States is one of the reasons for the poverty of these States. They are found there in twice the number of men, while at the same time they do not, through training, support any of the necessary activities . . .[14]

The critical view of the status of women in conservative Islamic society expressed here by Ibn Rushd finds an echo with most of the Muslim modernisers.

The mystics have also adopted a liberal stance towards the position of women. In the *Mathnawi*, Rumi laid stress on the equality of men and women. Sufi orders have admitted women as participants in the spiritual life of the *zawiya*. They are also allowed to be present during sessions of Sufi music and dancing. In civil life, their freedom of choice is respected. In Sufi circles they are permitted freely to choose their spouses and to decide of their own free will whether to work or study, without obligation to seek permission from a male guardian. They are also regarded as qualified to act in positions of high political and social responsibility. Ibn al-Arabi is reported to have said that even among the 40 *abdal* in the world – the most elevated of the Sufi saints – women were to be found, a fact of which even some Sufis were ignorant.[15] Ibn al-Arabi also said that women's contemplation of God was the most perfect. Rumi followed his lead when he said that 'woman's beauty reflects that of God'.[16]

In the nineteenth century, both Jamal Ad-Din Al-Afghani and Muhammad Abduh took a close interest in the status of women in the Muslim world. As they saw it, the struggle for independence and against imperialism should be accompanied by female emancipation. They took the view that the struggle for emancipation was an integral part of the general fight against injustice in the Muslim world. In addition, Muhammad Abduh spoke out against polygamy, and in favour of women's employment in Egyptian government service. He attempted to prepare the way for this by agitating for women to be educated and initiated into public life. He personally oversaw the introduction of a programme of civic and spiritual education targeted specifically at Muslim women.[17]

It was thanks to Muhammad Abduh's support that Egyptian women were the first to achieve emancipation. His exhortations soon bore fruit. Huda Shaa'rawi played the leading role in a group of intellectuals that provided the vanguard for an Egyptian feminist movement. In 1923, on her return from an international women's meeting in Rome, she greeted her native soil by throwing her veil on the ground as a gesture of protest against the restrictions imposed on Muslim women. This symbolic gesture was copied throughout the Islamic world, where women demanded enhanced rights and began to organise politically in order to throw off the yoke of discriminatory practices.

The issue of whether or not women should be veiled has been a major source of controversy in the Muslim world. Traditionalists have taken the view that the veil is part of the cultural heritage of the Muslim countries, while secularists and liberals have argued that women are free to choose to what extent to cover themselves. However, with the rise of Islamism, various factors have contributed to an increase in the prevalence of the veil. The exclusion and impoverishment of certain sections of the population, as well as hostility to female covering from some westerners, as well as by Muslim ultra-secularists, have contributed to the radicalisation of some Muslims and to their adoption of the veil as a symbol of resistance.

The issue of the veil also divides Muslim immigrant society in the West. In France, as well as in Switzerland, in the name of the French concept of 'laïcité' (the secularity of the state), the authorities have forbidden the wearing of Islamic head coverings by Muslim pupils in schools, as part of a general ban on what are described as conspicuous religious symbols. It is also argued that Muslim female attire is oppressive and an indication of inequality between the sexes.[18] Muslim modernisers, taking a similar view, have contended that the veil is the symbol of an ideology based on 'sexual apartheid' which can only intensify the isolation and exclusion of women.[19] They add that 'nothing in the Qur'an indicates that women are under any obligation to cover themselves, since the Qur'anic injunction relates only to the women of the Prophet's family and the wives of believers, which is taken to signify the wives of the Prophet's companions'.[20]

Those who take the view that women have the right to cover themselves as they choose reject these arguments. They point out that the authorities in France and Switzerland seem less punctilious on the issue of 'laïcité' when pupils appear in class wearing Christian crosses or the Jewish kippa. Such contrarians also ask what would be the reaction of French educationists if they were asked themselves while visiting Muslim states to wear the veil, the regulation beard and local costume, on the grounds of respecting local Islamic custom. Finally, such supporters of women's right to wear the veil maintain that women must be permitted the freedom to wear what they choose, on the grounds that interference with a woman's choice of dress is also interference 'with her honour and dignity'.[21]

The Rector of the Mosque of Bordeaux, Tareq Obrou, insists on the possibility of a compromise that would resolve such disagreements over women's dress. His proposed solution is one that could be profitably considered by both Muslims and westerners. He proposes that Muslim women and men should think carefully about the necessity of head-to-toe covering, and points out that there are precedents for the wearing of more practical covering. He notes, for example, the custom of Muslim women in the earliest days of wearing less cumbrous garments while, for example, caring for the wounded after a battle. Less extravagant coverings may well, he says, be perfectly modest. He also wonders whether covering the head is strictly necessary in modern circumstances, and suggests it should not necessarily be the first thing a woman should think of covering. He concludes:

> A woman who does not cover her head is not gravely at fault and may be one of the best of Muslims. For a woman not to cover the head is on a par with a man to shave off his beard or to wear tightly fitting trousers or shorts, as men in physical employment may well do. In the logic of *fiqh* (legal exegesis) the two are virtually equivalent.[22]

It should be pointed out, perhaps, that while the focus is on the plight of Muslim women, the situation of women in the West is not altogether without its own difficulties, and that they have had to struggle to gain their right to live in dignity. Meanwhile, despite that struggle, studies have shown that western women, even in the twenty-first century, are far from achieving financial equality with men.[23] In the United Kingdom, for example, it was estimated a few years ago that a woman earns £241,000 less in the course of her lifetime than a male colleague. If she has children, she is penalised yet further, losing another £140,000. In addition, western women are too frequently confined to subordinate positions, though there is no doubt that they are capable of taking on greater responsibilities.[24]

Nevertheless, it must be admitted that the situation of women in the West has little in common with that of Muslim women, who need to make even greater efforts to put themselves in a position to win freedom, emancipation and equality with men. Female emancipation will depend on education and dialogue, and the effort to obtain it should be made without loss of dignity. Muslim women should strive to gain the right to education and work, rather than devoting themselves to domestic tasks such as the care of children. They should lay claim to the right to marry whom they choose, to refuse polygamous marriages, and to spread out or limit pregnancies by the use of contraceptive techniques. They should also demand full personal legal rights and no longer be obliged to submit to the authorisation of parents or relatives when they are legally adult.

Their struggle should take its direction from their own culture and environment. Such action will take its effect, little by little, on the thinking of the most reactionary of men, who will in the end be obliged to accept what will have become an established fact. They will learn to show greater respect to women, whose emancipation will lead them towards greater equality, both in law and in fact.

THE PSYCHOLOGY OF SEXUAL BEHAVIOUR

For the Muslim rationalists, both the idea and the practice of sexuality follow the rules laid down in the earliest generations.

For every Muslim, issues related to sexuality are approached with a great degree of modesty. Such knowledge is passed down from one generation to the next according to well-established practices. Women are discreetly educated by other women in regard to all issues concerning sex, menstruation and traditional ideas of midwifery. Men learn from other men the rudiments of sex, as well as myths relating to virility. It is instilled into them that any insufficiency or deviance in this respect will bring them social disgrace and opprobrium. As the anthropologist and psychoanalyst Malek Chebel has put it:

> Muslims have made sexuality a zone both of interpersonal contact and of individual development, both moral and physical. But, in addition to the relegation of women to a secondary role, the notion of autonomous action is missing.[25]

It was the Sufis who attempted to lift the ritual taboos that surround Muslim sexuality. They were misunderstood, and were wrongly accused of being libertines and of abandoning the conventions of Islamic modesty. For them, in fact, sensual love is a necessary stage towards the achievement of true mystic love. They often employ the metaphor of love to symbolise their search for God. Rumi said, 'When the flame of love is ignited, it consumes all it touches save God',[26] and 'The beauty of woman reveals the beauty of God.'[27] The Sufis take a liberal approach to life, but their behaviour does not signify that they endorse fornication or lasciviousness. In their approach to the world, love and the beauty of art are only a means of seeking interior peace and of attaining the mystical ecstasy of mingling with God.

THE SUFI AND RATIONALIST
ATTITUDE TO ARMED CONFLICT

The Sufis and rationalists appear to adopt ideas in this field in conformity with the two first generations of Islamists. The humanitarian 'Ten Commandments' of Islam, set out in Part One, Chapter 5, are their guide. Ibn Rushd places humanitarian principles to the fore whenever conflict occurs, but in any case Ibn Rushd was more inclined towards spirituality than Jihad, and believed Islam should be spread through peaceful means.[28]

By the nineteenth century, the neo-Sufis, such as Muhammad Abduh and the moderate clerics who were of his persuasion, no longer saw armed Jihad as constituting in all circumstances an obligation on Muslims in modern times. The Azhar Mosque, as reformed by Muhammad Abduh, no longer spoke of armed Jihad (*jihad al-musalla*) as relevant to the duties of modern Muslims. Bassam Tibi has remarked that Al-Azhar began to place the emphasis on what it called the non-military Jihad, against such ills as ignorance, hunger, poverty and ill health and injustice.[29] These were indeed the objectives of the modern Jihad as conceived by moderate Muslims, rationalists and Sufis. They exclude all resorts to violence, except in the case where Muslims are unjustly attacked.

PART THREE

10

NATIONALISM, SUFISM AND RELIGIOUS FUNDAMENTALISM: EGYPT, TURKEY AND ALGERIA

In much of North Africa, Eurasia and Africa proper, religious fundamentalism and Sufism coexist, either in uneasy cohabitation or outright conflict. In some countries, such as Algeria, Tunisia, Egypt and Turkey, for historical reasons that have never been fully examined, there has been hostility to the Sufi orders. The results were soon to be seen. The vacuum left by the withdrawal of the Sufis was swiftly filled by other expressions of Islam, often of the most hard-line Islamist variety. On the other hand, countries that have taken the more judicious option of promoting the natural expansion of Sufism and its integration into civil society – such as Tanzania, the countries of West Africa and Morocco – seem up to the present little troubled by Islamic radicalism.

Following the two World Wars, nationalist movements in most Muslim countries made the mistake of emulating the erstwhile antagonism of the colonialists towards the Sufi brotherhoods. Like the colonists against whom they fought, these nationalists believed that popular support for the brotherhoods interfered with their own policies and constituted an obstacle to civilisation and progress. Such western-style nationalism, based on modernising liberalism, was exemplified by Mustafa Kemal's secularism in Turkey after the First World War, as well as by the Baath Party in Syria and Iraq, and Nasserism in Egypt in the 1950s. In North Africa, the philosophy of President Habib Bourguiba in Tunisia was another instance, as was the 'Etoile Nord-Africaine', founded in 1926, which was the precursor of the Algerian National Liberation Front.[1]

As early as 1897, Jules Cambon, one of the leading Islamologists of the colonial era, averred that in North Africa and in Turkey, 'the religious brotherhoods could represent a grave danger for the civilising mission on which Europe has embarked ... They are making giant strides within the lines of the existing colonial frontiers from Cape Verde in Senegal to the island of Zanzibar,' and he identified the enemy as 'the principal Sufi brotherhoods, the *Qadiriyya*, the *Sanoussiyya* and the *Shadhiliyya*'.[2] This theorist of the French and British colonial enterprise expressed his preference that colonial governments should work only with the traditional *ulema*. He believed that the *ulema* would be more accommodating than the Sufis towards the new 'Christian' government, which would respect their privileges and uphold their authority in the mosques. Jules Cambon and his fellow proponents of colonialism were convinced that little was to be expected from the 'Sufi orders and the dervishes, whose watchword is always "we are the law".'[3] Colleagues of Cambon who took a similar view were the Arabist military establishment such as Colas and Arnaud. The nationalists in these countries learned their lesson well from the colonialists, allying themselves with the *ulema*, even before they achieved independence, to exclude the Sufis. Their efforts were, however, in vain.

EGYPT

Egypt and Turkey are the states where Sufism historically reached its highest point. The Egyptian Mamluk Sultans in the fourteenth century promoted the mystical persuasion within Islam, and Sufism, with its freedom and its religious tolerance, achieved wide popularity, gaining a high degree of acceptance across the social classes through the Sufi religious festivals known as *mawalid* (singular, *mawlid*) associated with the Sufi saints. Among the long-established Sufi orders in Egypt are the Badawiyya, founded by Sayyid Ahmed Al-Badawi, who died in 1276, which has a link with the Rifaiyya, and, going further back, the order founded by the outstanding Sufi personality Dhul-Nun Al-Misri, who died in 861, to whom all the chroniclers of his day attributed miracles. For example, Misri was supposed to have 'replaced a tooth that had fallen out, moved about his room in his bed, and to have recovered a child from the belly of crocodile'.[4] Such suppositions, like the Sufi philosophy of life in general, were not at all in accordance with the dogmatic vision of the traditional *ulema* of the religious university of Al-Azhar, for whom such beliefs were no better than sorcery (*shawada*).

In the mid-nineteenth century and again in the twentieth century, the colonialists attempted to destroy Egypt's Sufi institutions, which were targeted because they constituted a real challenge to mercantilist materialism and the 'official' religion that had accommodated itself to the foreign presence.[5] Under Muhammad Ali, who ruled Egypt from 1805 to 1848, whose objective was the construction of a modern Egyptian state, the Sufis were at first accepted, but later came under attack and were left in a weak position.[6] A century later, in 1947, King Farouk once more targeted the Sufi leadership, turning instead to the religious doctrines of the *ulema* of Al-Azhar, who were by now seeking to purify Islam and return to the principles of the ancestors (the *salaf*).[7]

In the course of the twentieth century, the Egyptian Sufi orders had moments of triumph but also experienced periods of rejection and persecution. They came particularly under attack from the radical reformists, whose goal was the return to fundamentalism.[8] Their property was repeatedly confiscated, and their schools and hospitals were closed, as well as the canteens and kitchens they used to feed the poor and for their *mawlid* celebrations. This gave an advantage to their radical competitors, notably the Muslim Brotherhood. The spiritual leadership the Sufis were obliged to relinquish was frequently taken up by the fundamentalists, especially the supporters of Hassan Al-Banna and Sayyid Qutb. In 1952, President Nasser was the first Arab nationalist to attempt to bring a change to this situation, when he rehabilitated the Sufi orders, which he believed could be a bastion against the opposition of political Islamism. He revived the concept of a mystical Islam that would be conducive to personal development but free of political ambition. His reconciliation with the Sufi Sheikhs of Egypt also enabled him to re-establish links with the powerful Sufi orders in Syria, Sudan, Morocco and deeper into Africa. Nasser deliberately cultivated some of the Sufi orders, and Sheikhs from Nigeria, Mali, Senegal and Ghana became involved along with Sheikhs from Egypt itself in the preparation for a world Sufi conference that was intended to be held in Cairo. This plan was conceived in 1961, during a visit to Cairo by the Senegalese Tijani Sheikh, Ibrahim Niass.[9]

Sufism was by now restored to its rightful place both in the eyes of the Egyptian population at large and of the country's intellectual elite. In Tanta, near Cairo, the Sufi *mawalid* reached an unprecedented intensity under the auspices of the Badawiyya, the Rifaiyya, the Shadhiliyya and the Burhamiyya. At their festivals, these orders set up whole villages of tents to accommodate their guests and in the spirit of *khidma* (service) offered food and hospitality to all.[10] Egypt's social and religious scene was profoundly altered by the expansion of the Sufi orders. In 1976, the legal status of the orders was confirmed with the passage of the *Qanun Al-Turuq Al-Sufiyya* (Sufi Brotherhoods Act). By 1987, the number of members of orders had grown to six million, organised into 70 separate brotherhoods recognised by the authorities and a further 50 or so without official status.[11]

With its different religions and spiritualities, including not just the Sufis but also fundamentalists and secularists, and the Christian Coptic community, Egypt is a varied and contrasting community within whose society all these tendencies find expression. This multiconfessional mosaic has meant that Egypt has not been fundamentally destabilised by violence that could have undermined the institutions of the state. Had this occurred, Egypt would have been profoundly affected, losing first its foreign communities and then its Coptic Christians.

TURKEY

Turkey is the Muslim country most imbued with Sufi philosophy. The Sufi order best known to the general public in the West is that of the *mevlevi* (the 'Whirling Dervishes' of Jalal Al-Din Rumi). However, there is in fact a wide variety of orders, many of them with roots in the history of the Ottoman Empire, going back especially to the fourteenth and fifteenth centuries. Ahmet Yasar Ocak, a Turkish scholar who has studied the subject, offers this analysis:

> If we examine the history of Sufism in the Ottoman Empire, we see that it enjoyed a propitious start in terms of its relationships both with the central power and with the public. This intriguing story began with a curious fact: a group of Sufis belonging to a fringe movement known as *baba'*, who were rebels against the Seljuks, played a substantial role in the birth of the Ottoman Empire. The Ottoman *beylik* was founded in the early fourteenth century in north-western Anatolia, on the frontiers of the Byzantine Empire, and was supported by heterodox Sufis known as *bab'i Abdalan-i Rum* (otherwise known as the 'Rum Abdallari').[12]

Over time, other Sufi orders established themselves in Ottoman territory. The principal orders were the Rifaiyya, the Mawlawiyya, the Khalwatiyya and the Naqshbandiyya, and later the Bektashiyya. From the fifteenth century, however, after the revolt of the Sufi Bedr Ed-Din, the mystics were placed under surveillance, and to some extent harassed by the authorities and the *ulema*, who backed the official religion. In the sixteenth century, the persecution of the Sufis intensified. They were accused of stirring up insurrections in Anatolia, and of responsibility for religious dissent directed against the *ulema* of Istanbul and the established authorities.[13] It should be added that throughout Turkish history, the puritanical *ulema*, taking their lead from the strict interpretations of Islam offered by Ibn Taymiyya, never accepted the Sufis, and in particular Jalal Al-Din Rumi and his *mevlevi* order of dervishes. Ahmet Yasar Ocak comments on this anti-Sufi stance:

> By blaming Sufi circles for all religious 'disorder' and 'deformation' within Ottoman society at the time, this anti-Sufi spirit aimed to purify the people of all the 'heretical and satanic' elements introduced by the Sufis.[14]

Education was an important field in which the struggle between the strict conservatives inspired by Ibn Taymiyya and the more innovatory Sufis was acted out. The conservatives favoured the classic Qur'anic schools, the *madrasas*, while the Sufis pursued their own form of education in the *tekke*, or *zawiya*. From the nineteenth century, many Turks had taken up the Sufi way, including the liberal educational curricula associated with Rumi and Ibn Al-Arabi which dominated the Sufi schools.[15] Even philosophy and the arts were not excluded, while the traditional *madrasas* totally ignored such subjects, placing the accent rather on the Shari'a, the memorisation of the Qur'an and the promotion of strict social morality. Up to the present day, the contrast between these two styles of education has remained unaltered throughout the Islamic world.

In 1923, when Kemal Ataturk founded the secular Turkish Republic, he drew little distinction between the Sufis and the fundamentalists in his antagonism towards Islam. The sudden move towards secularism and in favour of western influence led to the dissolution of the Sufi orders and closure of the *tekke* in 1925.[16] This misunderstanding, highly characteristic of Arab and Muslim nationalists, led to the opposite effect from that intended. The outcome was that a section of the Turkish population, cut off from its way of expressing its Islamic identity, was driven to turn towards Salafi Islam. Though the Turkish authorities allowed the *tekke* to resume their activities in the 1950s, the moderate Salafi Islamist movement continued to gain strength in the country. The victory of the Islamist Justice and Development Party (the AK Party) in the Turkish elections of 2002 and its return to power in greater strength in 2007 was part of this historical process. In 2008, the confrontation between the AK Party government and the forces of Kemalist secularism was still the most important factor in Turkish politics. It should be borne in mind, nonetheless, that there is still a large proportion of Sufi sympathisers in Turkey. The *mevlevi* dervishes have a wide following and the Alevi population is largely organised around the Bektashi order. The Alevis have more and more attached themselves to this Sufi brotherhood, founded by Haci Bektash (1210–70).[17] The Alevis are perhaps 20 per cent of

Turkey's population of 75 million and live mainly in central Anatolia. Their version of Islam is liberal and tolerant. Like their co-religionists in Syria, for example, the women do not veil themselves and take part in public life.[18]

It would be incorrect, therefore, to assume that fundamentalist Islamism is a dominant factor in Turkish life: on the contrary, all varieties of Islam are to be found. Turkish accession to the European Union would no doubt be conducive to greater internal tolerance between the various forms of religious observance and expression. Were Turkey to be refused membership, on the other hand, it might turn in upon itself, with a reinforcement of religious radicalism that would inevitably tend to exclude the more liberal tendencies, among them the Sufis.

It should also be noted that liberal Turkish-style Sufism is also present in Central Asia and in the Balkans and is also represented in the moderate Islam practised by sections of the populations of Chechnya and Daghestan. From the thirteenth century, the Sufis have consistently suffered from devastating attacks by Tsarist Russia and the Cossacks. The Muslims of the region have been gradually radicalised and have distanced themselves from Sufi pacifism. In a war-torn region, families have been devastated by alcoholism and prostitution, which made their appearance under Russian rule.[19] Russian and Soviet policy have not been propitious for the development of Sufism in Chechnya and Daghestan, which has left room for the emergence of Islamist elements of the most radical kind. In spite of these misfortunes, Sufism has not disappeared and remains solidly based in the countries of the Caucasus as a whole.

In the Balkans, meanwhile, especially in Bosnia-Herzegovina and in Kosovo (Pristina), Sufism spread as the result of the efforts of Turkish dervish masters. The Balkan peoples have always displayed a spirituality that is tolerant and open to the western world, which the orthodox *ulema* have attempted to suppress. For example, the principal of the Qur'anic *madrasa* in the region of Has, in the neighbourhood of Prizren, complained that a dozen villages had ceased to ask for imams to lead their prayers during Ramadan, which might be regarded as an example of the liberalism and religious flexibility of the Balkan Sufi brotherhoods.[20] While the Balkan wars of the 1990s led a section of the Muslim population to seek its roots in a return to the origins of Islam, it is no less true that liberal and tolerant Sufism remains a constant factor among the peoples of the region. It is certainly the Sufis who hold the key to the development of a version of Islam adapted to the modern world which will be able to live in harmony with both the West and the East.

ALGERIA: RISING FROM THE ASHES

The Algerian Sufi movement originated long before the spread of the North African Almoravid and Almohad dynasties in the twelfth and thirteenth centuries, and was hence well entrenched before the Turkish and French colonisations of North Africa. The specifically Algerian culture of the *zawiya* was linked to the country's rich civilisation and to the powerful Berber federal structures (the *arsh*) which had been the form of government from Massinissa and Jugurtha, through the heroine Kahina and up to the Emir Abd el-Kader in the nineteenth century, and which are still reflected in Algerian society today. Colonial historians, in common with some Arab authors, have tended to discount the ancestral federal structures and the mystic tradition in Algeria with which they were linked.

It is not by chance that such legendary Algerian heroes as Kusayla and Kahina were mystics. Kusayla was a Berber chieftain who converted to Islam but nevertheless halted the advance of the Ummayad armies under Uqba Ibn Nafi in 682. He was killed in 690, attempting to resist another wave of Arab invaders in what was perhaps the last act of Berber resistance. Kahina was a mystic and alleged sorceress who took up the banner of Berber resistance after Kusayla and finally died in battle in the 690s.

The Sufi orders began to spread in North Africa after the Arab conquest, with a particular period of growth during the expansion of the Berber Almohad dynasty in the eleventh and twelfth centuries.[21] As in other countries, the Algerian Sufis found themselves in conflict with the rigid doctrines of the *ulema*, who represented official Islam. They also developed a real tradition of resistance to external oppression. They were the sole force to oppose Turkish colonialism, which the *ulema* justified in terms of Islamic legitimacy. The Sufi Sheikh Ahmad Tijani, born in Algeria in 1737 at Laghouat, was forced to migrate to Morocco after struggling against the presence in Algeria of the Ottomans. The Tijaniyya eventually spread throughout the whole of Africa.[22] Only after Tijani's death in 1815 were his sons able to return to Algeria to organise their passive resistance against the Turkish regime.[23] The Algerian Sufis, it should be noted, adopted non-violence, like that of Mahatma Gandhi against the British Raj in India. In the face of Ottoman intransigence, however, the Tijanis allied themselves in 1827 with the fighters of the Beni Hashem, who belonged to the redoubtable Qadiriyya order, to launch an attack on the major Turkish garrison at Mascara, in western Algeria.[24]

In the nineteenth century, the Emir Abd El-Kader, who also belonged to the Qadiriyya, took up the struggle when he in turn fought Algeria's new invaders, the French, who invaded Algiers in 1830 and soon drove the last remnants of the Turkish regime from the country. The Treaty of Tafna, concluded on 20 May 1837, recognised Abd el-Kader's regime, but the French generals, advised by their locally recruited intelligence agents, abrogated the agreement in 1839 and embarked on total war with the Algerians. General Bugeaud's scorched-earth policy finally obliged Abd el-Kader to surrender in 1847.[25] The Sufi opposition did not end, however. In 1870–1, it burst out into the open again with the Rahmaniyya order, a branch of the Khalwatiyya, which inflicted serious defeats on the colonialist regime.[26]

When the modern Algerian nationalist movement began to take shape, however, the nationalists chose, notwithstanding the brave history of Sufi resistance, to strike up a tactical alliance with the *ulema* movement of Sheikh Ben Badis. Ben Badis claimed to be a reformer, but actually favoured a measured return to the *salafiyya*. From the 1930s onwards, it could be said that the *ulema* hounded the Algerian Sufis without mercy. Even after independence in 1962, and especially under President Boumedienne, efforts were made to exclude the Sufis. As has been seen in other cases, the political and religious vacuum left by the Sufis was soon filled by radical Islamists. Algeria's troubles arose from the absence of an Egyptian-style equilibrium between the Sufis, the *ulema* and the ethnic and secular minorities. On the role of the Sufi orders in post-independence Algeria, Bouziane Daoudi has commented:

> In independent Algeria, Sufism has long been shunned by official Islam, which has inherited the attitudes of the orthodox doctrine espoused by the *ulema* in the colonial period. For three decades, Algerian state Islam attempted to throttle the Sufi *zawiyas* on the grounds that they had collaborated with the colonial power. The brotherhoods were disconcertingly popular, and were seen as nests of ignorant marabouts contaminating the 'true' faith with superstition. This marginalisation to a great extent opened the way for Islamism, as the authorities in the end understood. The first national meeting of the *zawiyas* in Algiers did not happen until 1991, the year when the FIS had their victory in the parliamentary elections, which was too late.[27]

According to informed observers, the balance was gradually tilted back towards the Sufis after 1996. Since then, there has been a resurgence of Sufi practices. The Alawiyya of Mostaganem, the most respected brotherhood today, has tens of thousands of members and stretches from the mountains of the Rif as far as Damascus and Paris.[28] The largest brotherhood is the Rahmaniyya, of Kabyle origin, founded by Sidi M'hamed Boukobrine, whose name is to be found on two memorials, one in Kabylie and the other in Algiers. The number of adherents affiliated to *zawiyas* in Algeria is estimated at 60,000.[29]

President Bouteflika has been more sensitive to the Sufi movement in Algeria than was Houari Boumedienne. He went in person to the funeral of a great Sufi Sheikh from southern Algeria, and according to the journalist Boubker Belkadi, the Algerian authorities appear to wish to restore to the *zawiyas* the social and charitable role they should rightfully enjoy.[30] In the same report, Belkadi claims that President Bouteflika has made it known that he would like to see the *zawiyas* become 'bulwarks against fundamentalism, . . . calling upon them to correct false ideas about Islam and to inform public opinion, and particularly that of the young people, about Sufism as they practise it'.[31]

In conclusion, it is significant that Algeria is today taking the same route as did President Nasser in 1960, when he deliberately sought to diversify religious sentiments through the establishment of an international organisation of the Sufi *turuq*, whose headquarters this time will be in Algeria.

11

AFRICA: THE STRUGGLE FOR PEACEFUL MUSLIM SPIRITUALITY

SUFISM IN WEST AFRICA

Islam has always adapted itself to the sociological specificities of the countries in which it takes root. For example, though the laws of the Qur'an forbid the consumption of alcohol and pork, such pre-Islamic practices continued unaltered in the Sufi regions of China, the Caucasus and Africa.[1] These Sufi communities have continued to eat pork, drink alcohol and also to smoke opium. Other groups maintained animist religious practices which have come down to them from their ancestors, despite the condemnation of strict Muslims. Though the fundamentalist theologians never abandoned their ambition fully to Islamise these African and Asian peoples, they found themselves opposed by the Sufi orders, who favoured a more subtle and liberal interpretation of Islam, better adapted to the social circumstances and to the differing manners of countries converted to Islam relatively recently. In West Africa, Sufism began its expansion in the eighteenth century, with the spread of the Tijaniyya, Qadiriyya and Alawiyya orders from the Maghreb, where they were strongly represented. These orders initiated local Sufis, allowing them to keep their own customs and the rituals practised by their ancestors.

At the same time, however, Islamist missionaries were attempting to transform local practices in such countries as Senegal, Mali, Niger, Nigeria and Sierra Leone, among others. They met strong resistance from the local populations, who were powerfully attached to local practices rooted in Black African civilisation. Meanwhile, the flexibility and freedom of interpretation on offer from the Sufis had already attracted many Africans, encouraging

189

them to enter the Sufi orders in large numbers. In Senegal alone, for example, the two largest Sufi brotherhoods, the Tijaniyya and the Mouridiyya, included half the country's seven million Muslims.[2] In other words there were 3.5 million African Sufi Muslims who represented an important element in the political, economic and social structures of the country. According to other sources, there were in the 1980s as many as two million followers of Sheikh Tijani alone.[3]

SUFI INTEGRATION INTO WEST AFRICAN SOCIETY

West Africa's encounter with the Sufi orders and the absorption of the ideas of Sufism produced a spiritual culture of an original kind. The Sufis embraced and adapted the existing African social structures, including initiation rites, ancestor worship and the freedom of women. The Sufi approach was characterised by respect for existing social structures.

When the Sufi missionaries and the fundamentalists arrived in West Africa, they found a pre-existing society founded on a solid basis of tradition. The population was divided into three broad classes. At the head of the hierarchy were the nobles, including chiefs, wise men and warriors. Then came the broad working mass of the people who were engaged in agriculture, looking after flocks and herds or cultivating the land, together with those who worked as artisans in a variety of professions. Finally there existed a slave underclass, some of them prisoners from various conflicts, others born in captivity and others freed but still not full members of society. The fundamentalists attempted to adapt these structures to the Islamic Shari'a, placing religiously endorsed rulers (known as Emirs or Sultans) at the head of the hierarchy, with the *ulema* below them and everyone else at the bottom. The slave class was in theory abolished.

Neither the existing nobles nor the artisans were happy with the restructuring of society on Islamic lines. The traditional chiefs were insulted by their relegation to a subordinate class. The artisan class rejected the idea of a position at the bottom of the social hierarchy, on a par with the now freed slaves. A particular problem arose with blacksmiths, for example, who formerly held a ceremonial position and were credited with being able to communicate with the earth spirits. The result was that the African population, over time, rebuffed all attempts made to install a religion-based hierarchy out of touch with their ancestral religious structures. In contrast, they turned eagerly to the Sufi orders, who from the outset showed their willingness to respect the indigenous social hierarchy with its existing castes, with the one exception of institutionalised slavery.

THE SUFI VIEW OF LOCAL RITUALS

Initiation Ceremonies

The importance of initiation ceremonies in African society is well known. Among such ceremonies, those which contain the element of a period spent in a 'Sacred Grove' or other place of retreat seem especially solemn. Such rituals involve in general what anthropologists refer to as 'age sets', groups born in the same year who are therefore initiated simultaneously as adults. They are often subjected to some form of survival test. The Islamic fundamentalists tried to abolish these rites and to replace them with other tests tending to favour powers of memory and physical activities, so that young men would be challenged to memorise the Qur'an and to perform feats of physical exercise conducive to prowess at riding and archery, the forms of equestrian combat recommended by the Prophet Muhammad. The Sufis, on the other hand, retained the indigenous rites of passage, including the 'Sacred Grove', which was identified with the Sufi practice known as *khalwa*, in which all Sufi postulants were obliged to undergo 40 days of spiritual isolation on a mountain, in a forest or in some challenging and secluded spot.

The Cult of Ancestors

Among the rites that African populations were often anxious to retain was the ritual of visiting sacred tombs and the cult of

191

veneration of ancestors. African peoples often also showed great respect for what they regarded as holy idols, to which they attributed spiritual powers. Dancing and music were also part of their natural environment. The Sufis retained all these elements, to the extent that they resembled the Sufis' own practices, like the visits to the tombs of saints. In addition, the Sufis shared with the Africans the idea that the magic of music and dancing facilitated communication with benevolent saints and even with God himself. In contrast to this, the African fundamentalists, particularly the alumni of the Wahhabi *madrasas*, sought to abolish all these practices. Their view was that the cult of ancestors and saints, holy images and music and dancing were all tainted with heresy and should be excluded from Islamic society. The sub-Saharan expert Jean-Louis Triaud makes this comment:

> In the sub-Saharan region, these beliefs have been challenged over the last 30 years by new arrivals who emulate the Wahhabi model, though they purport to refuse the label. These movements are profoundly opposed to the brotherhoods, whose alleged ignorance, superstition and innovation (*bid'a*) they condemn. They are especially hostile to the Tijaniyya, whose claim to be an exclusive channel to salvation they regard as a heresy. The new arrivals claim to be the sole authentic 'Sunnis' (which is what they choose to call themselves) and wage energetic ideological war against the local Islamic establishments, pressing into service local anti-western sentiments and making an appeal to Arab culture.[4]

The Status of Women

In many African societies, a woman is the lynchpin of the family and the tribe. She is often the principal breadwinner of her family, thanks to her work in the fields or elsewhere. In many African societies, women are viewed as mother figures and as channels of wisdom inspired by the gods. In this capacity, respect and veneration is women's due in society. The manner of dress and attitude towards mixing with men displayed by African women is utterly at variance with that of traditionalist Muslim women.

The African woman is unveiled, mixes freely with men, and is able to travel alone and without permission from any man. The Wahhabis tried to change this situation, but met strong resistance from the women themselves, who jealously guarded the freedom they exercised, except in certain Islamic provinces of northern Nigeria. The Sufis, on the other hand, lent their support to continued freedom for women, while defending the rights they had enjoyed for many generations within African society.

CONCLUSION

The Islamists and the Sufis each interpret Islam in their own way, and do not share the same idea of its influence in African society. Nonetheless, in contrast to what has happened in the countries of North Africa, the Sufis and the Islamists have been able to coexist within African society and to live together. Neither of the two groups has dominated at the expense of the other.

The nationalist African regimes that have emerged from the process of decolonisation have refrained from allowing themselves to be persuaded by the traditionalist *ulema* to try to stamp out the brotherhoods, as was the case under President Bourguiba in Tunisia, and President Boumedienne in Algeria. The unintended consequence of Boumedienne's policies was to complete the work begun by Sheikh Ben Badis, who had persecuted the remaining bastions of liberal Sufism in Algeria which could have been ramparts against religious extremism. The Sufi brotherhoods have also had setbacks elsewhere. In Sudan, for example, it has been estimated that there are four million members of the Mahdist Sufi brotherhood: an impressively large figure.[5] However, the Sufis are held in a pincer movement by the government of Hassan Omer Al-Bashir in the north, and the southern SPLM movement. Sudanese Islamist extremism has turned its back on what is indubitably the country's major religious movement and chaos has predictably increased.

Nevertheless, in other countries with major Sufi representation, the outcome has been different. Thanks to the sterling efforts of the Mouridiyya, the Tijaniyya and the Qadiriyya, Africa has achieved modernity, a liberal outlook and religious tolerance. The African model has brought about harmony between pious Muslims, Christians, Jews and Hindus. Instances abound, in both West Africa and East Africa, from Senegal to Tanzania, both of which are salutary models. In these countries, no opening has been left for religious extremism to gain a foothold.

EPILOGUE

Relations between the East and the West are scarcely a cause for optimism. The two cultures have found it difficult to identify a basis for an effective dialogue aimed at reducing the tensions that poison their relationship. What is needed is an exchange of views, followed up by practical measures. Civil society, intellectuals, the clergy and organisations directed towards peace should all be involved. The barrier between the West and the East is primarily psychological. The problem arises from each party's belief that its culture is superior to that of the other.

In common with the Muslims, Christians are also haunted by memories of the wars of religion their ancestors were obliged to fight. Certain intellectuals, who have chosen to identify themselves with the global military and industrial lobbies, have sought to perpetuate the divisions between the Christian, Muslim and Jewish communities and the other religions of Asia and Africa, perpetuating their antagonism and rejection of coexistence. World powers should listen less to their security advisers and pay more attention to scholars and others who have studied the anthropology, the history and the social psychology of the peoples of the Third World. There is still time to halt the culture of religious and racial hatred. Those concerned with peace in the countries of the West, as well as in the Third World, should ponder the errors of the past and seek to promote strategies to avoid their recurrence. Only thus can future generations eschew the path of prejudice, and refrain from hatred and mistrust of other religions and races who have been arbitrarily defined as the enemy.

The errors of the past are exemplified by the hostility shown by certain westerners to the Orient, and vice-versa. One instance was that of the well-known author Ernest Psichari, the grandson of the Orientalist Ernest Renan and a fervent French nationalist.

195

Psichari underwent a personal conversion to Christianity while serving as a French soldier in Africa in the years before the First World War. In his book, *Le voyage du centurion*, his starting point is the superiority of the Christians over the Muslims, for whom he proposes wholesale conversion in order to raise their cultural level. This would require a will of iron on the part of the colonialists. To convince his readers, he emphasises the superiority of Christian values, which he says will sooner or later win the Muslims over:

> We are the victors and they the vanquished. What else is necessary? There is one thing we possess, however, that is more rich and true. This is the awareness we on our side have of both our worth and our unworthiness. These two feelings exist within us and neither can be false. Only with the mystery of Christianity are they conceivable.[1]

This jaundiced view of the Muslims, expressed by Psichari before his death at the western front in 1914, gained acceptance over time across wide sections of western society. There were Christians, even among those of Arab origin, who were persuaded of the view that Muslims had no conscience, ethics or dignity. In their eyes, these handicaps meant that they were unable to understand the values of the West, and in particular that they failed to perceive the difference between the servitude in which they lived and the freedom that the West was offering them. They also apparently believed that, in contrast to the Muslims, who were 'shivering slaves' and motivated by selfishness, Christians were by nature charitable and at all times expressed the love which was within them. These values, such Christians thought, were to be acquired only through the grace of Jesus Christ.

There were also politicians who were not shy of expressing their utter abhorrence of the very idea of Islam. Others again attempted to deconstruct the identity of the Arabs, in order to ensure that they would not become an effective political adversary and to provide a justification for colonialisation, investing the Arabs with deficiencies allegedly characteristic of their race.[2] At the close of the nineteenth century, Auguste Pomel, a writer who was also a member of the French National Assembly, described what he saw as 'Muslim obscurantism'. Two anthropological commentators offer this summary of Pomel's observations:

> The tyrannical administration of families and tribes, the base selfishness of individuals, the blatant exploitation of girl children: these are the intrinsic attributes of the race. The race is debased because it is cut off from the outside world and has failed to adapt because it is unproductive, predatory and impotent. It is impervious to influence because it has taken a stand against progress and civilisation. It is a barbarous and childish people, that takes refuge in the false memory of past glory and loses itself in futile dreams of a 'Moulay-Saa' [the master of the hour, who will come to redress present failures], and has defects that France cannot counter with a frontal attack.'[3]

Auguste Pomel, in his own words, does not stint his apparent contempt for the Muslims:

> Muhammadanism seems to be best adapted to societies whose social development has come to a halt at what might be described as the phase of barbarous patriarchy. Arab society is the most typical of this form of political organisation, to which the Arab race seems permanently subjected. The entire family is subject to the will of its oldest member, who is the sole proprietor and jealous guardian of his possessions . . . [There exists] a theocratic form of government of which absolutism is the lynchpin and fatalism the criterion. Society is divided into three types. The first of these is the base, hypocritical and idle cleric, a hereditary marabout whose influence is founded on his ignorant fanaticism. The second is the noble, a flea-bitten aristocrat for whom productive activity is abhorrent, in contrast to stupid or destructive fuss, which is highly honourable. The third is that of the impoverished peasant who is obliged to feed these two masters but is himself left to starve, if he will, on a fifth of what he produces.[4]

Pomel concludes in the same racist and splenetic vein:

> The Arab is the most inept exploiter of the land. He is incapable
> of anything but waste and destruction of the riches of nature ...
> This appears to be an inevitable result of the regime of patriarchal
> barbarism under which he agrees to live.[5]

Meanwhile, in the guise of an exercise in Islamology, Ernest Renan also offers a somewhat startling vision of Islam:

> Islam is the most complete negation of European values. It is
> fanaticism; it spurns science; it suppresses civil society. It is the
> stunning simplicity of the Semitic mind, which atrophies the power
> of the brain, closing it off from all subtlety of ideas and nobility
> of emotions, while blocking all attempts at rational inquiry in
> favour of the tautology, God is God. The future therefore lies with
> Europe and Europe alone. Europe will conquer the world and
> universally disseminate its faith: a religion in which there is
> something of the divine in the very midst of humanity.[6]

Sadly, views of this kind have not been confined to the colonial period. To point to just one example from the twenty-first century, the commentator Oriana Fallaci has chosen to publish a book full of racist prejudice against Islam. In a style worthy of the anti-Semitic literature of the 1930s, she drags the reputation of Islam and Muslims through the mud. She describes Islam as a 'fake culture' and the Muslims are represented as 'scowling, mincing, hostile, snarling, full of hate, bestial'.[7] In an article in an Italian newspaper, she fantasises that the fall of the United States would be followed by the fall of Europe. Then, as she puts it, 'we should have the muezzin instead of church bells; chadors for miniskirts; and camel's milk would have to do duty for a snifter of brandy'.[8]

It must be admitted in the interests of impartiality that, among Muslims, there has historically been no lack of prejudice against Christianity and other religions. A Syrian writer, Osama Ibn Munqidh, who first encountered westerners in the twelfth century, had a low opinion of those he met. In his view they were:

like animals whose only virtues were courage and sole accomplishments were in the military arena ... They have no nobility of feelings; their medicine is rudimentary and primitive compared with that of the Arabs; and their legal system is as stupid as it is outlandish.[9]

Much later, in the eighteenth century, the well-known Arab scholar Al-Jabarti, who accompanied the Emperor Napoleon during his expedition to Egypt from 1798 to 1801, remarked that 'the French were drunkards, and their women comported themselves in a shameful manner'.[10] Even in our own times, Muslims not infrequently entertain bizarre ideas concerning Christians and Christianity. The mental pictures constructed of each other by various civilisations can be unfortunate. Such preconceived opinions are passed down from one generation to the next. The only way of overcoming such entrenched prejudices is by rebuilding a minimum of trust between the different civilisations.

CONFIDENCE-BUILDING MEASURES BETWEEN ISLAM AND THE WEST

First, there must be tolerance towards the values of the other, which must be respected. The means of acquiring the necessary respect are through the educational system, within the family or through religious institutions. Responsibility for such education, whose goal is peace and inter-religious tolerance between Muslims, Christians, Jews and other believers, must be taken by families, clerics and educators themselves. Institutions for religious knowledge and education should develop and compare their curricula in the light of the promotion of tolerance, friendship and mutual sympathy. No person should be asked to deny his own religion, but their respect for dignity and for the beliefs of others can be developed by placing the emphasis on the unifying factors that religions have in common, such as belief in God, morality, charity and so forth. Some initiatives have already been taken in this direction, but they are so far on a low level and have received insufficient political support. For example, programmes have been undertaken by the Ecumenical Council of Churches in Geneva, and by the Catholic Church, whose efforts at dialogue have been models worthy of interest.[11]

The media, the family and the school all have a crucial role in the field of tolerance and the exchange of information between the Islamic, Christian, Jewish, Hindu and other religions. If success is to be achieved, the media war on Muslims and the crusader spirit that is prevalent in certain western religious circles must end once and for all. The construction of an ethical code that will put human dignity to the fore, and exclude discrimination based on affiliation to any given race or religion, as international human rights organisations demand, must be undertaken by appropriate international and regional organisations. These include the United Nations, UNESCO, the International Committee for the Red Cross and the Red Crescent, the European Union, the African Union, the Organisation of the Islamic Conference, the Ecumenical Council of Churches and others.

It is also time to halt the surreptitious promotion within schools and families of negative images of Islam, Christianity and Judaism. One long overdue practical example would be the exclusion from the curricula of certain Islamist educational establishments of the so-called 'Protocols of the Elders of Zion', a fictional document that was intended to prove the existence of a Jewish plot to dominate the world. The western media should also refrain from perpetuating the image of Muslims as identified with criminality: violence, theft and rape. A classic study of western media and images in the twentieth century has shown that Muslims are too often shown as perfidious, fatalistic and mendacious.[12]

A reading of the Arab press and the western press in English and Arabic leads to the observation of two complementary attitudes which reflect and nourish mutual racism. In some western journals, the Arab origin of any miscreant is always explicitly mentioned. For example, it was always carefully mentioned that Zacarias Moussaoui, accused of participation in the attacks of September 11, 2001, was 'of Moroccan origin'. On the other hand, if the person accused is not of Muslim Arab origin, this detail is omitted. In the Arab press, meanwhile, there is a tendency to insist on the Jewish origin of the subjects of stories. For example, in a story in *Al-Hayat* we read that the 'Jewish commentator' William Safire commented on the Palestinian President Arafat in 2003. Such insistence on the ethnic origin of persons mentioned in the media is common. Though sometimes not intentional, this subtly evokes racist emotions on the part of readers.

THE CLASH OF CIVILISATIONS

Peace between Christians and Muslims is everywhere neglected, and has so been since the start of the crusades, but seems able to withstand the final break. The threat of a clash between civilisations is not a new one. For Muslims, it is a reality to which they have become accustomed in the course of attempting to coexist with other religions over the course of history. They attribute the responsibility for the clashes they observe to the nature of different civilisations and the prophetic traditions on which they are based, which place little stress on the values that conduce towards unity between human communities.

As the Muslims see it, clashes between civilisations have always been the responsibility of westerners, whether under the crusades, the Napoleonic expeditionary force or French and British colonialism. On the other hand, strenuous efforts are made today to present the Muslim countries as engaged in a plan to invade the West in the name of Jihad. A deliberate confusion is created between the position of those radical minorities that have called for Jihad ever since Ibn Taymiyya, and the views of the silent majority of the Muslim world which wants no more than to live in peace and harmony with the rest of the world. Such a position is taken by all moderate believers, as well as by the Sufis and secularists, for all of whom Islam is an individual faith that identifies them with a society whose values are entirely peaceful and spiritual.

History shows that everything depends on the will of the religious and political leadership of the West and the East. They have sometimes chosen confrontation, but at other times they have opted for coexistence and co-operation in mutual respect. Thus, the world has already experienced such moments of bloody confrontation as the crusades, and the advance of the Muslim armies up to Poitiers in France. Meanwhile, there have also been periods of peace and mutual respect between Muslims and Christians, such as the relationship between Charlemagne and the Abbasid Caliph Harun Al-Rashid.

Today, some sections of the military–industrial lobby and the petroleum industry have thought it appropriate to revive the theory of the clash of civilisations and use it to interpret the world. This has had the consequence of reigniting hostility, violence and the spirit of religious confrontation. The Muslims suspect the intention of these lobbies is to justify intervention inside the frontiers of Muslim countries in order to profit from their rich resources and to suborn their governments to impose globalised economic and cultural systems upon the Muslim population. To counter these suspected threats, Muslim communities have resisted by means of non-governmental action, which has to some extent been able to ward off the perceived danger and prevent confrontation with the West from spreading.

In 1991, for example, at the time of the first war waged by the Americans and their allies against Iraq, the Islamic world rose up almost as one against the westernisation that threatened the heartland of the Two Sanctuaries of Mecca and Medina. Total war between the civilisations, including that of Judaism, did not follow but was only narrowly averted. The second war against Iraq, in 2003, plunged the Muslim world again into disarray and hostility towards the West. Radical tendencies of all kinds emerged, and though international terrorism was more or less defeated, religious fundamentalism continued to make inroads among peoples that were disappointed by the attitude of the western political establishment. Fundamentalism finally began to gain the support of even moderate Muslims, who were the victims of frustration and political disagreements with the United States and Europe. What is at present a confrontation between Muslim and Christian puritan tendencies could degenerate into something worse. Populations whose governments are supported by the West may yet begin to lean towards the side of Islamic radicalism.

The only means of avoiding a total rupture of the fragile

relationship which at present exists between the West and the Muslims will be, as soon as possible, to open a dialogue involving the entire spectrum of political and religious standpoints in the Islamic world. This exchange of views should be undertaken in a spirit of even-handedness and should be accompanied by practical steps. Tangible programmes should be set in motion to assist Muslim populations to stand on their feet once more and to restore their hope that they may be allowed to live in dignity, free from the moral and material deprivations they suffer at the present time.

The attitude of the Anglo-American coalition in the offensive against Iraq, however, has undermined the already minimal level of trust of the West felt by the Muslim countries. It is to be hoped that in the post-war period, the Muslims will nevertheless be able to take a new approach to their situation, and will be able to install democratic institutions and to inaugurate of their own free will a programme of sustainable development. With the crucial benefit of international aid, the Muslim countries should be able to nourish political, artistic and cultural talents whose existence has up to now been unsuspected. They will be able once more to enjoy real freedom of speech and thought, together with a return to the humanistic virtues for which they were known during the golden age of Muslim civilisation.

GLOBAL RELIGIOUS DIPLOMACY

SHOULD THERE BE DIALOGUE WITH THE ISLAMISTS?

The rise of racism, intolerance and religious extremism in the world leads to the supposition that the clash of civilisations is inevitable. However, much depends on the will of the religious and political leaders of the various camps. Historically, these have sometimes opted for confrontation, and at other times have chosen coexistence and co-operation in a framework of mutual respect. Notwithstanding the pessimism of Samuel Huntington's thesis on the clash of civilisations, which first appeared as an article in the journal *Foreign Affairs* in 1993,[13] total war between the blocs identified as civilisations has not ensued.

One reason for this has been the development and utilisation of the concept of 'soft power'. A concept originated by the Harvard political scientist Joseph Nye, the expression describes the ability to exercise influence and achieve goals through persuasion and attraction, rather than coercion.[14] In recent years, especially following the occupation of Iraq in 2003, there have been various initiatives aimed at dissipating the peril of a conflict between civilisations that would involve the entire world. In discussion of these initiatives, reference may be made to a further concept, that of 'soft diplomacy'.

I would like to propose a further concept, related to both 'soft power' and 'soft diplomacy', which might be described as 'global religious diplomacy'. This new type of diplomacy attempts to develop fresh kinds of dialogue within the context of a global religious and spiritual network. This new approach to international relations, by way of what might be called 'spiritual dialogue', has helped to preserve the fragile relationship between the West and the Muslims. Those taking part in global religious diplomacy have made the effort to open a dialogue, by way of the institutions of civil society, whose goal has been to involve all the Islamic world's religious and political tendencies.

The network engaged in global religious diplomacy has included various actors in the field of international relations, with links to civil society. These include a variety of NGOs, such as Amnesty International, Médécins sans Frontières, Caritas and Sant'Egidio, as well as UNESCO, UNICEF, the Red Cross and Red Crescent, think tanks of various persuasions, the churches, and both Muslim and western intellectual lobbyists. In the last five years, since 2003, all these participants have been involved in the preparation of a basis for dialogue between Muslims, Christians, Jews and other religious faiths. On the other hand, their efforts have been unco-ordinated and might seem almost incompatible.

I would like to present here various practical and theoretical proposals, drawn from my own experience in the field, to support the advancement of networks that work for global religious diplomacy, which will, I hope, continue to be able to defuse the tension and hatred that sadly exist between different communities. I should like to begin by putting forward some ground rules, and will then go on to draw some lessons from initiatives that have taken place in connection with the Muslim communities of Africa. Finally, I shall lay stress on the importance of taking account of the structure of factional power, rooted in the faith and passions of Muslims in the real world, whether Arab, African or Asian.

GROUND RULES

1) Actors within the dialogue should refrain from hostility, and in particular any temptation to use information they may have acquired in order to undermine or disempower any particular religious group. They should remember that they are not engaged in conflict. Contacts should be undertaken in a spirit of mutual respect.

2) Contacts should have as their sole objective the initiation of a preventive dialogue, whose intention is the avoidance of any resort to arms or repressive action.

3) The actors in any dialogue should keep at the forefront of their minds the evils of racism or discrimination of whatever sort which has as its objective the affirmation of the pretended superiority of any specific race or religion.

4) These actors should accept unreservedly the implications of the injustices that result from past history, such as slavery, colonisation, deportation, genocide (including the Holocaust), and encourage all participants in dialogue to proceed in the light of the principles of non-violence and dignity.

5) Attempts should be made to go beyond the simple juxtaposition of religious positions which is the rule at the moment in encounters between clerics. So far, clerics have not engaged in constructive dialogue but have contented themselves with mutual statements of their religious convictions and with mega-conferences. For example, 300 delegates, including 150 political figures as well as clerics and experts from 56 countries, attended a two-day conference hosted in Cordova by the Organisation

205

for Security and Co-operation in Europe. However, no follow-up in the Muslim countries was provided for. Though the conference initiated useful contacts, the absence of follow-up mechanisms meant it was likely to remain without effect on the situation on the ground. For example, it may be seen as ironic that Spain refused to allow Muslims to pray in the Cathedral at Cordova, though it is a former mosque.

LESSONS FROM THE PRACTICE OF GLOBAL RELIGIOUS DIPLOMACY

The outcome of any dialogue depends on the methods employed. In this respect certain religious NGOs have developed new practices, and UNESCO in particular has made great efforts, holding major conferences in 2003 and 2004 in New Delhi, Yemen and Australia.[15]

THE INCLUSIVE APPROACH TO RELIGIOUS FACTIONS

What follows is drawn from an experiment undertaken in various Muslim African countries. A participant in global religious diplomacy should be prepared to engage without prejudice in a dialogue with representatives of all religious factions, without discrimination. I would add that, speaking in my personal capacity, I believe that Al-Qa'ida should also be included in any such dialogue, given the institutional, ideological and political evolution in which it is engaged. The approach consists of giving a hearing to the representatives of each faction, responding with a statement of the common humanitarian values universally recognised by the international community, by Islam and by other religions. In this manner, an attempt may be made, for example, to convince an interlocutor that Islamic doctrine unequivocally rejects attacks against civilians.

Once initiated, contacts should be followed up, if possible without allowing the groups of interlocutors to become larger, since enlargement often disrupts the building of mutual confidence.

I would say further that during the initial phase of contact, the organiser of the dialogue is under an obligation to make a close study of the cultural subtleties of his interlocutors. All contacts should be undertaken, for preference, through verbal exchanges, since many contacted cultures are essentially oral and rely on oral tradition rather than documentation. It is therefore advisable to limit the amount of written correspondence and to develop direct oral contacts.[16]

INVOLVING THE 'ELDERS'

Experience shows that in place of the organisation of mega-conferences, like the meeting in Spain mentioned above, a better plan is the multiplication of small-scale meetings, informally organised and involving only between seven and nine participants, carefully chosen and delegated by local religious groups. Such small-scale encounters allow spiritual leaders, preferably those regarded as 'elders', to speak freely without being mandated on specific lines by their communities. It is easier in small-scale encounters to go beyond the level of the simple exchange of religious positions, and local leaderships are in addition encouraged to transcend religious, ethnic and sectarian divisions. Experience shows that when these conditions are satisfied, local leaders are able easily to identify the unifying cultural values between their different religions and to move on without difficulty to the next level of dialogue.

One result may be that such an encounter results in the diminution of tension and an end to violence, as with the meeting under the auspices of Christian Solidarity Worldwide between Imam Muhammad Nurayn Ashafa and the Reverend James Movel Wuye in Nigeria in 2004.[17] A further outcome may be a return to a basic concept of social justice, with a fairer distribution of resources, together with the devolution of democratic participation over matters of concern to a wide variety of ethnic and religious communities. The 'Elders' represent the most efficient mechanism for the reduction of religious tension. Certain 'Elders' operate in different spheres, acting not only as religious leaders but also as academic experts and as points of contact with violent 'takfiri' groups. It is crucial to persuade them to pass on the humanitarian message, as far as it is consistent with their religious values, as a means towards the re-establishment of dialogue and movement towards pacification or even lasting peace.

ADDRESS THE BASES OF ISLAMIC SOCIETY: FAITH, REASON AND FAMILY

Muslim society is still imbued with neo-feudal practices based on patriarchal values. However, the structure that underlies educational practice in the Muslim countries is essentially threefold. Three essential aspects contribute to the construction of the Muslim personality. These are moral education, faith and reason. The first aspect of a Muslim's basic education is essentially grounded in moral education. From his earliest years, a Muslim is initiated into respect for the sacral nature of blood ties and the maintenance of family alliances (*nissab*). His personality develops within the parameters of the extended family, the clan and the tribe, and eventually of his geographical territory or region. The young Muslim therefore grows up to respect his parents and his elders.[18] He is also expected to be ready to defend the honour (*'ird*) of his group. Vengeance (*thar*) must be exacted in response to any encroachment on this honour. Loyalty to the patriarchal family and clan solidarity are essential if a person is to exist and thrive in a situation where the material and security interests of the group take unquestioned precedence.

This moral education is complemented from childhood by initiation into the subtleties of language, poetic creation and an awareness of a mystical notion of divine love. The process culminates in a solemn avowal of commitment to the faith (*iman*) and to the tenets of Islamic doctrine (*'aqida*). These represent the second aspect of personal development, that of faith. Finally, the moral and doctrinal aspects are completed by the third element: the rational study of theology. A Muslim is thus encouraged to use his reason (*'aql*), without allowing it to overshadow his simple faith. This third educational phase often introduces complications, inasmuch as it addresses itself to the individual and is each individual's responsibility. According to Sura 6, verse 164 of the Qur'an, 'no soul shall bear the burden of another soul'.

Finally, it may be said that in the present transitional phase of the debate over Islam, it appears to be crucial that an attempt to establish a process of 'global religious diplomacy' should be made. To this end, rhetoric that tends to demonise Islam must be avoided. The initiative should be taken by means of a process of direct contact by interlocutors with Islamic movements, with no suspicion of any attempt to carry out 'espionage', which may have counter-productive results. Any such dialogue should be meticulously prepared and should take account of the cultural specificities and the institutions of those who exercise real power. Finally, it is crucial to refrain from promoting in any way the 'fear of the other', irrespective of whether the 'other' is identified with the Christians, the Jews or the Muslims.

GENERAL CONCLUSION AND SIX RECOMMENDATIONS

What would the necessary conditions be for the Muslim world to flourish once more? What can Muslims and the West do, within and across their frontiers, to avoid confrontation? The reply to these questions implies a fundamental change of attitude, and also six positive steps which, in conclusion, I shall propose.

1) RADICAL REFORM OF THE ISLAMIC EDUCATIONAL SYSTEM

The state educational system in the Muslim countries is inadequate, often reserved for a select group, and frequently shunned by large sections of civil society. Many religious associations have set up their own educational facilities, creating a kind of parallel school system that provides religion-based education. Most of these institutions are beyond state control: for example the *madrasas*, which employ antiquated teaching methods. Such schools are breeding grounds for one-dimensional minds closed to modern subjects such as science and philosophy. Their methods of teaching need radical reform, modelled on the proposals of the classic Muslim philosophers, such as Ibn Rushd, Ibn Al-Arabi, Ibn Sina and Al-Ghazali, adapted to modern circumstances. The Muslim countries should encourage projects on the lines of the 'pedagogy of liberation', such as the ideas developed in Brazil by Paulo Freire.[19] This should embody what might be described as Sufi liberation theology, and ought to be able to avoid repeating the disasters of a traditional educational system ill adapted to the modern world.

In the margins of the basic educational system, teaching should also include the principles of non-violence and the means of self-assertion, including passive civil resistance and individual spiritual power. Well-implemented, peaceful and spiritual resistance is quickly seen to be more effective than violence. In addition, the modern and liberal teaching to be found in the Sufi *zawiyas* or *tekke* should be freed from the administrative shackles placed on it by some states. Such institutions should be allowed naturally to resume the position they held in the Muslim golden age. The time has come to halt the persecution of Sufis, as well as the Ismailis and Alevis, and the Sufi orders of the Shi'ite world.

The Muslim intellectual world should also break free from the sterile cycle of traditional thought and open itself to new disciplines and modern methods of research in anthropology, sociology and comparative religion. Rational thought should again be allowed to take its place in Muslim society, while avoiding the excesses of materialism and individualism that have been exaggerated by some in the West. For these reasons, sight should not be lost of the sociological realities of the Islamic nation. In the words of Mohammed Al-Jabri,

Some Muslim intellectuals blindly emulate the characteristics of European modernity, apparently unaware, whether genuinely or not, of the vast chasm that divides our condition from that of the West. It is true that in the industrial West, rationalism is all-pervasive in individual and collective existence and holds undisputed sway over human relations and conceptions about

the world, ideas and behaviour. Rational organisation in the fields
of the economy, administration, the machinery of state and
institutions in the West has come to be reflected in all spheres.[20]

For Al-Jabri, Muslim rationalism should hold back from the
excesses of individualism that have beset western society. A traveller
on the road that leads to rationalism, liberty of thought and
modernity should not lose sight of the sociological realities of the
Islamic *umma*.

2) THE CREATION OF A FEDERAL STRUCTURE TO ACCOMMODATE ETHNIC AND RELIGIOUS SPECIFICITIES (RESPECTING HUMAN RIGHTS)

While maintaining its special place in society, religion should
cease to assume the role of the unique vehicle for thought about
collective life: the institutions of politics, family law, work and the
economy. Only a federal state, responsible for defence, security
and external relations, can ensure that any particular state, whatever
its own specificities, accepts the universally recognised norms of
human rights. Other responsibilities should be devolved to the
federated components, who will legislate in accordance with the
Islamic sensibilities of the regions, democratically expressed.
Consider the example of Nigeria, whose federal laws should be
better respected, with the result that condemnations to death for
apostasy or adultery should be automatically annulled by the Head
of State, who is the guarantee of the supremacy of federal law.

The Muslim states of today have diverse populations, with
different beliefs regarding the nature of Islam, but no
accommodation is made to allow minority groups to live
autonomously and in accordance with their beliefs. These
centralised states, which expect their populations to behave in a
uniform fashion, insist on applying legal systems that take no
account of the ethnic and religious sensibilities of the people they
govern. Their only route to survival is federalism, which will at
least enable them to retain control of their federal armed forces,
internal security and foreign affairs, while leaving local authorities

211

a margin of manoeuvre for the conduct of local affairs in accordance with principles laid down at the federal level.

3) THE PRIORITISATION OF INDIVIDUAL FREEDOMS, AND THE RIGHTS OF WOMEN

The place of individual freedoms in Muslim society must be restored to the centre of the stage. Freedom of thought and religion must be absolute and not conditional on restrictive religious interpretations, as is the case today. In addition, a particular status must be accorded to women. A woman must have the opportunity to determine her own place in society, without restrictions. Women's responsibility may be enhanced through a process of education, and through the extension to women of the same rights as those enjoyed by men.

4) THE MUSLIM POPULATION MUST BE CONTROLLED

Muslim clerics should take steps to render the population as a whole more aware of issues relating to the environment and to demography. Population in the Muslim world is growing at the rate of 6.4 per cent, according to United Nations figures. If the Muslim countries fail to take steps to limit their population growth to a reasonable figure, they will suffer dire consequences. The *umma* today has no need of population in quantity: what is required is quality. If demographic growth and the destruction of the environment continue at their present rate, Islam will be unable to enter into competition with other civilisations. Population growth will lead inevitably to the collapse of states into anarchy and self-destruction.

5) THE *UMMA* MUST RECOGNISE ITS CULTURAL ANTECEDENTS

The Muslim *umma* emerged from a past in which Greek, Christian, Pharaonic, Hindu, Hebrew, Hispano-Mauresque, Berber, Zoroastrian and animist cultures all had their part to play. Without in any way renouncing its Islamic nature, the *umma* should recognise this heritage. While maintaining intact its enthusiastic Islamic faith and the tolerance associated with it, the Muslim *umma* should display the courage to reconcile itself with its complex ethnic and cultural past, and in addition embrace rationalist thought, Sufism and the arts. These are unexploited or dormant treasures, the rediscovery of which cannot fail to revitalise the Muslim world and enable it to escape from its one-dimensional intellectual prison. Islam must take care not to annihilate its own memory, and its historical associations with the non-Arab Occident and Orient. The rediscovery of these aspects of the Muslim past, followed by a return to freedom of thought, will endow the Islamic world with the grandeur it knew in the past.

6) ABOLISH TYRANNY

First of all, corruption in government must be stamped out. Mutual tolerance between the adherents of various religions and sects must be promoted, and secular nationalists should reach an accommodation with the religious authorities. The Muslim states should endeavour to redistribute wealth and halt the decline of the standard of living of the poorest. Civil society should learn from the institutional practices of the West with a view to halting despotism, injustice and corruption on the part of Muslim leaders and the parasitic oligarchy within the Muslim states. Only a long period of apprenticeship in democracy and human values will permit the realisation of such measures. Popular checks and balances will also need to be put in place, under a federal model, which alone allows different ethnic and religious elements to express themselves peacefully.

MUTUAL UNDERSTANDING

On the western side of the equation, the image of Muslims has been tarnished in recent decades. Some have flatly identified Muslims with barbarous and bloody terrorism, an image fostered by parts of the western media. In parallel, many young Muslims make no secret of their admiration for Osama Bin Laden. In their eyes, Bin Laden is the sole champion prepared to fight what they see as 'sinners' and 'infidels', in addition to which he appears the antithesis of the despotic and corrupt Muslim governments by which they are ruled.

It is therefore as urgent for the West as for the Muslims to put in place a strategy for communication and a partnership intended to reveal the true face of the peaceful and tolerant majority within Islam, followed by a complementary humanisation of the image of the West in the eyes of young Muslims. This will require the deployment of competent international organisations, drawn from both sides of the divide. Meanwhile, Islam's increasing geographical dispersion across the world has seen it take root in a plethora of dismal and unwelcoming slums outside its original lands. Whatever action may have been taken against terrorism, there remains the possibility that social disturbances may once more occur in these areas, and new forms of violence may emerge in the future from such zones of urban deprivation.

In this precarious and unstable environment, action can be taken against prejudice, and an effort to produce a change of attitudes, both by the NGOs and international organisations active in the field and by communicators and the media. Through their involvement and the creativity of their efforts, together with the recruitment of participants from the Muslim countries as well as those of the West, they will certainly succeed in laying down benchmarks of tolerance and mutual understanding. The involvement of Muslims, from the Middle East, Asia and Africa, as well as other figures from the countries of the Third World, is of key importance. Many Arab and Muslim personalities have told me of their concern at the lack of representation of Muslims in the NGOs and international organisations. There is also a lack of Muslim individuals from Muslim populations resident in the west. Such elements could provide a bridge between the Orient and the Occident and be useful as interlocutors.

The NGOs and international organisations, intervening in a humanist and spiritual sense, will no doubt make their mark in history, and will help to ward off new 'clashes of civilisations'. These, for the moment, appear likely, in fact, to take the shape of what might be described as 'clashes of puritanism'. Their activities cannot fail to promote tolerance in the world. As Louis Massignon, the great French mystic, has put it:

> We must never tire of the insistence that we must pray together, Christians, Jews and Muslims, for the advent of the peace which we desire and which has been so tardy in making its appearance. Any initiative in the economic and even the cultural field that is not seen to come from hearts united in the Faith of Abraham, father of all believers, will only arouse the suspicion of the Third World . . .[21]

Within the countries of the Third World, it will remain true that particular attention must be paid to the problem presented by Islam. There may once more be a grave threat to world peace in the Persian Gulf. It is in view of this that I have presumed to offer my recommendations for the handling of future crises. Not all Third World countries, however, are beset by problems arising from Islamism. Other civilisations also demand more sustained attention on the part of the international community, as other areas of the world may yet have their surprises to offer. I refer to China, Korea and even to Russia, as well as to countries in Africa and South America that are, for the moment at least, regarded as stable.

NOTES

PART ONE

INTRODUCTION

1   J. Ismaël, 'Les sources du complot', *El Moujahid*, nos 28 and 29, vol.3, shaaban/ramadan 1992 (AH 1411) p.21.

2   Jacques Le Goff provides further details on these ways to combat the Muslims. He speaks of Peter the Venerable, Abbot of Cluny (1109–56) as follows: 'While in Spain for a tour of inspection of the Cluniac monasteries which had made their appearance at the time of the *reconquista*, Peter the Venerable developed his first notions of how to combat the Muslims by intellectual means rather than on the field of battle. The idea was that their doctrine should be understood if it is to be refuted. This idea, which seems obvious to us, was boldly original at the time of the crusades.' J. Le Goff, *Les intellectuels au moyen âge*, Paris: Seuil, 1985, p.20; see also the study by Michel Ballard, *De Cicéron à Benjamin*, Paris: PUF, 1992, p.76

3   A fatwa is a legal ruling issued on a point of Shari'a law by a Mufti or a member of the body of learned clergy (the *ulema*), or among the Shi'ites by an Ayatollah. The individual who has asked for the fatwa is at liberty either to follow it or to ask for a piece of contrary advice, a 'counter-fatwa'. The most binding fatwas are those that are confirmed by the consensus of a college of clerics competent and qualified so to do.

4   See Francesco Gabrieli, *Mahomet et les grandes conquêtes arabes*, Paris: Hachette, 1967, p.12ff.

5   The statistics for the number of Muslims in the world vary somewhat according to whether they are derived from United Nations data or from specialised agencies that take their information from western

embassies across the world. For instance, the table given by David B. Barrett of the United Nations, quoted by the *Almanach populaire catholique* gives for 1998 the figure of 1,164,622,000 Muslims around the world, while other sources based on the *CIA Factbook* estimate the number at 1,678,442,000. For 2000, the *CIA Factbook* gives the figure of 1,902,095,000. See www.religion.qc.ca/themes/statistics/releve.htm; and www.bostani.com/musul-mond.htm. The figures relate to broad confessional groups rather than to the strict practice of Islam.

6   Elsa C. Arnett, Knight Ridder News Service, widely quoted but see for example www.thedivinereligion.com

7   France, Ministry of Foreign Affairs, Religion in France factsheet, http://www.ambafrance-au.org/article.php3?id_article=462&var_recherche=religion, 2007.

8   Jonathan Petre (religious correspondent), *Daily Telegraph*, 'Muslims to outnumber traditional church goers', 26 March 2008.

9   'Muslims in Britain, 2007', European Council of Religious Leaders, http://www.rfp-europe.eu/index.cfm?id=125945

10   www.islamicpopulation.com

11   Craig Smith, 'Europe fears threat from its converts to Islam', *International Herald Tribune*, 19 July 2004.

12   Sarah Lyall, *International Herald Tribune*, 17 August 2006. Estimate from Yahya Birt.

13   Zentralinstitut Islam-Archiv-Deutschland Stiftung, Nachrichten 2005, www.islamarchiv.de

14   See the report by Association Culturelle des Femmes Musulmanes en Suisse, 'La Suisse et la présence des musulmans'. See also figures from the Swiss Federal Office of Statistics quoted in Antoine Menuisier, 'Qui sont les musulmans de Suisse?' *Hebdo*, 24 October 2002.

15   By 'Islamologists' (*islamologues*) I mean to specify those who make a special study of Islam, as distinct from 'Orientalists', whose field of study includes many subjects appertaining to the East.

16   E.W. Said, *Orientalism*, New York: Pantheon Books, 1978 passim.

17   The word 'algebra' derives from *al-jabr*, coined by the renowned Arab mathematician al-Khawarismi (c. 780–850).

18   William McGuckin de Slane (trans), *Prolégomènes*, 3 vols, Ibn Khaldoun, Paris/Algiers: Imprimerie Impériale, 1863–8. Also William McGuckin de Slane (trans), *Histoire des Berbères et des dynasties musulmanes de l'Afrique septentrionale*, Algiers: Imprimerie du Gouvernement, 1852–6. In English. F. Rosenthal, *The Muqaddima*, 3 vols, Princeton University Press, 1958.

19 R.A. Nicholson (editor and translator), *The Mathnawi of Jalaluddin Rumi*, Cambridge University Press, 1926.

20 Louis Massignon, *La passion d'al-hosayn ibn-mansour al-hallaj, martyr mystique de l'islam, executé a Bagdad le 26 mars 922*, 4 vols, Paris: Paul Geuthner, 1922.

CHAPTER 1

1 Al-Tabari, *History of Prophets and Kings (Muhammad at Macca)*, Albany: State University of New York, SUNY Press, vol.6, parts 2 and 3, 1988.

2 See Ibn Ishaq, *Muahhamd*, translated by Abd Al-Rahman Badawi, Beirut: Albouraq, 2001, p.60.

3 Ibn Khaldun, *Peuples et nations du monde* (extracts from the *Kitab al-Ibar*), translated from the Arabic and annotated by Abdesselam Cheddadi, Arles: Sindbad et Actes Sud, 1995, p.296.

4 Francesco Gabrieli, *Mahomet et les grandes conquêtes arabes, op. cit.*, p.36.

5 Henri Lammens, 'Qoran et traditions: comment fut composée la vie de Mahomet', *Recherches de science religieuse*, no.1, Paris 1910, pp.25–61.

6 According to Odon Vallet, 'Les arabes et l'Europe', *La Croix-L'Evènement*, Paris, 23–24 November 1986, '[Ernest Renan] made the same accusation against both Jews and Muslims, that the semitic peoples suffered from a lack of curiosity and from intolerance and were troublemakers. He therefore called for the "destruction of Islam": "War will only cease," Renan said, "when the last son of Ishmael [the brother of Isaac, the ancestor of the Arab tribes of the north] is either dead or has been driven into the depths of the desert."'; see also Ernest Renan, *L'avenir de la science*, Geneva: Bibliothèque de l'Humanité, 1961, pp.77–82.

7 Francesco Gabrieli, *op. cit.*, p.82.

8 Ibn Khaldoun, *Discours sur l'histoire universelle*, Paris: Sindbad, 1997, p.293.

9 *Ulema* is the plural of *alim*, which literally means 'scholar'. In its western usage, it refers to Muslim religious clerics.

10 Chafik Chehata, *Etudes de droit musulman*, Paris: PUF, 1971, p.15.

11 Markus Hattstein, *Les grandes religions*, Cologne, 1997, p.97.

12 Anne-Marie Delcambre, *Mahomet, la parole d'Allah*, Paris: Découvertes (collection Religions), 1981, p.119.

13 'Abu Lahab' was the nickname of Abdul Uzza, an uncle of the Prophet: the name means literally 'The Father of Flame'. His wife had reportedly taken pleasure in strewing thorn bushes where she knew the Prophet might wish to walk.

14 Malek Bennabi, *Le phénomène coranique: essai d'une théorie sur le Coran*, Paris: no publisher given, 1976, p.39 (original edition: Algiers: En-Nahdha, 1946). For a more recent analysis see Alfred-Louis Prémare, *Les fondations de l'Islam, entre écriture et histoire*, Paris: Seuil, 2002.

15 Malek Bennabi, *op. cit.*, p.39.

16 Ibid. p.14.

17 See Ibn Khaldun, *op. cit.*, 1977, p.291.

18 It should be kept in mind that the different Islamic dynasties had their origins in two distinct blood-lines of the tribe of Quraysh. One descended from Muhammad's grandfather, Hashim, from whom come the Hashemites. This line also includes Ali, the cynosure of the Shi'ites, Fatima, after whom the Fatimids are named, and Abbas Hussein, the father of the Abbasids. The other line descends from the brother of Muhammad's great-grandfather, whose son was Umayya, from whom the Umayyad dynasty takes its name. The Caliphs Mu'awiya and Othman were from the Ummayad clan.

19 The word Shi'a means 'partisan' or 'follower'. This term is applied to the followers of Ali and their descendants, among whom were his sons Hassan and Hussein. See Ibn Khaldoun, *op. cit.*, p.302.

20 See Yves Thoraval, *Dictionnaire de la civilisation musulmane*, Paris: Larousse, 1995, pp.213–14.

21 Francesco Gabrieli, *op. cit.*, pp.217–18.

22 Evariste Lévi Provençal, *Histoire de l'Espagne musulmane*, vol.1, Paris: Maisonneuve et Larose, p.96ff.

23 The Islamists accused Ataturk of having suppressed the Turkish nation's Islamic heart. They also took him to task for secularising education, liberating women and replacing the Arab alphabet of the Qur'an with western script.

24 Yves Besson, *Ibn Sa'ud, roi bédouin: la naissance du royaume d'Arabie Saoudite*, Lausanne: Editions des Trois Continents, 1980, p.166.

25 See also S. Naef, in Husayn Ahmad Amin, *Le défi du fondamentalisme islamique*, Genève: Labor et Fides, 1988, p.67ff.

26 See Said M. Laham, *La quintessence du Sahih Al-Bokhari*, Beirut: Dar al-Fikr, 1993, Hadith 3455, p.36.

27 Ali Abderraziq, *L'islam et les fondements du pouvoir*, (trans Filali Ansary), Paris: La Découverte/CEDEJ, 1994, p.22; Louis Gardet, *La cité musulmane: vie sociale et politique*, Paris: Librairie Philosophique J. Vrin, 1975 p.355ff.

28 See Tore Kjeilen, Looklex Encyclopedia, 'Ibadi Islam', http://i-cias.com/e.o/ibadi.htm

29 Yves Thoraval, *op. cit.*, p.101.

30 Jean Béraud-Villars, *L'Islam d'hier et de toujours*, Paris: Arthaud, 1969,

p.86; see also Farhad Daftary, *The Ismailis: their History and Doctrine*, Cambridge University Press, 1992.

31 See Bernard Lewis, *The Assassins: a Radical Sect in Islam*, London: Weidenfeld and Nicholson, 1967.

32 According to the *CIA Factbook*, the population of Pakistan was just short of 165 million, based on a July 2007 estimate (www.cia.gov/library/publications). The Shi'ites represented some 20 per cent of the population, with a very approximate figure of something less than a million Ismailis (www.asianInfo.org).

33 Yves Thoraval, *op. cit.*, p.101.

34 Hugh Pope, Syria's political changes threaten Alawites' power, *Wall Street Journal*, 14 June 2000, cited at www.likud.nl/press18.html. See also *CIA Factbook* (Syria) (www.cia.gov/library/publications)

35 For a full study of the Alawis, see Joseph Azzi, *Les nousaïrites alaouites: histoire, doctrine, coutumes*, Paris: Publisud, 2002. On the relation between Druze and Alaoui beliefs, see Fuad I. Kuri, *Imams and Emirs: State, Religion and Sects in Islam*, London: Saqi Books, 1990, p.132ff.

36 See Sayyid Abu'l Ala Mawdudi, *Towards Understanding Islam*, Lahore: Islamic Publications Ltd, 1960, pp.143–5. Mawdudi cites statistics for the four schools specified above, which have of course substantially changed since publication in 1960.

37 Joseph Schacht, *Esquisse d'une histoire du droit musulman*, Paris: Librairie orientale et américaine, 1953, p.64.

38 Muhammad Talbi, 'Une communauté de communautés, le droit de la différence et les voies de l'harmonie' *Islamochristiana*, no.4, 1978, p.11.

39 William Zartmann, 'Pouvoir et Etat dans l'islam', *Pouvoirs*, no.12, 1980, pp.5–14.

40 René Kalinsky, *Le Monde arabe: L'essor et le déclin d'un empire*, Paris: Marabout, 1968, p.131.

41 Vincent Monteil, *Clefs pour la pensée arabe*, Paris: Seghers, 1974, p.24.

CHAPTER 2

1 Henri Laoust, *Essai sur les doctrines sociales et politiques de Taki-d-Din Ahmad b. Taimiya*, Institut français d'archaéologie orientale, Le Caire, 1939, p.132.

2 Henri Laoust, *op. cit.*, p.171.

3 Henri Laoust, *Le Traité de droit public d'Ibn Taimiya*, Institut français de Damas, 1948, pp.125–6. (This book is a complete translation of the text of Ibn Taymiyya, *Siyasa shar'iya*.)

4 Ibid. p.126.

5   *Encyclopédie de l'Islam*, Leiden and Paris: Brill/Maisonneuve et Larose, 1971, vol.3, p.978.

6   Ibn Taymiyya, *Majma' al-Fatawa al-Kubra* (Fatawa 4/319), Riyadh: Editions direction générale pour le Da'wa et l'orientation, n.d., vol.4, pp.319–22.

7   Henri Laoust, *op. cit.*, p.117.

8   Ibn Taymiyya, *Siyasya shar'iya, op. cit.*, p.173.

9   Eric Geoffroy, *Le soufisme en Egypte et en Syrie*, Institut français de Damas, 1995, p.446ff.

10 Ibid., p.446.

11 *Encyclopédie de l'Islam, op. cit.*, p.461.

12 Ibn Taymiyya, *op. cit.*, pp.5–6. See also Albert Hourani, *Arabic Thought in the Liberal Age*, Cambridge University Press, 2001, p.21.

13 Henri Laoust, *Essai sur les doctrines, op. cit.*, p.39.

14 Ibid., p.41

15 Ibid.

16 Yves Besson, *Ibn Sa'ud, roi bédouin: la naissance du royaume d'Arabie Saoudite*, Lausanne: Editions des Trois Continents, 1980, p.24.

17 Ibid., p.25.

18 Ibid., p.88.

19 Mohamed-Chérif Ferjani, *Islamisme, laïcité et droits de l'homme*, Paris: L'Harmattan, 1991, p.167.

20 *Le Monde*, 2 June 1996. The same observation is quoted by Ghassan Salamé, 'L'Islam en Arabie Saoudite', *Pouvoirs*, no.12, 1980, p.125.

21 Ghassan Salamé, *op. cit.*, p.126.

22 In other words, placing the emphasis on *tawhid* – the unity and oneness of God.

23 Sherif Hussein, who had declared himself King of the Hejaz, took the title of Caliph when it was abolished by the Turkish National Assembly in March 1924 but was himself deposed on 5 October 1924 by Ibn Saoud, in a decision endorsed by the notables of Mecca and Jedda. See Yves Besson, *op. cit.*, p.172ff.

24 Christophe Ayad, 'Arabie Saoudite. Le wahhabisme, une arme à double tranchant', *Libération*, 21 September 2001; see also, for a study of the World Islamic League, Faez Ajjaz, *Cette Terre d'Allah*, Beirut: Presses Islamiques, 1967, p.226ff.

25 Ibid.

26 Islamic groups around the world were financed by means of the privately controlled resources of the Saudi Islamic charitable organisations. Wahhabi youth found itself a new international role to play. Most of the perpetrators of the events of September 11, 2001 in New York were Saudi citizens under 25. Together with Egyptian and

North African Islamists, Saudis made up the senior officials of
international Islamic organisations.

27   See also Jalal Bennani Boubker, *L'islamisme et les droits de l'homme*,
     Lausanne: Editions de l'Aire, 1984, p.46.

CHAPTER 3

1   Rochdy Alili, *Qu'est-ce que l'islam?* Paris: La Découverte, 1996, p.323.
2   Olivier Carré and Gérard Michaud, *Les frères musulmans: Egypte et
    Syrie, 1928–1982*, Paris: Gallimard, 1983, p.37.
3   Muhammad Shawqi Zaki, *Al-ikhwan al-muslimin wal-mujtama al-misri*
    (The Muslim Brotherhood and Egyptian Society), Cairo: [no publisher]
    1952, cited by Tariq Ramadan, *op. cit.*, p.214.
4   See Tangi Salaun, 'Egypte: le pari social des Frères musulmans',
    Le Figaro, 5 July 2005.
5   Rachid Ridha, in Emile Dermenghem, *Les plus beaux textes arabes*,
    Paris: La Colombe, 1951, p.360.
6   For an account of the armed resistance and terrorism undertaken by
    the Brotherhood, see Richard P. Mitchell (foreword by John Voll), *The
    Society of the Muslim Brothers*, Oxford University Press, 1969, p.75ff.
7   Richard P. Mitchell, *op. cit.*, p.153.
8   Regarding the symbolism of the Qur'an and the swords of the *ikhwan*,
    see the excellent doctoral thesis of Yves Besson, *op. cit.*, p.85.
9   Mohamed-Chérif Ferjani, *op. cit.*, p.167.
10 Johan Cartigny, *Cheikh Alawi, documents et témoignages*, Paris: Les amis
    de l'islam, 1984, p.36ff.
11 For a discussion of affiliated groups, see Richard H. Dekmejian, *Islam
    in Revolution: Fundamentalism in the Arab World*, Syracuse University
    Press, 1995, p.63ff. and p.67. See also the Muslim Brotherhood
    homepage: www.ummah.net.uk/ikhwan/
12 Ibid.
13 Ibid.
14 Sayyid Qutb, *Islam, religion de l'avenir*, Riyadh: International Islamic
    Federation of Student Organizations (IIFSO), 1994, p.141.
15 Muhammad Qutb, *Islam, the Misunderstood Religion*, Kuwait: Darul
    Bayan Bookshop, p.21.
16 Sayyid Qutb, *L'islam par le martyre*, Riyadh: IIFSO, 1994, p.28.
17 Ibid., p.28.
18 Ibid., p.34.
19 Sayyid Qutb seems yet more radical than Ibn Taymiyya on the issue
    of God's absolute prerogative. According to Qutb, this must be the

sole basis for the institutions and law of all Muslim communities. Ibn Taymiyya takes a more moderate position, accepting that under certain circumstances Imams can legislate. Qutb rejects this.

20   Sayyid Qutb, *op. cit.* (*L'islam par le martyre*) pp.34–5.
21   Sayyid Qutb, *L'islam, religion de l'avenir, op. cit.*, p.7.
22   Ibid., pp.85–6.
23   Ibid., p.87.
24   Ibid., p.53.
25   Sayyid Qutb, *Islam, the Misunderstood Religion, op. cit.*
26   Muhammad Qutb, *Islam, the Misunderstood Religion, op. cit.*, p.21.
27   Ibid., p.8.
28   Ibid., p.12.
29   Ibid., p.12.
30   Sayyed Abul Ala Mawdudi, *Towards Understanding Islam*, preface by Khurshid Ahmed, web edition www.witness-pioneer.org/vil/Books/M_tui/editors.html, 1990.
31   Tariq Ali, *The Clash of Fundamentalisms: Crusades, Jihads and Modernity*, London: Verso, 2000, p.174.
32   See for example the law promulgated by General Zia on the application of the Shari'a in Pakistan, which reinstated *zakat* and the Islamic courts. In addition, the consumption of alcohol, theft and illicit sexual relations were punished by lashing or amputation. See Bannani, *op. cit.*, p.64ff.
33   Sayyed Abul Ala Mawdudi, *Towards Understanding Islam*, preface by Khurshid Ahmed, web edition: www.witness-pioneer.org/vil/Books/M_tui/editors.html; print edition, Leicester: The Islamic Foundation, 1981 (revised edition) reprinted 2004, p.110.
34   Ibid., p.110.
35   Ibid., p.110.
36   Ibid., p.113.
37   Ibid., p.114.
38   Ibid., p.115.
39   Ibid., p.115.
40   Ibid., p.116.
41   Ibid., p.125.
42   Ibid., p.125.
43   Ibid., p.125.
44   Ibid., p.125.
45   Fathi Yakan, *Problems Faced by the Da'wah and the Da'iya*, Riyadh: WAMY, 1992, p.108.
46   Bedreddine Manaa, 'Enquête – El Qaïda: l'armée secrète de Bin Laden', *Le Soir d'Algérie*, 24 September 2001.

47 Farid Zemmouri, 'Logique de Guerre', *Le Nouvel Afrique-Asie*, no.110, November 1998, p.31.

48 An entirely Judaeo-Christian term unknown to Muslims.

49 Hassane Zerrouky, *La Nébuleuse islamiste en France et en Algérie*, Paris: Editions No.1, 2002, p.329ff.; and Bedreddine Manaa, *op. cit.* See also MedIntelligence at www.medintelligence.free.fr/bdterror4.htm#GIA. Finally see the present author's unpublished and forthcoming work, *Islamisme et Evangéliques*, 2009.

50 Bin Laden's famous fatwa of 23 February 1998 specifying the legitimate targets for attack by Jihadists is quoted in full in Antoine Sfeir, *The Columbia World Dictionary of Islamism* (English edition translated and edited by John King), New York: Columbia University Press, 2007, p.86.

51 Rapport d'information de l'Assemblée nationale française, no.3460, 12 December 2001, p.14.

52 Zidane Meriboute, *op. cit.*

53 John Esposito, 'Le fondamentalisme islamique', SIDIC, vol.32, no.3, 1999, at www.sedos.org. See also François Burgat, *L'islamisme au Maghreb*, Paris: Payot, 1995.

54 See the statutes of Ennahda and the FIS, www.ezzitouna.org. See also La Tribune d'Octobre, no.11, Paris, 25 July 1989 (pullout section entitled 'FIS: le Programme').

55 Abdessalam Yacine, 'L'islam ou le déluge', *Courrier international*, 27 January 1994, no.169, p.11.

56 See the positions taken by Karkar and Belhadj in *Courrier international*, *op. cit.*, pp.10–12.

57 Rochdy Alili, *op. cit.*, p.334.

58 See Azzam Tamimi, *Rachid Ghannouchi: a democrat within Islamism*, Oxford University Press, 2001.

59 *Courrier international*, *op. cit.*, p.12.

60 See the interview Ben Ali gave to the *Financial Times*, 27 July 1994.

61 *Courrier international*, *op. cit.*, p.10.

62 Quoted by Pierre Guillard, *Ce fleuve qui nous sépare: lettre à l'imam Ali Belhadj*, Paris: Loysel, 1994, p.218.

63 Ibid.

64 Ibid.

CHAPTER 4

1 See 'Organisation of Islamic Conference's Human Rights Confab: Islamic Declaration of Human Rights, potential rallying point for Moslem world', *Tehran Times*, 4 January 1990.

2 Henri Laoust, *Essai sur les doctrines, op. cit.*, p.167.
3 Louis Gardet, *La cité musulmane: vie sociale et politique*, Paris: J. Vrin, 1976, p.56.
4 See for example L. Bakhtiar (ed.), *Encyclopedia of Islamic Law: a compendium of the major schools*, Chicago: Kazi Publications, 1996, p.291ff.
5 These are known in Arabic as the *hadd* transgressions, and are: banditry or insurrection; slander; theft; fornication and the consumption of alcoholic drinks. The Wahhabis also regard apostasy as a *hadd* crime.
6 A.R. Doi, *Shari'a: the Islamic law*, London: Ta Ha Publishers, 1984, p.289.
7 *Encyclopédie de l'islam*, Paris: Maisonneuve et Larose, 1991, vol.6, p.452.
8 Qur'an, Sura 2, verse 223.
9 Louis Milliot, *Introduction à l'étude du droit musulman*, Paris: Recueil Sirey, 1953, p.98; cited in *Encyclopédie de l'islam, op. cit.*, p.452.
10 Quoted by Muhammad Hamidullah, *Introduction to Islam*, New Delhi: Kitab Bhavan, 1992, p.185.
11 *La femme musulmane, ses droits et ses devoirs*, Saudi Arabia: WAMY, Dar Al-Elm Printing, 1997, p.3.
12 Nikolaus Rhodokanakis, in *Proceedings of the Twenty-Second Congress of Orientalists*, Istanbul, 1951, Leyden 1957; see also *Encyclopédie de l'islam, op. cit.*, p.458.
13 Nikolaus Rhodokanakis, *op. cit.*, p.7; see also *Encyclopédie de l'islam, op. cit.*, p.459.
14 Nikolaus Rhodokanakis, *op. cit.*, p.9; Qur'an, Sura 4, verses 128–30.
15 Nikolaus Rhodokanakis, *op. cit.*, p.5.
16 Nikolaus Rhodokanakis, *op. cit.*, p.11.
17 Qur'an, Sura 4, verse 19.
18 See *Encyclopédie de l'islam, op. cit.*, p.455ff.
19 Abu al-Faraj al-Isfahani (ed.), Ahmad Al-Shanqiti, *Kitab al-Aghani*, Cairo: Matba'at Al Takkadum, 1905–6, p.58 and p.150; see also *Encyclopédie de l'islam, op. cit.*, vol.6, p.455.
20 Abd Al-Ati Hammuda, *Islam in Focus*, Riyadh: WAMY, n.d.
21 Ahmad Fakhri, *Al-Yaman Madiha Wa-Diruha*, Cairo: 1970, p.110, quoted in *Encyclopédie de l'islam, op. cit.*, p.460.
22 *Encyclopédie de l'islam, op. cit.*, p.460.
23 Ibid.
24 Muhammad Hamidullah, *Initiation à l'islam* (a publication of the 'Amicale des musulmans en France'), Paris: Imprimeries de Carthage, 1963, p.95.

25   Will Durant, *Histoire de la civilisation (La Judée, la Perse, l'Inde)*, vol.2, Paris: Payot, pp.95–6, quoted by Ayatollah Morteza Motahari, Teheran: Organisation for the Propagation of Islam, 1993, pp.12–13.

26   Morteza Motahari, *op. cit.*, p.12ff.

27   Jawharlal Nehru, *Glimpses of World History*, New Delhi: Oxford University Press/J. Nehru Memorial Fund, 1989, p.148.

28   Qur'an, Sura 33, verse 59.

29   See the relevant comments of Tariq Ramadan in *Le Courrier* (Geneva), 10 September 2002. It should be noted, however, that Tariq Ramadan has also suggested that lapidation should be the object of a moratorium, rather than an outright ban, which shocked western intellectuals. See www.lexpress.fr/actualite/societe/religion/extraits-exclusifs_488295.html

30   Qur'an, Sura 4, verses 7–12.

31   See Dominique and Janine Sourdel, *Dictionnaire historique de l'islam*, Paris: PUF, 1996, p.347.

32   The Shi'ite tradition may be found at: http://users.skynet.be/yassine/fadak1.htm. The Shi'ite Hadith can be found at Usul-Kafi, Bab al-Fayi', Al-Anfal wal-Khums, Hadith 1400. A contrary Sunni opinion, from Mufti Taqi Usmani and Sheikh Muhammad Sarfraz Khan, can be found at http://perso.guetali.fr/mohmdpat/fadak1.html. See also Abdulaziz A. Sachedina, *The Just Ruler: the Comprehensive Authority of the Jurist in the Imamite Jurisprudence*, Oxford University Press, 1988, p.9ff.

33   Qur'an, Sura 17, verse 26.

34   See above: note 31.

35   See Abdel Wahab Boudhiba, *Sexuality in Islam*, London: Routledge and Kegan Paul, 1985.

36   *La Quintessence du Sahih Al-Bokhari, op. cit.*, p.168, Hadith 499.

37   Michel Random, *Mawlana Djalal-ud-Din Rumi*, Tunis: Sud Editions, p.118.

38   Qusta Ibn Luqa, *The book of characters*, edited and translated by Paul Sbath, *Bulletin de l'institut d'Egypte*, 23 (1940–1), pp.103–39. See also J. Boswell, 'Revolutions, Universals, and Sexual Categories' in Martin Duberman, Martha Vicinus and George Chauncey, Jr., *Hidden from History: Reclaiming the Gay and Lesbian Past*, New York: Meridian, 1989, available at http://www.hem.passagen.se/nicb/boswell.htm

39   See Qusta Ibn Luqa, *op. cit.*, p.112ff.

40   A. Reza Arasteh, *Final Integration in the Adult Personality*, Leiden: E.J. Brill, 1965.

41   Muhammad Hamidullah, *Documents sur la diplomatie musulmane du Prophète et des khalifes orthodoxes*, Paris: Maisonneuve, 1935, p.24.

42 Qur'an, Sura 9, verse 6.

43 Abdul-Rahman Arabi, *L'islam et la guerre à l'époque de Mahomet*, unpublished thesis, Université de Lausanne, 1955.

44 Qur'an, Sura 9, verse 6.

45 Marcel Boisard, *L'humanisme de l'islam*, Paris: Albin Michel, 1979, p.177.

46 Ibn Taymiyya, *Majmu'at ar-rasa'il al-kubra*, Cairo: Al-Manar, 1924, vol.1, p.229. See also Henri Laoust, *Essai sur les doctrines, op. cit.*, p.266.

47 Hélène Vandevelde, *Cours d'histoire du droit musulman et des institutions musulmanes*, Algiers: Office des Publications Universitaires, 1983.

48 Rodrigo de Zayas, *Les morisques et le racisme d'Etat*, Paris: La Différence, 1992; see also the same author in *Le Monde Diplomatique*, March 1997.

49 Louis Gardet, *Les hommes de l'islam – approche des mentalités*, Paris: Complexe, 1977, p.98.

50 Ibid.

51 See Badria Al-Awadi, *International Law*, Kuwait, 1979.

52 Louis Gardet, *Les Hommes . . .* , *op. cit.*, p.99; Said Ramadan, *Le shari'a – le droit islamique, son envergure et son équité*, Paris: Al-Qalam, 1997, p.154ff.

53 Abdel-Rahman Ghandour, *Jihad humanitaire – enquête sur les ONG islamistes*, Paris: Flammarion, 2002, p.32ff.

CHAPTER 5

1 Hamed Sultan, 'La conception islamique', in *Dimensions internationales du droit humanitaire*, Paris: Pedone, 1986, p.47.

2 Abubaker Djaber Eldjazairi, *La voie du musulman*, vol.2, Medina: Aslim Editions, 1986, pp.531, 534.

3 Attributed to the Caliph Abu Bakr, and quoted in Marcel Boisard, *L'humanisme de l'islam*, Paris: Albin Michel, 1985, p.259.

4 Abdur Rahman Doi, *Shari'a: the Islamic law*, London: Ta Ha Publishers, 1984, p.221.

5 Abubaker Djaber Eldjazairi, *La voie du musulman*, vol.2, Medina: Aslim Editions, 1986, p.544.

6 Ibid., p.543.

7 Qur'an, Sura 16, verses 126–8. On the Muslim doctrine relating to peace, war and prisoners of war see the excellent treatment by Abu Yusuf Yaqub Ibn Ibrahim Al-Ansari Al-Kufi (745–93), an Iraqi-born adviser to the Caliph Harun Al-Rashid, in his *Kitab Al-Kharaj*, translated by Edmond Fagnan, *Le livre de l'impôt foncier*, Paris: Paul Geuthner, 1921. The classic treatment by the Hanbali theologian Ibn

Qudama is to be found in Henri Laoust (translator and ed.), *Précis de droit d'Ibn Qudama*, Beirut: Institut français de Damas, p.268ff.

8   Ameur Zemmali, *Combattants et prisonniers de guerre en droit islamique et en droit international humanitaire*, Paris: Pedone, p.418ff.

9   Ibn Taymiyya, *Lettre à un roi croisé*, translation Jean Yahya Michot, Lyon: Tawhid, 1995.

10 Ibid.

11 Salah al-Din al-Munajjid (ed.), *Muhammad ibn Ahmad al-Sarakhsi, Commentary on Muhammad ibn al-Hasan al-Shaybani: Sharh Kitab al-Siyar al-Kabir*, Cairo: Institute of Manuscripts: League of Arab States, 1971, p.43 ff. On these issues, see also Ameur Zemmali, *op. cit.*, p.109ff., and John A. Williams, *Themes of Islamic Civilization*, University of California Press, 1972, p.262; and Sohail H. Hashimi, 'Interpreting the Islamic Ethics of War and Peace', in Terry Nardin, *The Ethics of War and Peace*, Princeton University Press, 1998, p.161. On the precise issue of the protection of monasteries and synagogues, see Abu Yusuf Yaqub, *op. cit.*, p.213ff.

12 Shawgi Dayf, *L'universalité de l'islam*, Rabat: ISESCO, 1998, p.33ff.

13 Henri Galland, *Essais sur les mo'tazelites*, Doctoral Thesis, Geneva, printed W. Kundig, 1906, p.24. *Kalam* or *Ilm Al-Kalam* (the science of disputation) was employed by the Islamic rationalists.

14 For the statements by the Prophet Muhammad and by Omar, see Abu Yusuf Yaqub, *op. cit.*, p.110, and Hamed Sultan, *op. cit.*, p.58.

15 Hamed Sultan, *op. cit.*, p.54.

16 Said El-Dakkak, 'Le droit international humanitaire entre la conception islamique et le droit positif', *Revue internationale de la Croix-Rouge (RICR)*, March–April 1990, p.111ff.; M Abuzalma, 'la théorie de la guerre en Islam', *Revue égyptienne de droit international*, 1958, p. 30.

17 Yadh Ben Achour, 'Islam et droit international humanitaire', *RICR*, March–April, p.9.ff.

18 Tarikh Al-Tabari, New Cairo Edition, vol.3, 1962, pp.226–7, translated in John A. Williams, *Themes of Islamic Civilization*, University of California Press, 1972, p.262; see also Sohail H. Hashimi, 'Interpreting the Islamic Ethics of War and Peace', in Terry Nardin, *The Ethics of War and Peace*, Princeton University Press, 1998, p.161.

19 Sayyid Qutb, *Islam, religion of the future, op. cit.*

20 Sayyid Qutb, *Islam par le martyre*, Riyadh: International Islamic Publishing House, 1994, pp.103, 116, 151ff.

21 On Bin Laden's position, see the text of Bin Laden's policy statement, document no.5 in Roland Jacquard, *Les archives secrètes d'Al-Qaïda*, Paris: Jean Picollec, 2002, p.237 ff. For the GIA and Hattab, see *Le Matin* (Algeria), 18 September 2001; El-Djamaa, no.13, 1997 (the secret

GIA bulletin); and AFP, 26 August 1997, quoted in Hassane Zerrouky, *La nébuleuse islamiste en France et en Algérie*, Paris: Editions 1, 2002, p.274ff. and p.360, n.28ff. See also report no.3460, *Les conséquences pour la France des attentats du 11 Septembre* 2001, submitted in December 2001 to the National Assembly of France.

22   On Al-Banna's concept of Jihad, see Bassam Tibi in Terry Nardin, *The Ethics of War and Peace*, Princeton University Press, 1998, p.138ff.

23   See Muhammed Essam Derbala, writing in *Sharq Al-Awsat*, 16 January 2004.

24   Abdullah Azzam, *Fil-Jihaad: Adaab wa Akhaam*, Beirut: Al-Hazm and Maktabat al-Jil al-Jadid, 1992. Extracts appear in www.islamicawakening.com. See also *Military Studies in the Jihad against the Tyrants*, published in English on the site of the United American Civil Taskforce (UACT), www.uact.1.com

25   *Le Matin,* 19 September 2002, www.lematin-dz.net/19092002/jourilyaquatreans.htm

26   See Muhammed Sifaoui, *Mes 'frères' assassins – comment j'ai infiltré une cellule d'Al-Qaïda*, Paris: Le Cherche-Midi, 2003, p.86.

27   *International Herald Tribune,* 22 May 2003.

28   See the study by André Andries, 'Rapport sur les sciences humaines et crimes de guerre', *Revue de droit militaire et de droit de la guerre*, 30, 1992, p.14ff. See also Jean-Pierre Chrétien, *Le défi de l'ethnisme: Rwanda et Burundi, 1990–1996*, Paris: Karthala, 1997, p.395; and Isaac Ngema, *Review of the Commission on Human and Peoples' Rights*, vol.4, 1994, p.60ff.

CHAPTER 6

1   Louis Gardet, *Les hommes de l'islam* . . ., *op. cit*, p.201ff.

2   Louis Gardet, *La cité musulmane, vie sociale et politique*, Paris: Vrin, 1954, quoted by Hélène Vandevelde, *Cours d'histoire du droit musulman . . .*, *op. cit.*, p.98.

3   See William Zartmann, 'Pouvoir et Etat dans l'islam', *Pouvoirs . . .*, *op. cit.*, p.8.

4   Ibid., p.5.

5   Ibid., p.11.

PART TWO

INTRODUCTION

1 Aziz Nasafi, *Maqsad-i Aqsa*, appended to Jami, *Ashi'at l-Lama'at*, Teheran: H. Rabbani, 1973. This is quoted in Lloyd Ridgeon, *Aziz Nasafi*, Richmond: Curzon Press, 1988, p.83. See also Lloyd Ridgeon (translator and ed.), *Aziz Nasafi, Persian Metaphysics and Mysticism, selected Works of Aziz Nasafi*, Richmond: Curzon Press, 2002; and Aziz Nasafi, *Kitab al-insan al-kamil*, French translation from the Persian by Isabelle de Gastines, Paris: Fayard, 1984.

2 The concept of 'reform', which implies an innovative approach, would more naturally be applied to the rationalist philosophers, such as the mu'tazilites, and to Ibn Rushd and Ibn Sina, as well as Jamal Ad-Din Al-Afghani and Muhammad Abduh in more recent times, as well as to the Sufi schools of Ibn Al-Arabi and Rumi.

3 Dominique Urvoy, *Les penseurs libres dans l'islam classique: l'interrogation sur la religion chez les penseurs arabes indépendants*, Paris: Flammarion, 2003, p.217. For a treatment of Ibn Al-Muqaffa, see ibid., p.29ff.

4 Ibid.

5 Sarah Stroumsa, *Free Thinkers of Medieval Islam: Ibn al-Rawandi, Abu Bakr al-Razi and their impact on Islamic thought*, Leiden: Brill, 1999.

CHAPTER 7

1 The texts and sermons of Wasil Ibn Ata in Arabic and German are introduced with a commentary in *Islamic Philosophy and Theology*, vol. 2, Leiden: E.J. Brill, 1988. Wasil Ibn Ata's views are reported by a classic chronicle writer named Al-Mas'udi in *Moroudj al-Dhahab (Meadows of Gold)*, Arabic text edited and translated by Charles Barbier de Meynard and Able Pavet de Courteille, Paris: Société Asiatique, 1861–77, vol.6 p.22ff.

2 Baron Bernard Carra de Vaux, *Les penseurs de l'islam*, vol.1, *Les souverains, l'histoire et la philosophie politique*, Paris: Paul Geuthner, 1921, p.8.

3 Henri Laoust, *Les schismes dans l'islam*, *op. cit.*, p.102.

4 For more details, see Louis Gardet and George Chehata (M–M) Anawati, *Introduction à la théologie musulmane*, Paris: J. Vrin, 1948, p.49.

5 Ibid., p.791.

6 Henri Terrasse, *Islam d'Espagne: une rencontre de l'Orient et l'Occident*, Paris: Plon, 1958, p.65.

7   Louis Gardet, *op. cit.*, p.307.

8   www.sunnah.org/sources/Hadith_utlub_ilm.htm

9   www.sunnah.org/ibadaat/albani.htm

10 See the collection of Hadith compiled by A.R.I. Doi, *Introduction to the Hadith*, Zaria: Hudahuda Publishing Company, 1983, p.95ff.

11 See Anna Alter, *L'événement*, Paris, 11–17 February 1993, and the same author, 'L'islam et la science: le problème de la *qibla*', *La Recherche*, Paris, February 1987.

12 See 'Ibn Sina', in *Encyclopédie de l'islam, op. cit.*, vol.3, p.967.

13 Al-Farabi's original text on the 12 qualities of the imam of the virtuous city may be found in *Idées des habitants de la cité vertueuse*, translated by Youssef Karam, J. Chlala and R.P. Janssen, Beirut and Cairo: Commission libanaise pour la traduction des chefs-d'oeuvre, Institut français d'archéologie orientale, Librairie Orientale, 1980, p.93ff.

14 See Dominique and Janine Sourdel, *op. cit.*, p.482, and Yves Thoraval, *op. cit.*, p.159.

15 Ibn Sina, *Al-shifa*, vol. 9: *Al-Ilahiyat*, ed. Anawati and Zaid, Cairo: 1960, p.431, quoted in Meryem Sebti, 'La distinction entre intellect pratique et intellect théorique dans la doctrine de l'âme humaine d'Avicenne', in *Philosophie arabe*, Paris: Editions de Minuit, p.43. See also *Encyclopédie de l'islam, op. cit.*, p.968.

16 Louis Gardet, *Etudes de philosophie et de mystique comparées*, Paris: J. Vrin, 1972, p.43. See also *Encyclopédie de l'islam, op. cit.*, p.958.

17 Al-Ghazali, *Tahafut al-falasifa*, Cairo: Dar Al-Ma'arif, 1961, p.1ff. See also Dominique and Janine Sourdel, *op. cit.*, p.312ff.

18 See Abd Al-Rahman Badawi, *Averroès (Ibn Rushd)*, Paris: J. Vrin, 1998, p.9ff.; Roger Arnaldez, *Averroès: un rationaliste en islam*, Paris: Balland, 1998, p.15ff.

19 See Dariush Shayegan, *Qu'est-ce qu'une révolution religieuse?* Paris: Les Presses d'Aujourd'hui, 1982, p.94.

20 *Encyclopédie de l'islam, op. cit.*, vol. 3, p.935.

21 Ernest Gilson, *La philosophie du Moyen Age*, vol.1, Paris: Payot, 1976, p.359.

22 See Ibn Rushd's original text in *Averroès, discours décisifs*, translated by Marc Geoffroy and Alain de Libera, Paris: Flammarion, 1976, p.117. See also *Averroes, Commentary on Plato's Republic*, edited and translated by E.J. Rosenthal, Cambridge University Press, 1956, p.117. In addition, see Ernest Gilson, *op. cit.*, p.359.

23 Ernest Gilson, ibid.

24 Roger Arnaldez, *Averroès, op. cit.*, p.68. See also *Encyclopédie de l'islam, op. cit.* p.939.

25 *Encyclopédie de l'islam, op. cit.*, p.941; Ernest Gilson, *op. cit.*, p.366ff.

26 Ernest Lavisse, *Histoire de France depuis les origines jusqu'à la Révolution*, Paris: Hachette, 1901, vol.3, p.392.

27 Ibid.

28 Henri Corbin, 'En Orient, après Averroès', in *Multiple Averroès; actes du colloque international à l'occasion du 850e anniversaire de la naissance d'Averroès*, ed. Jean Jolivet, Paris: Les Belles Lettres, 1978, p.326.

29 Ernest Renan, *Averroès et l'averroïsme, essai historique*, Paris; 8th edition, p.111; Henri Corbin, *op. cit.*, p.323.

30 On the ideas of Ben Badis, see Ali Merad, *Le réformisme musulman en Algérie de 1925 à 1940: essai d'histoire religieuse et sociale*, Paris: Mouton, 1967. For an assessment of Sheikh Al-Alawi, see Khaled Bentounes, *Le soufisme: coeur de l'islam*, Paris: La Table Ronde, p.92ff. and p.225ff.

31 For a discussion of Muhammad's spiritual legacy to Ali, see Henri Laoust, *Essai sur les doctrines sociales et politiques de Taki-d-Din Ahmad B. Taimiya* [Ibn Taymiyya], Cairo: Institut français d'archéologie orientale, 1939, p.201.

32 Ibn Khaldun, *Discours sur l'histoire universelle: Al-Muqaddima*, trans. Vincent Monteil, Paris: Sindbad, p.171.

33 See Ibn al-Arabi, *Les illuminations de la Mecque*, an anthology edited by Michel Chodkiewicz, Paris: Albin Michel, 1997.

34 For further details on monasticism in Egypt, see Otto Meinardus, *Monks and Monasteries of the Egyptian Desert*, Cairo: American University in Cairo Press, 1989.

35 Translated by Henri Corbin, *L'imagination créatrice dans le soufisme d'Ibn al-Arabi*, Paris: Flammarion, 1977 (2nd edition), p.109. See also Claude Addas, *Ibn al-Arabi ou la quête du soufre rouge*, Paris: Gallimard, 1989, pp.252–3.

36 Ali Hudjwiri, *Kashf al-mahdjub*, quoted in Michel Random, *op. cit.*, p.134.

37 See *Islamic Spirituality: Manifestations*, ed. Seyyed Hossein Nasr, New York: The Crossroad Publishing Company, 1977, p.22.

38 See the extensive study of Al-Hallaj by Louis Massignon, *La Passion d'Al-Husayn Ibn Mansur Al-Hallaj, martyr mystique de l'islam exécuté le 26 mars 922*, Paris: Gallimard, 1922, new edition in 4 vols.

39 Daniel Massignon, *Présence de Louis Massignon: hommages et témoignages*, Paris: Maisonneuve et Larose, 1987, p.114.

40 See 'Al-Hallaj' in *Encyclopedia of Islam*, Leiden: Brill, 1986, vol.3, p.100.

41 See Yves Thoraval, *op. cit.*, p.126.

42 See 'Qaramita' in Ian Richard Netton, *A Popular Dictionary of Islam*, London: Curzon Press, 1992, p.203.

43 Boubker Philip Bennani, *L'islamisme et les droits de l'homme*, op. cit., p.42.
44 Louis Massignon, *op. cit.*, pp.56–7.
45 Ibid., p.676.
46 Michel Random, *op. cit.*, p.57 and p.80.
47 Titus Burckhardt, introduction to Michel Random, *op. cit.*, p.6.
48 Michel Random, *op. cit.*, p.44.
49 From *Mathnawi*, quoted in Coleman Barks, ed. and trans, *The essential Rumi*, London: Penguin Books, 1995, p.49.
50 Rumi, *Mathnawi*, Eva de Vitray-Meyerovitch and Djami Mortazawi, Paris: Editions du Rocher, 1990, (couplets 2330–40), p.434.
51 On Afghani and Abduh's Sufism, see Nikki Keddie, *Sayyid Jamal ad-Din al-Afghani: a political biography*, Berkeley: University of California Press; and Muhammad Abduh, *Rissalat al-Tawhid*, translated by B. Michel and M. Abdel Razik, Paris: Geuthner, 1925.

CHAPTER 8

1 Simone Van Riet, *Introduction à l'histoire contemporaine*, Brussels: MMC-initiations, 1962, p.47.
2 Ibid.
3 See A. Belkziz, *The State in Contemporary Muslim Thought* (in Arabic), Beirut: Centre for Studies in Arab Unity, 2002, p.44ff.
4 Homa Pakdaman, ed. and trans, *Djamal-ed-Din Assad Abadi dit Afghani* (texts by and about Al-Afghani), Paris: Maisonneuve et Larose, 1969, p.194 and p.312.
5 Ibid., p.195.
6 Amélie-Marie Goichon, *Jamal ad-Din al-Afghani: réfutation des matérialistes* (translation of *Risalat al-Radd ala al-Dahriin* 'The Refutation of the Materialists'), Paris: Paul Geuthner, 1942, pp.166–7.
7 Jamal Ad-Din Al-Afghani, *Madalat-e Jamaliyye* (in Persian), French translation of the text annexed to Homa Pakdaman, *op. cit.*, p.279.
8 Amélie-Marie Goichon (trans), *Réfutation des matérialistes*, op. cit.
9 Introduction to *Risalat al-Tawhid* by Muhammad Abduh, translated by B. Michel and M. Abdel Razik, *op. cit.*, p.xxiii.
10 Amélie-Marie Goichon (trans), *Réfutation des matérialistes*, op. cit., p.42.
11 Ibid., pp. 67, 73, 82.
12 Ibid., p.5.
13 Ibid., p.85.
14 Ibid., p.126.
15 Ibid., p.138.

16 Ibid., p.73ff.
17 Ernest Renan, *L'islam et la science* (avec la réponse d'Al-Afghani), Montpellier: L'Archange Minotaure, 2003, p.9.
18 Henri Laoust, *Les schismes* . . . , *op. cit.*, p.346.
19 Dominique and Janine Sourdel, *Dictionnaire historique, op. cit.*, p.17.
20 Henri Laoust, *Les schismes* . . . , *op. cit.*, p.347.
21 Ibid., p.347.
22 See Muhammad Abduh, *Risalat al-Tawhid, op. cit.*; see also A. Belkziz, *op. cit.*, p.48ff.
23 Muhammad Abduh, *op. cit.*, p.27ff.
24 Ibid., p.42.
25 Ibid., p.xliv.
26 Ibid., p.77.
27 Ibid., p.lxxx and p.116.
28 Ibid., p.116 and p.125.
29 Ibid., p.129.
30 Ibid.
31 See Bernard Lewis, *The World of Islam: Faith, People, Culture*, London: Thames and Hudson, 1992, p.333.
32 For details on these reformers, see R. Alili, *Qu'est-ce que l'islam?* Paris: La Découverte, 2000, p.308ff.
33 Abd Al-Rahman Al-Kawakibi, *Taba'i al-istibdad wa masari' al-ist'ibad* (in Arabic), Beirut: Centre for Arab Unity Studies, 1995, p.430; quoted in A. Belkziz, *op. cit.*, p.35.
34 Abd Al-Rahman Al-Kawakibi, *op. cit.*, p.438ff.; see also A. Belkziz, *op. cit.*, p.55ff.
35 A. Belkziz, *op. cit.*, p.68.
36 Abd Al-Rahman Al-Kawakibi, *Umm Al-Qura*, the full text is given in the study by Jamal Tahan, Aleppo: Dar Al-Awal, 2002.
37 Ibid., p.30, p.26, and p.154ff.
38 Ibid., p.29ff.
39 Ibid., p.155ff.
40 Ibid., p.156.
41 Ibid., p.31 and p.161.
42 Ibid., p.177 and p.205 ff.
43 For a longer list of names, see Louis Gardet, *Les hommes de l'islam, op. cit.*, pp.329ff.
44 See Abd Al-Rahman Badawi, *La transmission de la philosophie grecque dans le monde arabe*, Paris: Vrin, 1968.
45 Adel Darwish, 'Abdel Rahman Badawi: free-thinking existentialist philosopher', *The Independent*, 7 August 2002.
46 Ali Abderraziq, *L'islam et les fondements du pouvoir, op. cit.* See also

Abdou Filali-Ansary, *Réformer l'islam? Une introduction aux débats contemporains*, Paris: Le Découverte, 2003, p.95–112; and Louis Gardet, *op. cit.*, p.355ff.

47 Samir Amin, *Eurocentrism*, London: Zed Books, 1989.

48 Nawal Saadawi, *The Hidden Face of Eve: women in the Arab world*, Boston: Beacon Press, 1982.

49 Abdallah Laroui, *L'histoire du Maghreb: un essai de synthèse*, Casablanca: Centre Culturel Arabe, 1995.

50 See Abdou Filali-Ansary, *op. cit.*, pp.127–40.

51 Ibid., pp.167–73, 221–9.

52 See for example, Muhammed Arkoun, *L'humanisme arabe, IVe-Xe siècles*, Paris: Vrin, 2005 (3rd edition); and *Pour une critique de la raison islamique*, Paris: *Islam d'hier et d'aujourd'hui*, vol. 24, 1984.

53 Edward W. Said, *Orientalism*, New York: Pantheon Books, 1978.

54 For a more complete list of Muslim modernists, see Abdou Filali-Ansary, *op. cit.*, p.1ff., and the same author writing in *Courrier de l'Unesco*, November 2001, p.40.

55 Ziad Hafez, 'De nouveaux penseurs', *Le Monde Diplomatique: Manière de voir*, 64, July–August 2002, p.89.

CHAPTER 9

1 Henri Laoust, *op. cit.*

2 On the views of the Mu'tazilites regarding the punishment of serious misdemeanours, see Si Hamza Boubakeur, *Traité moderne de théologie islamique*, Paris: Maisonneuve et Larose, 1985, p.378ff.

3 Abol Hassan Bani Sadr, *Le Coran et les droits de l'homme*, Paris: Maisonneuve et Larose, 1989, p.68.

4 Leïla Babès and Tareq Oubrou, *Loi d'Allah, loi des hommes*, Paris: Albin Michel, 2002.

5 Salman Rushdie, *The Satanic Verses*, London: Viking Penguin, 1988.

6 Ruthven, Malise, *A Satanic Affair: Salman Rushdie and the Rage of Islam*, London: Chatto & Windus, 1990.

7 *Time*, 21 September 1998.

8 Louis Gardet, *Les hommes de l'islam . . . , op. cit.*, p.98.

9 Choucri Cardahi, 'La conception et la pratique du droit international privé dans l'islam', *Recueil des cours de l'Académie de droit international*, vol.60, The Hague, 1937, part 2, pp.511–642.

10 See Yves Thoraval, *op. cit.*, p.1.

11 Eric Geoffroy, *Le soufisme en Egypte et en Syrie sous les derniers Mamelouks et les premiers Ottomans*, Institut français de Damas, 1995, p.70.

12   Louis Gardet, *L'islam, religion et communauté*, Paris: Desclée de
     Brouwer, 1967, p.340.

13   Maurice Flory and Robert Mantran, *Les régimes politiques des pays
     arabes*, Paris: PUF, 1968, p.138, and Hélène Vandevelde, *Cours d'histoire*,
     op. cit., p.231.

14   E.I.J. Rosenthal (ed.), *Averroes' Commentary on Plato's Republic*,
     Cambridge University Press, 1956, p.166. See also E.I.J. Rosenthal,
     Political Thought in Medieval Islam, Cambridge University Press, 1958,
     p.191.

15   Javad Nurbakhsh, *Sufi Women*, New York: Khaniqahi-Nimatullah
     Publications, 1983, p.22.

16   Michel Random, *op. cit.*, p.118.

17   See Louis Gardet, 'Notion et principes de l'éducation dans la pensée
     arabo-musulmane', *Revue des études islamiques*, 44, 1976, pp.1–13.

18   For an account, see *Jeune Afrique*, November 1997, no.1887, p.43.

19   Hanifa Cherifi, 'Le voile est un piège qui isole et marginalise',
     Le Monde, 16–17 December 2001.

20   See Leïla Babès and Tareq Oubrou, *op. cit.*, p.181ff.

21   Ibid., p.202.

22   Ibid.

23   See for example, 'Why can't a woman be (paid) more like a man?'
     The Observer, 20 January 2002.

24   According to a study summarised in the *Sunday Times*: 'Freedom has
     its price, girls', *Sunday Times*, 7 April 2002.

25   Malek Chebel, 'Sexualité, pouvoir et problématique du sujet en Islam',
     in 'Sexualité et sociétés arabes', *Confluences Méditerrannée*, 41, Spring
     2002, p.17. Also in www.ifrance.com/confluences/numeros/41.htm.
     See also the same author's *Encyclopédie de l'amour en Islam*, Paris:
     Payot, 1995.

26   Eva de Vitray-Meyerovitch, *Rumi and Sufism*, Sausalito, CA: Post
     Apollo Press, 1987, p.101.

27   Michel Random, *op. cit.*, p.118.

28   Chérif Bassiouni, reviewing Hilmi M. Zawati, *Is Jihad a Just War? War,
     Peace, and Human Rights under Islamic and Public International Law*,
     Lewiston, NY: Edwin Mellen Press, 2001, in *The American Journal of
     International Law*, vol.96, 2002, p.1001.

29   See Bassam Tibi, in Terry Nardin, *op. cit.*, p.138.

PART THREE

CHAPTER 10

1   See Paul Balta, *L'islam dans le monde*, Paris: La Découverte, 1986, pp.25–6.

2   See Jules Cambon, introduction, Octave Depont and Xavier, *Les confréries religieuses musulmanes*, Alger: Editions Jourdan, 1897, p.xiv. See also General Pierre-Jacques André, *Contribution à l'étude des confréries religieuses musulmanes*, Alger: La Maison de Livres, 1956.

3   Cambon, ibid., p.xiv.

4   Emile Dermenghem, *Vie des saints musulmans*, Paris: Editions d'Aujourd'hui, 1981, p.95.

5   Sayyed Hossein Nasr, *Islamic Spirituality, op. cit.*, p.198.

6   Ibid., p.203.

7   Frederik de Jong, 'Tasawwuf', in *Encyclopedia of Islam*, Leiden: Brill, 2000, p.324.

8   Ibid., p.324ff.

9   Ibid.

10 Henri Chambert Loir and Claude Guillot, *Le culte des saints dans le monde musulman*, Paris: Ecole française d'Extrême-Orient, 1995, p.76.

11 Rachida Chih, 'Les confréries soufies dans l'Egypte contemporaine', *MARS Revue de l'institut du monde arabe*, 8, 1997, p.33.

12 A. Yasar Ocak, 'Opposition au soufisme dans l'Empire Ottoman aux xvème et xvième siècles', in F. De Jong and B. Radtke (eds), *Islamic Mysticism Contested: thirteen centuries of controversies and polemics*, Leiden: Brill, 1999, p.603ff.

13 Ibid., p.607.

14 Ibid., p.610.

15 *Encyclopedia of Islam*, vol.10, *op. cit.*, p.333.

16 Ibid.

17 See Irène Melikoff, *Hadji Bektach, un mythe et ses avatars – genèse et évolution du soufisme populaire en Turquie*, Leiden: Brill, 1998.

18 H.L. Kieser, *The Alevis' Ambivalent Encounter with Modernity: Islam, Reform and Ethnolopolitics in Turkey (19th and 20th centuries)*, conference paper, University of Wales, November 2001, forthcoming.

19 See Elizabeth Sirriyeh, *Sufis and anti-Sufis: the defence, rethinking and rejection of Sufism in the modern world*, Richmond, Surrey: Curzon Press, 1999.

20 Nathalie Clayer and Alexandre Popovic, 'Les courants anticonfrériques dans le Sud-Est européen à l'époque post-ottomane (1918–1990): les cas de la Yougoslavie et de l'Albanie', in F. De Jong and B. Radtke

(eds), *Islamic Mysticism Contested: thirteen centuries of controversies and polemics*, Leiden: Brill, 1999.

21 See Abdallah Laroui, *L'histoire du Maghreb, op. cit.*

22 See René-Luc Moreau, *Africains musulmans*, Paris: Présence africaine, 1982, p.175; and senegalmaur.ifrance.com/islamnoir.html

23 Elizabeth Sirriyeh, *op. cit.*, pp.30–1.

24 Ibid., p.31.

25 Malise Ruthven, *Islam in the World*, 2nd edition, London: Penguin Books, p.291.

26 Elizabeth Sirriya, *op. cit.*, p.34.

27 Bouziane Daoudi, 'Inauguration of the series "Méditerranée; Méditerranées" at the Institut du Monde Arabe', 2002.

28 Ibid.

29 Boubker Belkadi in *Bulletin d'information sur l'Algérie*, May 2000.

30 Ibid. the same author is quoted expressing similar sentiments by Abdel Rahman Ghandour, *Jihad humanitaire*, p.92.

31 Ibid.

CHAPTER 11

1 Symposium on religion, Abidjan, 5–12 April 1961, reported in *Présence africaine*, 1961, p.119.

2 Abdel Rahman Ghandour, *op. cit.*, p.91.

3 Paul Balta, *L'islam dans le monde*, Paris: La Décourverte, 1986, p.259.

4 Jean-Louis Triaud, 'Islam et confréries en Afrique subsaharienne', *MARS Revue de l'Institut du Monde Arabe*, no.8, 1997, p.47.

5 Gérard Prunier, 'Le mouvement des Ansars au Soudan depuis la fin de l'Etat mahdiste (1898–1987)', *Islam et sociétés au sud du Sahara*, journal published by Editions de la Maison des Sciences de l'Homme, no.2, 1988, p.73.

EPILOGUE

1 Ernest Psichari, *Le voyage du centurion*, Paris: Louis Conard, 1947, pp.224–6. See also Philippe Lucas and Jean-Claude Vatin, *L'Algérie des anthropologues*, Paris: Maspero, 1979, p.178.

2 P. Lucas and J-C. Vatin, *op. cit.*, p.129.

3 Philippe Lucas and Jean-Claude Vatin, *L'Algérie des anthropologues*, Paris: Maspero, 1979, p.129. See also Auguste Pomel, *Des races indigènes de l'Algérie et du rôle que leur réservent leurs aptitudes*, Oran: Veuve Dagorn, 1871, p.5ff.

4   Ibid., p.130ff.
5   Auguste Pomel, *op. cit.*, pp.5–7
6   Ernest Renan, *De la part des peuples sémitiques dans l'histoire de la civilisation*, lecture to the Collège de France, 23 February 1862, Paris: Michel Lévy Frères, 1875.
7   Oriana Fallaci, *La rage et l'orgueil*, Paris: Plon, 2002.
8   Oriana Fallaci, *Corriere della Sera*, 29 September 2001.
9   H.A. Amin, 'Religious impediments to cultural exchanges in the Council of Europe' (Lecture, May 1991), Strasbourg: Editions du Conseil de l'Europe, 1991, p.1ff., duplicated typescript; see also Osama Ibn Munqidh, translated by P. Halsall, Fordham University Center for Medieval Studies, www.fordham.edu/halsall/source/usamah2.html
10 H.A. Amin, *op. cit.*, p.1.
11 See Henri Teissier (Archbishop of Algiers), 'Chrétiens et musulmans, cinquante années pour approfondir leurs relations', *Islamochristiana*, 26, 2000, Rome: Pontificio Istituto di Studi Arabi ed Islamistica, 2001.
12 Edward Said, *Covering Islam*, New York: Pantheon Books, 1981, pp.4–23.
13 Samuel P. Huntington, 'The Clash of Civilizations?', *Foreign Affairs*, Summer 1993.
14 See Joseph Nye, *Soft Power: The Means to Success in World Politics*, New York: Public Affairs 2004.
15 *Dialogue Among Civilisations*, New Delhi, 9–10 July 2003; *Dialogue Among Civilisations*, Sana'a, 10–11 February 2004; *Education for Shared Values for Interfaith Understanding*, Adelaide, 28 November–3 December 2004 (published 2005); proceedings published by Editions UNESCO, Paris. See also A. Wigger, 'Rencontres de points de vue dans certaines parties du monde musulman et leur impact sur l'efficacité du CICR', *Revue internationale de la Croix-Rouge (RICR)*, 858, Geneva, 2005.
16 Mutoy Mubiala, 'Les droits de l'homme dans les processus de paix en Afrique', *Revue Congo-Afrique*, Kinshasa, December 2005, p.535ff.
17 See www.cswusa.com/reports, Nigeria, 22 November 2004.
18 See H. Charabi, *Al nizam al-abawi wa ishkaliyat takhaluf al-mujtama al-'arabi* (The patriarchal system and the modalities of change in Arab society), Beirut: Centre d'Etudes de l'Union Arabe, 1993, p.60ff.
19 See Paulo Freire, *Pedagogy of the Oppressed*, London: Penguin Books, 1993.
20 Mohammed Abed Al-Jabri, *Introduction à la critique de la raison arabe*, Paris: La Découverte, 1995, p.28.
21 Louis Massignon, *Sur l'Islam*, Paris: Editions de l'Herne, 1995, p. 127.

INDEX

UNIVERSITY OF WINCHESTER
LIBRARY